David Caldwell was brought up in Ardrossan in Ayrshire. He studied archaeology at Edinburgh University and worked for the National Museums of Scotland for 38 years as a curator. He has long had an interest in the history and archaeology of the West Highlands and Islands, directing excavations at Finlaggan in Islay, the centre of the Lordship of the Isles, in the 1990s. He has already written two books on the Hebrides for Birlinn – *Islay, Jura and Colonsay: A Historical Guide* and *Islay: The Land of the Lordship.*

Mull and Iona

A HISTORICAL GUIDE

David H. Caldwell

BIRLINN

For Rex

First published in 2018 by
Birlinn Limited
West Newington House
10 Newington Road
Edinburgh
EH9 1QS

www.birlinn.co.uk

Copyright © David H. Caldwell 2018

The moral right of David H. Caldwell to be identified as
the author of this work has been asserted by him in accordance
with the Copyright, Designs and Patents Act 1988.

ISBN 978 1 78027 525 3

British Library Cataloguing-in-Publication Data
A catalogue record for this book is available
from the British Library

Typeset by Mark Blackadder

Printed and bound by Clays Ltd, Elcograf S.p.A

Contents

Acknowledgements

I am very grateful to family, friends and colleagues who have helped me, either directly or indirectly, in writing this book. In particular I would like to record my indebtedness and gratitude to many friends and colleagues who contributed to the Regional Archaeological Framework for Argyll created by Kilmartin Museum and due for publication in 2018, and to Historic Environment Scotland for inviting me to undertake a study of the medieval monuments of Iona and to the colleagues, particularly Nigel Ruckley, Simon Howard and Susy Kirk, who worked on the project with me. I am also very grateful to Nigel Ruckley for accompanying me on field-work undertaken in preparing the gazetteer and being a source of good ideas. I owe a great deal to the work of the Royal Commission on the Ancient and Historical Monuments of Scotland. Their published inventories of monuments in Mull and Iona are of the utmost importance, as is Canmore, the online database maintained by their successor organisation, Historic Environment Scotland. The text has benefited greatly from comments and advice by Hugh Andrew and two anonymous readers in Mull, as well as the editorial care and attention given to it by Andrew Simmons and Barbara Simmons of Birlinn.

D.H.C.

List of Plates

List of Illustrations

List of Maps

List of Genealogical Tables

Visiting Mull and Iona

This book has been written for those with a general interest in archaeology and history, particularly those keen to go and explore the many sites and monuments of these islands themselves.

Three ferry services connect Mull to the Scottish mainland. The main one connects Craignure with Oban on the Argyll coast, which has regular train and bus services to Glasgow. It takes vehicles, as do the ferry services across the Sound of Mull from Fishnish to Lochaline in Morvern and from Tobermory to Kilchoan in Ardnamurchan. Other ferries for foot passengers operate between Fionnphort and Iona and Ulva and the adjacent mainland of Mull. Gometra, with only a handful of inhabitants, can be reached by trekking across Ulva, and then crossing a bridge, or else directly by boat. Erraid, at the southwest tip of the Ross of Mull, is tidal, and can be easily reached by walking from Knockvologan when the tide is out. The Findhorn Community residents on Erraid operate their own boat service. Trips to Inch Kenneth, a privately owned island with a substantial holiday home, and uninhabited islands, especially Staffa and the Treshnish Isles, are organised by local tourist agents.

There is a range of accommodation all the year round on both Mull and Iona, including hotels, bed and breakfast establishments and accommodation to let. There is a hostel run by the Scottish Youth Hostel Association in Tobermory and another hostel at Lagandorain on Iona. The only campsite on Iona is for tents only since that island is a car-free zone, but campsites in Mull also cater for caravans and campervans. There are shops on both islands, some of which are open seven days. The range of food and other goods offered for sale may often seem rather limited, apart from in the main shopping centre of Tobermory. Tobermory is also well provided with restaurants and there are many other options for dining out elsewhere. Both islands are becoming increasingly popular as tourist destinations and it would be wise to make arrangements in advance at any time of the year for where to stay and eat.

These islands are of great beauty, with colourful, rugged landscapes, secluded glens and great vistas across hills and distant islands. There can be great days in any month for exploring the sites. It can also be windy and rainy at any time of the year. Whatever the weather, it is essential to have stout walking shoes or boots and good waterproof clothing. Even the more accessible sites can often only be reached by clambering over rough ground or through bogs. I have found a bicycle good fun and useful for going along tracks unsuitable for a car.

The selection of sites in the gazetteer reflects the writer's ignorance and enthusiasms. Nevertheless, places of interest which are reasonably accessible for the fit have been picked in preference to those involving epic walks off the beaten track or private boat hire. The island fortresses of Cairn na Burgh More and Cairn na Burgh Beg are included because of their importance, although few will have the opportunity to visit them. Sad to say, there are few historic sites which can be reached or fully enjoyed by those confined to a wheelchair.

Only four monuments in these islands are directly in the care of the State, maintained by Historic Environment Scotland. The ruined medieval chapel on Inch Kenneth is open all year round, but visitors have to make their own arrangements to get there by boat. The other three monuments in State care are on Iona. The nunnery and Maclean's Cross are accessible at all times, but the abbey is only open at certain, regular times on a daily basis. The Historic Environment Scotland website can be checked in advance for up-to-date information on opening hours and admission costs. The islands of Iona and Staffa, along with the Burg estate in Ardmeanach, are the properties of the National Trust for Scotland, and the mausoleum at Gruline, Mull, of Lachlan Macquarie, an early governor of New South Wales, is maintained by the National Trust of Australia. All the rest of the sites and monuments listed in this book are in private ownership. The restored castle of the Macleans at Duart is the property of the chief of the Macleans of Duart and is run as a tourist attraction with regular opening hours, gift shop and tearoom. The Duart Castle website provides information on opening times, fees and facilities.

The Mull Museum in the Main Street of Tobermory is a must. Although the exhibition space is relatively small, it is packed with interesting material on the prehistory and history of the island. Admission is free but it is only open in the summer season. Guides to Mull archaeology, history and genealogy are available for sale. There is also a library and archive of local material which can be visited by researchers all year by prior arrangement. The Ross of Mull Historical Centre is located in Millbrae Cottage in Bunessan, adjacent to the ruined corn mill. The centre produces a useful series of guides to historic walks in the Ross. Also in the south of the island is the Pennyghael in the Past Historical Archive and Cottage Museum (Balevulin, Glen Seilisdeir), and in the north there is the Old Byre Heritage Centre near Dervaig, with a video presentation on the island's history and models of early dwellings.

Apart from the historic sites, museum and facilities run by Historic Environment Scotland on Iona there is the Iona Heritage Centre, open each summer season, with its own exhibition of Iona history and life, a shop and café. All the ecclesiastical grounds and buildings on Iona were gifted to the Iona Cathedral Trust by the 8th Duke of Argyll in 1899 and the trustees have recently taken steps to curate and restore the small but valuable library at the abbey. The abbey is also the home of a Christian ecumenical group, the Iona Community.

Good maps, particularly the Ordnance Survey Explorer Series (1:25000, 2.5 inches to 1 mile), are an essential piece of equipment. Mull and Iona are covered by sheets 373 (Iona, Staffa and Ross of Mull), 374 (Isle of Mull North and Tobermory) and 375 (Isle of Mull East, Craignure). The Ordnance Survey Landranger Series (1:50000, 1.25 inches to 1 mile) is also of use, these islands being covered by sheet 47 (Tobermory and North Mull), 48 (Iona and West Mull, Ulva) and 49 (Oban and East Mull). The collection of historic maps in the National Library of Scotland Map Library can be accessed online. Apart from early editions of Ordnance Survey maps, the 1654 map of Mull by Joan Blaeu and the 1801 map of Argyll by George Langlands are of considerable importance.

Some areas of these islands are quite remote, with difficult terrain, and it would be wise to leave information on your intended itinerary before embarking on ambitious treks. Spellings of some place-names have varied considerably over the years. The author has tried to use those current on up-to-date Ordnance Survey maps. No doubt inconsistencies will be found for which he begs forgiveness. Variations will also be found in the spelling of surnames, which were often not spelled consistently, if at all, until recent times.

It should go without saying that it is important to behave responsibly when in the countryside – shut gates, avoid disturbing livestock and nesting birds, keep off crops, do not pick wild flowers, light fires or leave litter. Particular considerations for these islands are to avoid sheep during the lambing season and to be aware of the potential dangers of crossing moorland when there are parties of stalkers about. If in doubt about access to sites ask at the nearest farm or estate office.

Useful Addresses

The organisations and websites listed below are useful sources of information on monuments and finds from Mull and Iona. The National Museum of Scotland, based in Edinburgh, has many artefacts from Mull and Iona in its collections, by no means all on display. Historic Environment Scotland (HES) (recently formed from an amalgamation of the Royal Commission on Ancient and Historical Monuments of Scotland (RCAHMS) with Historic Scotland) maintains the National Monuments Record of Scotland in John Sinclair House in Edinburgh. It is open for public consultation, normally without any need to make an appointment in advance. It contains information, photographs and plans of many sites and monuments in Mull and Iona. Volume 3 of the *Inventory of Ancient Monuments of Argyll* by RCAHMS covers Mull, while Iona is dealt with in Volume 4 (see Further Reading section of this book for more information). Both are important and authoritative sources of information.

HES maintains *Canmore*, the online catalogue of Scotland's archaeology, buildings, industrial and maritime heritage. This is an essential source of information which is constantly being updated and added to. Between 2006 and 2011 RCAHMS managed *Scotland's Rural Past*, an initiative to encourage local groups to research, record and promote Scotland's vanishing historic rural settlements and landscapes. Several groups on Mull participated and recorded their results on the Scotland's Rural Past website, as well as feeding them into *Canmore*.

Historic Environment Scotland, as the public body charged with looking after the country's cultural heritage, has been instrumental in having many of the sites listed in this book protected by scheduling as important monuments. It is an offence to damage or alter a scheduled monument without permission from the Secretary of State. It is also forbidden to use a metal detector on a scheduled site. An updated list of scheduled monuments is maintained on its website. New archaeological discoveries and reports on progress with fieldwork and excavation projects are given yearly in *Discovery And Excavation in Scotland*, published by Archaeology Scotland. Back numbers are available online. Many archaeology reports relating to all parts of Scotland are published by the Society of Antiquaries of Scotland, especially in their *Proceedings* and series of *Scottish Archaeological Internet Reports*, both also freely available online. Their *Scottish Archaeological Research Framework* is designed to be the go-to resource for Scottish archaeology, one which provides an overview of the subject (by period) and also a set of useful and relevant research questions for everyone to use. Regional Archaeological Frameworks are now being developed, including one for Argyll. The Society of West Highland and Island Historical Research publishes a regular series of *West Highland Notes & Queries*, many of them relating directly to Mull history and genealogy.

Archaeology Scotland
https://archaeologyscotland.org.uk

Duart Castle
www.duartcastle.com

Historic Environment Scotland
Longmore House
Salisbury Place
Edinburgh EH9 1SH
Tel: 0131 668 8600
https://www.historicenvironment.scot
https://www.canmore.org.uk

Iona Cathedral Trust
http://iona-cathedral.org.uk

Iona Community
http://Iona.org.uk

Mull Museum
Columba Buildings
Main Street
Tobermory
Isle of Mull PA75 6NY
Tel: 01688 301100
www.mullmuseum.org.uk

National Library of Scotland, Maps Library
Tel: 0131 623 4660
https://maps.nls.uk

National Museums Scotland
Chambers Street
Edinburgh EH1 1JF
Tel: 0131 225 7534
http://www.nms.ac.uk

National Trust for Scotland
https://www.nts.org.uk

NWMAIG (North West Mull Archaeology Interest group)
www.nwmaig.btck.co.uk
bill_suzanne_patterson@hotmail.co.uk

Old Byre Heritage Centre
Dervaig
Isle of Mull PA75 6QR
Tel: 01688 400229
www.old-byre.co.uk

Pennyghael in the Past Historical Archive and Cottage Museum
Balevulin
Tiroran
Isle of Mull PA69 6ET
Tel: 01681 705261
pennyghaelpast@btinternet.com

Ross of Mull Historical Centre
Millbrae Cottage
Bunessan
Isle of Mull PA67 6DG
Tel: 01681 700659
www.romhc.org.uk

Scotland's Rural Past
www.scotlandsruralpast.org.uk

Scottish Archaeological Research Framework (ScARF)
www.scottishheritagehub.com/regionalresearch
(for the research framework for Argyll)

Society of Antiquaries of Scotland
https://socantscot.org

Society of West Highland and Island Historical Research
www.hebrideanhistory.com

Other useful addresses
For ferry services to Mull and Iona:
Caledonian MacBrayne
Hebridean and Clyde Ferries
The Ferry Terminal
Gourock PA19 1QP
Tel: 0800 066 5000
Email: enquiries@calmac.co.uk
http://www.calmac.co.uk

The site for Scotland's National Tourism Organisation:
https://visitscotland.com

For other useful tourist and local information:
www.isle-of-mull.net
www.welcometoiona.com
www.isleofulva.com
www.gometra.org
www.lochalinedivecentre.co.uk

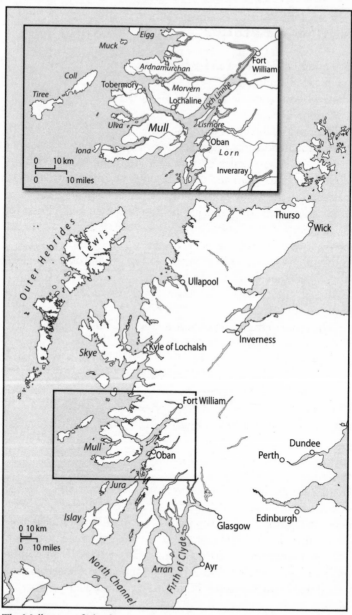

The Mull group of islands

The Geographical Background

Mull is the fourth largest of the Scottish Islands, after Lewis with Harris, the mainland of Shetland and the Isle of Skye. It has an area of 338 square miles (875km²). It stretches about 25 miles (40km) north to south and about 28 miles (45km) east to west. It is almost cut in two by Loch na Keal, a sea loch opening from the west, and extends westwards in a peninsula known as the Ross. To the northeast it is separated from the mainland area of Morvern by the Sound of Mull, in places only 1.5 miles (2.5km) wide, and to the southeast the 2.5 mile (4km) wide Firth of Lorne separates it from the island of Kerrera and mainland Lorn. Off its west coast lie several other smaller islands, including Gometra, Ulva, Inch Kenneth and Iona.

The geographical and political context of Mull has always been as one of the Hebrides, or Western Isles. These are sometimes distinguished as the Inner Hebrides (including Islay, Mull and Skye) and the Outer Hebrides (including Barra, the Uists and Lewis). In medieval times Mull was often grouped with Tiree and Coll to the west as the Mull group of islands. Now, administratively, it is within the local authority area of Argyll and Bute, with its head office at Kilmory, Lochgilphead, on the mainland.

The landscape of Mull is largely the result of a major phase of volcanic activity about 60 to 52 million years ago in the Palaeogene (Early Tertiary) Period. There was a large volcano in the southeast of the island, now eroded to its roots. Deep layers of lava were deposited, giving a stepped appearance to many areas of the island. Where these lavas cooled rapidly and can be inspected in section a columnar structure is evident, as most famously at Fingal's Cave on the island of Staffa. Basalt dykes, originally molten lava that welled up through fractures in the crust, can also be traced across Mull.

Within these layers of lava are sediments and plants, notably the Ardtun Leaf Beds (NGR NM 378 248), exposed in coastal cliffs to the north of Bunessan. Included are fossils of plane, hazel, oak and maidenhair fern leaves. Visually much more striking is the tree, MacCulloch's Fossil Tree (named for an early 19th-century geologist), embedded upright in lava flows at the western tip of the Ardmeanach Peninsula, on the Burg Estate belonging to the National Trust for Scotland (NGR NM 403 278).

Traces of earlier geological times are visible in some areas, like the sandstone of the Jurassic Age (199 to 145 million years ago) visible at Carsaig Bay on the south coast of the island. The Ross of Mull is composed of distinctive red granite that was intruded in Silurian times, more than 400 million years ago. Even older rocks, Lewisian gneisses, amongst the earliest visible anywhere on the surface of the planet, compose much of the landmass of Iona. They were formed over 1,700 million years ago by the metamorphosis of igneous and sedimentary rocks.

These early rocks and later lavas have been subjected to a very long period of weathering and erosion, culminating in a period of glaciation from about 2.6 million years ago. The most recent glaciation from about 12,500 to 11,700 years ago, resulted in many of the surface features we see today, including cliff faces and hills scoured by the slow passage of deep sheets of ice, as well as hummocks and spreads of gravel left by melting glaciers. Another effect of the retreat of the ice was a lifting of the land relative to sea level, resulting in raised beaches, for instance on the east side of Iona, occupied by the medieval abbey and modern village, Baile Mor.

The post-glaciation landscape was initially tundra, mostly grasses and sedges. From about 8,800 years ago tree cover was taking over much of the surface of the island, made up of mixed woodland including hazel, elm and oak. From about 5,000 years ago there was an expansion of heathland, grass and heather moorland, along with the development of peat bogs. This was largely down to climatic changes but also, at least partially, the result of land clearance by humans to create space for their farming activities.

Mull now has more than 200 'wet days' per year. The climate is oceanic, with temperatures generally slightly cooler in summer than elsewhere in mainland Britain but relatively little frost or lying snow in winter around the coasts of the island. Winds are mainly westerlies.

Mull nowadays can be divided into five main landscape types. Much of the south and east is mountainous and relatively uninhabited. The highest peak is Ben More with an elevation of 966m (3,169 feet). The peninsula to the south, separated from this mountainous region by Lochs Buie, Uisg and Spelve, is composed of craggy upland, lower lying moorland with rounded knolls. The Ross of Mull has boulder strewn moorland with granite and quartzite tors. Much of the rest of the island, including Brolass, Ardmeanach, Torloisk and Treshnish, is also largely moorland, but with distinctive stepped slopes and sheer basalt cliffs.

The main lowland areas are situated along the north and east of the island, extending from the north side of Calgary Bay round by Tobermory and down beyond Duart Castle to the north side of Loch Don. They extend across the middle of the island from the head of Loch na Keal in the west to Salen in the east, and further fingers of lowland cross the Ross of Mull from Bunessan southeastwards to the south coast and along the south shore of Loch Scridain. There is a narrow strip along the west coast, including some of Ulva, extending northwards from Loch na Keal, and further pockets in the south at Carsaig Bay and the head of Loch Buie. Much of this lowland is also moorland, but there is, or has in the past been, farming activity on some of it, and this is where the majority of islanders have settled. Iona is characterised by low upland moor and rocky outcrops, along with some pastureland. Crops were grown, particularly on the raised beach around the abbey.

The soils that have been cultivated can generally be characterised as humus-iron podsols, mostly on the raised beaches. Podsols are very acidic soils, often developing in areas of heavy rainfall. They require the administration of a lot of lime and fertiliser to produce good crops. They are regarded by soil scientists as only class 4 land in terms of their suitability for growing crops. Now much of this farmland is covered by grass. The moors and high lands are clad with purple moor-grass, fescue, bent and heather. Mull was probably largely treeless by medieval times through a combination of climatic changes and human depredations.

Limited areas of natural woodland including birch, oak and ash, have survived, often showing evidence of coppicing in order to provide the wands used in traditional house building. Many areas of the island have also in relatively recent times been planted with large conifer forests.

Animal life should be much in evidence to anyone walking through the Mull countryside. Farming activity is concentrated on the raising of beef cattle, including distinctive horned, Highland cattle, and sheep. Feral goats will be found in more remote places, especially Ardmeanach and along the south coast. Red deer abound in the hills, as well as other animals including rabbits and hares. Otters and seals are to be seen around the coasts. There are, however, no badgers, foxes or squirrels.

Bird life is diverse and includes several birds of prey, notably golden eagles, buzzards and recently reintroduced sea eagles. There are vast numbers of other sea birds, especially around the coasts and on smaller islands and rocks around Mull – gulls, puffins and shag amongst them. Hooded crows, corncrakes and wrens are just a few of the others that may be encountered.

The human population of Mull peaked at over 10,000 in the 1820s but now stands at about 3,000. The mainstay of the economy is tourism, catering for several thousand visitors each summer. Farming, fishing and forestry also offer employment, and there is one whisky distillery at Tobermory, the main settlement on the island. In the 19th century the quarrying of granite in the Ross of Mull was a significant industry.

The town of Tobermory has a population of about 1,000. There are also substantial villages at Dervaig, Salen, Bunessan and Fionnphort, and Baile Mor in Iona.

Almost all the roads are single track with passing places. There are cars, taxis, bicycles and electric bicycles available for hire on the island, and West Coast Motors operate bus services from Craignure to Salen and Tobermory, and Craignure to Bunessan and Fionnphort.

Archaeological and Historical Research on Mull and Iona

Until quite recently Mull had not been so well researched archaeologically as some of the neighbouring islands and other parts of Argyll despite the thorough recording of sites and monuments by RCAHMS in their inventories of 1982 and 1984. Now, thanks to the enthusiastic and very able fieldwork being undertaken by local groups, many inspired by the Scotland's Rural Past initiative, Mull has more than caught up.

In 1989–91 Clive Bonsall of Edinburgh University excavated a cave in Ulva (1.1) with Mesolithic occupation, while Steven Mithen has more recently undertaken fieldwork and excavation at some sites as part of a much bigger project looking at the Mesolithic in the Inner Hebrides. There is little archaeological work on Neolithic and Bronze Age sites to report except the research and excavations by Clive Ruggles and his team on short stone rows and their astronomical significance. In 1960 Horace Fairhurst of Glasgow University excavated an Iron Age dun at An Caisteal near Bunessan (3.14). In recent years there have been community archaeological projects, especially the excavations of a medieval chapel at Baliscate near Tobermory (5.1), under the leadership of Clare Ellis, with Mull-based volunteers, many of them associated with the Mull Museum. Ross of Mull Historical Centre, Pennyghael in the Past and the North West Mull Archaeology Interest Group are undertaking important work surveying and recording sites across the island including farming townships abandoned or cleared in the 19th century. There is an ongoing recording programme and associated publications of memorial inscriptions in burial grounds.

The seas around Mull have been a graveyard for many ships, including a ship of the Spanish Armada (The Tobermory 'Galleon'), but most are unrecorded, leaving few or no traces on the sea bed. There have, however, been two exceptional underwater explorations of two 17th-century wrecks in the Sound of Mull off

Duart Castle, both by Colin Martin of St Andrews University. One, believed to be the *Swan*, is a Cromwellian warship that sank in 1653 (6.33). The other is HMS *Dartmouth*, a fifth-rate warship that went down in 1690 (6.34).

Iona has seen a lot more archaeological activity over the years than Mull, almost all concentrated on the abbey and its immediate vicinity and specifically aimed at elucidating the early history of the Columban monastery. In the years from 1956 to 1976 excavations by leading archaeologists, including Charles Thomas, were funded by the Russell Trust, though much of this work is still to be fully published. There have been several other excavations in more recent times, many of them government-funded rescue excavations. Notable amongst them were the excavations of 1979, directed by John Barber, which recovered water-logged deposits in the vallum (ditch) surrounding the early monastery, and evidence for other early structures.

A Note on Dates

Many of the dates given in this book are little better than guesses, even for medieval and modern times where there is a lack of documentation about buildings and few diagnostic features which can be closely dated by comparison with better-known examples elsewhere.

There are now a few radiocarbon (C14) dates for prehistoric monuments in Iona and Mull, the result of assessing the radioactive decay of carbon 14 in organic material like charcoal and bone. A full understanding of the reliability of these dates, which in any case have been the subject of several revisions, is a complex matter. In the text which follows the writer has used them, along with dating evidence from similar sites in neighbouring islands and parts of the mainland, to give a rough idea of when a site was occupied. For more information on radiocarbon dating see Edwards and Ralston 2008, 6–7, and Patrick Ashmore's contribution on how to interpret radiocarbon dates and a list of many of those from sites in Argyll in Ritchie 1997, 236–83.

PART I

From the Palaeolithic Period to the Present Day

1. Early Visitors and Settlers:
Palaeolithic and Mesolithic Hunters and Gatherers

It is probable that Mull was visited by bands of Palaeolithic (Old Stone Age) hunters and gatherers in warmer phases in the late Glacial Period. There is now evidence of their presence on the neighbouring islands of Islay and Tiree. The last Ice Age ended, relatively abruptly, about 9700 BC. The complex interrelationship between rising sea levels as the enormous ice-sheets melted, and rising land masses as the weight of the ice was lifted, is not yet fully understood for Mull, nor the processes by which the island was colonised by plants and animals.

The earliest actual evidence for human occupation of Mull comes largely in the form of assemblages of flint. These comprise the flakes and cores, sometimes present in their thousands, which were discarded in the process of making implements from flint pebbles. Many Mesolithic (Middle Stone Age) tools were composite, with several small retouched flint blades (known as microliths) being glued together in a haft to make a cutting edge, or mounted at the tip of an arrowshaft. Only the flint, however, has survived.

The flints have been recovered from locations believed to have been used as seasonal campsites. Many were coastal, like sites at Croig at the mouth of Loch a' Chumhainn. The earliest Mesolithic settlers would have been confronted by a densely forested landscape, with birch, oak and hazel. Small nomadic family groups probably ranged over large areas in their search for food and other resources. They would have followed seasonal rounds which exploited all available food resources in the form of mammals, including wild cattle, deer and elk, other fauna such as birds, fish, and molluscs, as well as edible plants, roots, berries and nuts. Some experts now believe that a significant draw would have been the opportunity to hunt seals, for their meat but particularly for their skins. They reason that the boats which must have been used to get from one island to another probably consisted of lightweight

frames made of branches and covered with seal skins. At Creat
Dubh near Dervaig a probable fireplace has been excavated, used,
on the basis of radiocarbon dating, between 6080 and 6440 BC.
On Ulva, as no doubt in many other locations, a cave, A' Chrannag
(1.1) was used for shelter. Here midden deposits containing large
quantities of seashells datable to about 6500 and 6000 BC have
been excavated. Elsewhere in mainland Britain house sites have
recently been excavated. They were circular and probably had a
framework of timbers clad with turf.

A hunting and gathering way of life continued for several thousand years, down to the early 4th millennium BC and the appearance in the Scottish archaeological record of farming, and for many
groups for a long time after that. So far very limited work in Mull,
for instance at Tenga, suggests that Mesolithic groups did not limit
themselves to the coasts but ranged across much of the island. On
the basis of comparisons with hunter-gatherer groups known in
other parts of the world in recent times it may be supposed that
the population density of Mull and Iona in Mesolithic times was
never any greater than nine persons per hundred square kilometres,
and often considerably less.

2. Early Farmers:
The Neolithic to the Bronze Age

THE NEOLITHIC AGE

From Mull itself there is as yet little direct evidence for the Neolithic Age (New Stone Age), during which one of the most momentous developments in human progress took place. This was the adoption of farming, especially the growing of cereal crops and the raising of cattle and sheep as the mainstays of life. Extrapolating from the results of archaeological research in neighbouring areas and islands we can suppose that farming was introduced to Mull late in the 5th millennium BC. To what extent this was through the arrival of significant numbers of migrants from mainland Britain, Ireland and further afield or the adoption of new ways by indigenous hunters and gatherers is not known. Archaeologists now recognise strands within the archaeological record suggesting that early farmers came from Brittany and the area around Calais in northeast France. There is also growing evidence for a spread of ideas, if not people, from Orkney southwards at the beginning of the 3rd millennium BC.

In general terms the archaeological record shows the development of animal husbandry and crop cultivation in the Near East at a much earlier date and the spread of these practices across Europe over a long period of time. Hand in hand with farming went a sedentary way of life and often the development of new technologies, most striking in the archaeological record being the use of pottery. Stone, especially flint, remained the main material for providing an edge or point to tools and weapons, but a significant addition to tool kits was the polished stone axe, necessary for chopping wood and cutting down trees. It is probable that much of the Mull landscape had to be cleared of forest cover to provide the space for growing crops and pasturing animals. Environmental evidence from Coire Cladach in central Mull shows the appearance of plantago (*Plantago laceolata*) about 3850 BC and a decline in oak and hazel. Plantago is a common weed on cultivated land.

Elsewhere in the British Isles there is evidence for the houses of Neolithic farmers, many of them large rectangular structures of timber. In Mull the presence of a Neolithic way of life is indicated by the recovery of pottery and stone tools, for instance sherds of so-called Unstan ware overlying the Mesolithic deposits in the Ulva Cave. A cave at Scoor (4.5) has cup-markings on its walls, a type of carving considered to date as early as the first half of the 3rd millennium BC. They occur widely in Britain, Ireland and Galicia. The reasons for carving them are not known, but their presence possibly shows that the cave at Scoor was occupied at this time. A handful of stone axes have also been recovered as stray finds, including one from Killiemor in the collections of Glasgow Life and one from Loch Peallach in the National Museums of Scotland (NMS). A third one, also in NMS, is from Loch Mingary, and is made from porcellanite from Northern Ireland.

The most important evidence for Neolithic farmers in Mull is the chambered cairn at Port Donain (2.11) for the burial of the dead. It was long and trapezoidal (32m by 11m in maximum width) in shape when built, heaped high with stones. It had a concave façade formed with upright stones, and a long narrow chamber formed of large slabs. Its erection would have involved a considerable amount of manpower, and it is believed that it was for the deposition of the remains of a community over a long period of time. It is probable that there would have been several small communities spread out over Mull and Iona at any one time.

The Port Donain cairn belongs to the Clyde group of chambered cairns, believed to date to about 4300 to 3800 BC. They are distributed from the Solway Firth to Argyll and the southern Hebrides. Characteristically Port Donain is of considerable length, with its burial chamber entered from the centre of its forecourt. Where such cairns have been carefully examined by excavation it has been shown that they are often of more than one phase of construction, sometimes also with secondary burials cut into the cairn material much later. That is the case here with a cist of stone slabs at the southwest end of the cairn. It may have been inserted in the Bronze Age at a time when the main chamber at the other end of the cairn had been sealed up. Grave goods were deposited with the interments, including pottery and stone tools. With the possible exception of the round barrow at Suidhe (2.12, Plate 1) in the Ross of Mull, no other chambered Neolithic tombs survive in Mull.

THE CHALCOLITHIC AGE

Archaeologists now distinguish a Chalcolithic or Copper Age, covering the years from about 2500 BC to the first use of bronze about 2200 BC. Bronze is a copper alloy, at its simplest involving the addition of a small percentage of tin to the copper. This expedient greatly improved the hardness and properties of the metal and is reckoned a significant technological leap forwards.

The local transition from the Neolithic to the Chalcolithic Age is marked in several ways in the archaeological record, most obviously by the adoption of new technology: tools made from copper. The earliest evidence for this in Mull is from Salen where a group of cist burials was discovered, one with a beaker, two flint implements and fragments of copper deemed to be the remains of a dagger. These finds are now in the National Museum of Scotland. Cist burials are typical of the Chalcolithic and succeeding Bronze Age, generally formed of stone slabs for the burial of one body alone, often crouched and sometimes with grave goods. Burials with daggers are also typical, as well as beakers. Beakers, handmade pots with an S-shaped profile, possibly for drinking, occur widely across Europe from *c.* 2500 to *c.* 1500 BC, and the one from Salen, with all-over cord decoration, is an early type. There is a lot still to be understood about burials like this one from Salen but it seems to represent a new world, perhaps shaped by the arrival into Mull of new immigrants or invaders. There is increasing evidence from early beaker burials elsewhere in Britain, including one from Sorisdale in the neighbouring island of Coll, of the presence of people who had grown up on the continent of Europe. This observation is made largely on the basis of scientific analyses of the strontium and oxygen isotope values in dental enamel.

Another cist burial at Callachally, Glenforsa, apparently contained two later beakers (Fig. 1), a fragmentary knife and a greenstone bracer (Fig. 2), all now in the National Museum of Scotland. Such bracers were to provide archers with protection to their wrist when firing a bow and, along with barbed and tanged flint arrowheads, are another typical artefact associated with

Figure 1. A beaker from a cist burial at Callachally, Glenforsa, now in the National Museum of Scotland (from *Catalogue of the National Museum of Antiquities of Scotland* 1892)

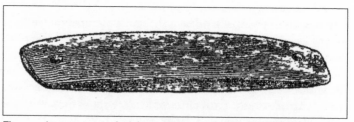

Figure 2. A greenstone archer's bracer from a cist burial at Callachally, Glenforsa, now in the National Museum of Scotland (from *Proc Soc Antiq Scot* 9, 1870–72)

beakers. Bows and arrows could be used for both hunting and warfare but the copper axes that appear in the Chalcolithic Age were probably primarily for use as tools, like ones from Glenforsa and Glengorm now in the National Museum of Scotland.

THE BRONZE AGE

With the adoption of a bronze technology about 2200 BC more and more metal implements were made and used, including more complex axes, adzes and chisels, halberds and swords, and items of personal adornment, some of gold, but these have yet to be discovered in Iona and Mull, all except a bronze bracelet recently excavated in Croig Cave in Mull (2.1). It had been deposited in a small pit about 950 BC along with an amber bead, perhaps for ritual reasons. The cave was used about that time for processing shellfish by people who also engaged in inshore fishing.

Burial of individuals in cists remained a typical way of disposing of the bodies of at least some of the population for much of the Bronze Age. Some, like a burial in a cist at Quinish (NGR NM 4150 5385), were buried with 'food vessels', pots known also to occur in domestic contexts (Fig. 3). Much of the equipment used by these remote ancestors would have been of organic materials, including animal skins and wood which would only survive in exceptional circumstances. Unfortunately, the remains of houses of the period in Mull and Iona have still to be located and excavated. On the basis of work elsewhere they will be round houses, 'hut circles' varying in diameter from about 7m to 12m, perhaps with low stone walls and conical roofs supported on upright timbers. A probable one has recently been identified at Torrans (2.2). Potential remains of others have been noted by Calgary Pier (NGR NM 3643 5151) and at Torness (NGR NM 6490 3253).

One of the most prevalent types of Bronze Age monument in these islands are circular burial cairns, some less than 5m in diameter, others over 15m. None has been scientifically excavated. A particular type of cairn, defined by a kerb of upright stones (Plate 2), makes an appearance in Argyll from about 1500 to 1000 BC. They also occur in the northeast of Scotland, Wales and Ireland

Figure 3. Bronze Age food vessel from a cist burial at Quinish, Mull, now in the National Museum of Scotland (from *Proc Soc Antiq Scot* 27, 1892–93)

and are associated with cremation burials. The change from inhumation to cremation burials at this time is probably the result of major changes in society or beliefs but there are few clues as yet to what they might have been.

Standing stones, mostly positioned individually (Fig. 4), but also in short rows or circles, are amongst the key monuments of ancient Mull. The Rev. McLauchlan published a paper in the 1860s in which he pointed out how many of the standing stones were strung out along a route from Fionnphort across the Ross of Mull, perhaps all the way originally to Grass Point (formerly known as Achnacraig), where there used to be a ferry to Kerrera and the mainland. He reasoned that these marked a pilgrim route to Iona and dated to a time after St Columba's death. While it is possible

Figure 4. Standing stone at Tirghoil in the Ross of Mull (2.25)

that some of these stones were useful way-markers for Christian pilgrims, there can be little doubt that most or all of them were first erected during the Bronze Age. Why is less clear, though it would not be surprising if some were always intended to be landmarks.

We are on slightly surer ground with other stone monuments, the 'short stone rows' that are such a feature of the Mull landscape. These consist of alignments of three to five standing stones, relatively close together, and are found in Brittany, Ireland and Britain, as far north as Orkney and Shetland, and especially in southwest Ireland and the west of Scotland. Recent archaeological research suggests that they date to the Late Bronze Age, perhaps mostly about 1800–1200 BC. A radiocarbon determination from charcoal in the pit of one of the stones at Ardnacross in Mull could indicate it was slightly earlier in date (calibrated date of 1260–920 cal BC).

The research on the Mull short stone rows, including those at

Ardnacross (Plate 3), Baliscate (2.16), Glengorm (2.19) and Dervaig (Plate 4), suggests that there were two important considerations for their builders, the first that there should be a prominent peak to the south or east associated with the southernmost rising of the moon, towards its major standstill limit. The second important factor was that there should be a relatively distant horizon to the south, as well as to the west of south. All this indicates that the builders were interested in making lunar observations. We can only speculate that this was so they could keep a track of and anticipate changes in the seasons.

Another megalithic monument on Mull for which astronomical claims have been made is the stone circle at Lochbuie (2.10, 2.21). Stone circles are another well-known feature of the Bronze Age. There are two at Hogh on Tiree, another at Cultoon in Islay, and several at Machrie Moor in Arran, and in the vicinity of Kilmartin on the mainland of Argyll. Lochbuie has also been seen as a potential local ritual centre, owing to the presence not just of the stone circle but also a kerb cairn and standing stones.

3. A Warrior Society: The Iron Age

The Iron Age is deemed in Argyll to have commenced about 700 BC. A deterioration in the climate about this time was probably largely responsible for the growth of peat over large areas of Mull and Iona, covering areas which had previously been farmed. Theoretically the Iron Age is marked by the arrival of a great technological step forward – the use of iron. There is no actual evidence for iron tools, weapons, etc., in Mull or surrounding areas for hundreds of years after 700 BC. The earliest evidence for iron smelting or smithing has recently been excavated in Croig Cave (2.1) in the form of a piece of slag and fragments of charcoal, deposited about 400 BC. Archaeologists are more aware of a change in the archaeological evidence from a preponderance of burial and ritual monuments to one of fortified sites.

The Iron Age culture of the region is probably largely a local development by a long-settled people. A shared architectural tradition of brochs and duns is evidence of links with elsewhere in the west and north of Scotland, and much of their material culture, way of life and technology was prevalent over much wider areas of Britain.

The characteristic monuments of the Iron Age in Mull and the neighbouring islands are defended settlements, normally positioned on hilltops or rocky outcrops (Plate 5). The defensive walls of many of these forts must originally have been very impressive, of considerable height and thickness. Destruction by the elements and the hand of man has left most of them as low mounds of stones and scatters of tumble. They mostly have a coastal distribution. At one end of the scale are forts, contained, normally, within a single rampart or drystone wall. Some also have minor outworks. Forts were large enough to give shelter to more than one family, but whether permanently, seasonally, or only when danger threatened, is not clearly understood. They were high-status locations, and may have functioned as communal centres where groups would gather for feasts or festivals. While some forts elsewhere in Britain and Europe are of immense size, classified as regional centres, or oppida, those in Mull are mostly small, with an area of less than half a hectare. On the basis of evidence from elsewhere, these forts would have contained round houses but so far traces of such structures have only been recorded in excavations at Creag a'Chasteil at Calgary (3.2) and at Dùn Cùl Bhuirg on Iona (3.3). The finds from the latter suggest it was occupied between the 1st century BC and the 3rd century AD. Other forts will undoubtedly turn out to be of earlier date.

Duns are smaller than forts, normally circular or oval, and surrounded by single drystone walls, of massive thickness compared to the area enclosed. Although they are found throughout the west of Scotland they are particularly densely distributed in Argyll, especially around the coasts. The working definition for them proposed by the Royal Commission on Ancient and Historical Monuments of Scotland suggests they enclose an area of $375m^2$ or less. There is, in fact, no exact distinction between a fort and a dun, and many forts, confusingly, have a place-name including the element *dùn*, the Gaelic for a fort. Although many duns in Argyll and the west were reoccupied in historic times or remained in use for a very long time, archaeological opinion, based on excavations, currently favours the view that many or most were originally constructed in the second half of the 1st millennium BC.

Duns may best be considered as falling into two types. First, dun enclosures, often larger in size and irregular in plan, like Dùn Aoidhean on Erraid (Plate 6), Cnoc na Sroine (3.18), Dùn a' Chiabhaig (3.19) and An Dùn at Torrans (3.15), all in Mull. They may not have been dissimilar in function to small forts and no doubt provided shelter to houses. Second, dun houses, of smaller, normally circular plan, capable of being roofed over, the roof timbers resting on the enclosing wall. Good examples, An Sean Dùn (3.16), Dùn Aisgain (3.21) and Dùn Bhuirg (Plate 7), have internal areas with diameters respectively of about 9m, 10.4m and 8.5m to 6.9m. The walls of dun houses are typically over 2m in thickness, and in some cases over 4m. Those of Dùn Aisgain still stand about 2.75m high. Most are reduced to remains of less than

ɪm in height. Many show evidence for entrance passages, sometimes checked for a door, galleries and chambers in the thickness
of their walls. Outer enclosures or other defensive works are not
unusual.

Dun houses may be thought of as the dwellings of single-family
units. Archaeologists see these dun houses as versions in stone of a
shared tradition of round house architecture – Atlantic round
houses – extending up and around the Atlantic seaboard. Also
included in this Atlantic round house tradition are brochs, circular
tower-like structures with galleries and stairs in the thickness of
their massive walls, and scarcements for supporting the floors and
roofs of structures in the interior space. They have courtyards from
about 5.8m to 13.5m in diameter. The most completely preserved
broch – Mousa in Shetland – stands to a height of over 12m, but
most may not have attained this height. The distribution of brochs
is predominantly in the Northern Isles and the north of the Scottish mainland, but there are two in Mull and others in the neighbouring islands of Lismore (Map 1), Tiree and Islay. The broch at
Dùn Mor Vaul in Tiree has been extensively excavated and appears
to have been built about 50 BC and to have been occupied until
about 250 AD. Neither of the brochs in Mull, An Sean Chaisteal at
Ardnacross (Plate 8) on the Sound of Mull and Dùn nan Gall on
the shore of Loch Tuath (Plate 9), are in a good state of preserva-
tion. Dùn nan Gall is the more complete of the two, though
severely encumbered with the debris from its own walls.

Crannogs, artificial islands made up of brushwood, stones and
peat, held in place by stakes, are also known to have been occupied
in Argyll in the Iron Age. Many have no doubt disintegrated or
sunk without trace; others may be obscured by later occupation
build-up or now only appear as natural islands. A timber from the
crannog at Eilean Ban in Loch Frisa (5.19) has produced a radiocarbon date suggesting it was built some time between about 400
and 60 BC, although its present form, with a drystone perimeter
wall and boat inlet, suggests a medieval or more recent date. There
are several other crannogs known or suspected in Mull, in Lochs
Assapol, Ba, Frisa and Poit na h-I, but their date is not known, and
some of them may have been built, or remained in use, in medieval
times. One found in Loch nam Miol about 2km to the southeast

of Tobermory (NGR NM 5185 5273) was discovered to have a stone causeway connecting it to the edge of the loch, with dug-out canoes adjacent to it, the largest over 5m long, when it was drained in the 1860s.

While forts, duns and crannogs must have been the residences of aristocrats or substantial farmers, the homes of lesser members of society have not yet been identified. Recent excavations at Kilninian in Mull have uncovered some evidence for an unenclosed domestic site. The artefacts included a glass bead which may have been manufactured here from reused Roman glass. The evidence for ironworking in Croig Cave (2.1) about 400 BC has already been mentioned, and sherds of early Iron Age pottery outside a cave at Reudle in Treshnish (NGR NM 3634 4563) suggest occupation there, at least on a casual basis.

There is clearly still a lot to be learned about the Iron Age in Mull and Iona. Although we are still dealing with a prehistoric era, there is a tantalising glimpse of an awareness of Mull in the work of the Alexandrian geographer, Claudius Ptolemy, in the early 2nd century AD. He notes that one of a group of five islands to the north of Ireland is called Malaois, possibly from the local Celtic language for 'lofty isle'. That is the earliest historical reference to Mull. Whilst the Lowlands of Scotland were subjected to direct or indirect Roman military control in the years from the late 1st to the 4th century AD, Argyll and the islands remained beyond their control. There may, nevertheless, have been a significant amount of Roman influence in Argyll. Roman coins and artefacts have been recovered from the area, including a bronze coin of 187 AD of the Emperor Diocletian from the garden of Gometra House.

4. From Saints to Sinners:
The Early Historic Period

THE KINGDOM OF DÁL RIATA

The traditional version of the early history of the Scots maintains that about 500 AD, Fergus Mor mac Eirc, king of the Dál Riata in Northern Ireland, came to rule in Argyll over a colony of Gaels from Ireland. Language experts have used the Gaelic place-names of Argyll to prove the influx of Gaelic speakers in such numbers as to cause the local tongue, presumably distantly related to Welsh, to die out.

This kingdom of Dál Riata in Argyll developed into one of the great and long-lasting European states, the kingdom of Scotland, but experts like the archaeologist Ewan Campbell and the historians David Dumville and James Fraser now question many of the assumptions derived from traditional sources on the origin and nature of the kingdom of Dál Riata. Archaeologists have had little success in uncovering evidence for the sudden arrival of large numbers of settlers in the southwest of Scotland and Argyll in the 5th and 6th centuries. Instead, there had probably been a two-way process over a long period of time of people in dribs and drabs moving for a variety of reasons, north and south, across the North Channel separating Ireland from mainland Argyll and the Hebrides. A gradual adoption of Gaelic as the language of the people of Argyll, starting long before 500 AD, may have been one of the most significant outcomes of these migrations.

There is overwhelming evidence that by the 7th century Gaelic was the dominant language used in Argyll. It was a language spoken in common with the people of Ireland, while many of the neighbouring parts of the Scottish mainland were inhabited by British (early Welsh) and Pictish speakers. It is also clear that the people of Argyll had many other cultural links with Ireland, which was more accessible to a people used to travelling by boat than much of the rest of Scotland. The most important evidence for this is the activities of Irish Christian missionaries like St Columba from the 6th century onwards.

Dál Riata may only have coalesced into an Argyll-wide kingdom about 700. It included several important peoples or kindreds: the Cenél nGabráin in Kintyre and the Cenél Comgaill in Cowal, both of which together formed the Corcu Réti, the Cenél nÓengusso in Islay and the Cenél Loairn in Lorn, and probably the Mull group of islands as well. The Cenél Loairn consisted of three main segments, the Cenél Salaich, Cenél Cathboth and Cenél nEchdach, but it is not known which of these was based in Mull and Iona. The main royal centre for Cenél Loairn was probably at Dunollie, the site of a later castle of the MacDougalls next to Oban. No royal centre or other important secular site of this period has as yet been identified in Mull.

The little that is known about the Cenél Loairn is largely derived from *Míniugud Senchasa Fher nAlban* (the explanation of the genealogy of the Men of Alba), a composite text with 7th-century origins, providing genealogical information and a survey of the military resources of the kingdom of Dál Riata in terms of the number of houses and the ships they were to provide. While the Cenél nÓengusso was reckoned as having 430 houses, the Cenél nGabrain had 560 (including the houses of the Cenél Comgaill) and the Cenél Loairn had 420. These houses were the holdings of the freemen and nobles. The actual residences no doubt included some of the crannogs, forts and duns, some newly built, others reoccupied, listed below. There is now also important evidence for a settlement of the period at Baliscate near Tobermory (5.1). Despite early writings about St Columba and Iona, the Early Historic Period for Mull is still largely a dark age.

Míniugud Senchasa Fher nAlban divides the houses into groups of 20, each of which had to supply 'two seven benchers', meaning two ships each with seven oars a side, thus 28 men per 20 houses for naval or military service, and the ships themselves. It has often been assumed that these ships would have been of curach construction, with a wooden framework covered with leather, but perhaps they were wooden, of clinker build like Viking ships. The fighting strength of the Cenél Loairn was therefore 588 men and 42 ships – quite a respectable force for the time.

Early Irish law-texts, which have a lot of relevance for Scottish Dál Riata, describe a society in which cattle were of the utmost importance, and stock raising is known to have been widely practised in Mull and the neighbouring islands throughout recorded times. Milk products were evidently one of the main elements in the human diet. Cattle were a means of measuring wealth and status, and of paying rent and fines, and the extent or productivity of land was measured in terms of cows.

Apart from the monuments on Iona (4.3) discussed below there is little to mark this period apart from the cross-marked stones at Lochbuie (4.4) and Calgary (4.1) and some of the carvings of crosses in the Nun's Cave at Carsaig (5.21) and the cave at Scoor (4.5). The excavations at Baliscate have produced evidence for an Early Historic burial ground and there was probably also a small church of this period. The small rectangular church in an enclosed burial ground, now reduced to its foundations, at Crackaig (4.2), may also turn out to date to Early Historic times.

Three bronze penannular brooches of the 9th or 10th century, two now in the National Museum of Scotland (Fig. 5), are known to have come from Mull.

Figure 5. Two bronze penannular brooches of the 9th or 10th century from Mull, now in the National Museum of Scotland (from *Proc Soc Antiq Scot* 13, 1878–79)

ST COLUMBA AND IONA

Mull is hardly ever specifically mentioned in Early Historic sources, but there is copious information on Iona. This island was called *Hí*, and so it often appears in later sources as Icolumcille ('Columba's Hí'). In Latin it was *Ioua Insula*, and the name Iona results from a later misreading of the Latin. The meaning of Hí is obscure. It is, however, nothing to do with Martin Martin's ingenious explanation given at the end of the 17th century:

> The natives have a tradition among them that one of the clergymen who accompanied Columbus [Columba] on his voyage thither, having at a good distance espied the isle, and cried joyfully to Columbus in the Irish language, 'Chi mi I', i.e., 'I see her' – meaning thereby the country of which they had been in quest – that Columbus then answered, 'it shall be from henceforth called Y'.

It was on Iona that Columba, having left his native Ireland in 563, founded a monastery, which was his main base until he died there in 597. Columba, one of the most significant figures of his age, was also a key figure in the expansion of Christianity in Europe and in the development of a Scottish state. He had an aristocratic background as a leading figure of the powerful Cenél Conaill in the north of Ireland. The world he was brought up in was largely pagan and underlying his emigration from his homeland may have been a desire to become a pilgrim in expiation of some role he may have had in a battle won by his kinsmen at Cúl Drebene in 560. Whatever the precise circumstances, he had been trained as a churchman and had a powerful vocation to spread the Gospel. He was preceded in Scotland by other Irish missionaries and there were several others of his and later times, mostly not well documented, who were also responsible for the Christianisation of northern Britain. Columba and Iona, however, were undoubtedly the two key elements in this process and the monastic centre in Iona became an important centre of learning and pilgrimage for a wider European world.

The monastic settlement that thrived in Iona from the 560s to the early 9th century has all but been swept away or obliterated with the passage of time. From a small beginning with Columba and his immediate followers it may, even prior to the saint's death in 597, have grown to a sizeable establishment, not just in terms of area, but also as a community, including many workers, craftsmen and others who supported the activities of the monks, and in a world without towns and cities would have turned it into a notable hub for religious services, education, administration, trade and industry. By analogy with other early monasteries there would have been a core area with churches, lodgings, storehouses, workshops, burial grounds, etc., and a surrounding area where crops were grown and animals raised. Incidental detail in the life of Columba written by Adomnàn, the saint's 7th-century biographer and successor as Abbot of Iona, fits with this picture, as does evidence from various archaeological excavations, much of which is still to be adequately interpreted and published. It is clear from these excavations that despite occupation of the site in the later Medieval Period by the Benedictine abbey (Plate 10) and other structures that there is considerable potential to discover more about the early monastery archaeologically.

Stretches of ditches, some quite substantial, 3m wide and over 2m deep with inner and outer banks, are still visible in the landscape and also known from aerial photographs and geophysical prospection. They have been identified as the remains of the monastic vallum, enclosing a large rectangular area. It is clear that there is more than one phase to this work and the area included in it changed with time. An area of high ground with rocky outcrops, Cnoc nan Càrnan, is enclosed within a well-preserved section of it, but Reilig Odhráin, the main Christian burial ground on Iona, lies just to the south of it (Fig. 6). One view is that at some stage the area of the enclosure may have been extended to take in not just Reilig Odhráin but land as far south as that occupied by the present day St Columba Hotel. The archaeologist John Barber, however, who excavated at Iona in 1979, takes the view that the original nucleus of the monastic settlement was probably in the area of Reilig Odhráin and spread northwards with time. Barber excavated part of the vallum ('ditch 1', not now obvious on the surface) which runs east–west just to the north of Reilig Odhráin. Pollen collected from peat deposits in its bottom suggest that the

Figure 6. The ruins of Iona Abbey in 1772 (from Pennant 1774, fig. XXI). On the far left is the roofless Tigh an Easbuig. The small hill, Tòrr an Aba, is to the right of the ruined abbey nave with beyond it Reilig Odhráin and St Oran's Chapel

local landscape was dominated by oak and ash wood prior to the land being cleared by the early monks for agricultural activities, including the growing of cereal crops. The ditch itself appears to have been dug about 600–635.

The monastic enclosure at its maximum extent would have extended from 150m or so north of the medieval abbey and southwards for over 300m. There is no trace of it along the seaward side, but the monastic boundary here may have coincided with the top of a natural scarp overlooking the foreshore, giving an extent of up to 250m east–west. A substantial stream flows through this area from the higher ground to the west, tellingly called the Sruch a' Mhuilinn (Gaelic, 'mill stream'). Excavations adjacent to the stream in 1991, just to the west of the road, identified the site of a horizontal water mill. No dating evidence was recovered but it is conceivable that there was a mill here as early as Columba's time.

Excavations to the south of the abbey church in 1957 uncovered walling which may be part of the semi-circular apse of an early stone church, and further afield, St Ronan's, the medieval parish church, has been shown to have replaced a smaller rectangular structure with clay-bonded walls, almost certainly a church. The only trace of an early church above ground is the heavily reconstructed St Columba's Shrine-chapel at the west end of the medieval abbey church (Plate 11). It has been identified as a reliquary church for containing the bones and relics of St Columba. Adomnàn describes how Columba's body was wrapped in linen and buried in a grave, with a stone, previously used by the saint as a pillow, alongside to act as a marker (Fig. 7). In the mid 8th century his bones were placed in a shrine, described as being of precious metals. St Columba's Shrine-chapel would have been the place to keep and display it. Opinions have changed amongst scholars as to its date, but now the Irish archaeologist Tomás Ó Carragáin has made a convincing case that it also dates to the mid

Figure 7. A boulder carved with a ringed cross, evidently an early grave-marker, perhaps of the 9th century. It is said to be the stone that St Columba used as a pillow (from *Proc Soc Antiq Scot* 10, 1872–74)

8th century. It reflects a knowledge of the Holy Sepulchre in Jerusalem, fulfilling a local need to give due honour and prestige to the saintliness of Columba. It acted as an inspiration for other shrine-chapels at religious centres in Ireland. In 825 Blathmac and his companions were martyred at Iona by Viking raiders searching for St Columba's shrine. The saint's bones had by then been 'lifted from [their] pediments' by the monks and buried for safety 'in the earth, in a hollowed barrow, under a thick layer of turf'. The Vikings failed to get Blathmac to divulge where this treasure was hidden and left empty-handed.

St Columba's Shrine-chapel may also be the church referred to in an account of the devastating raid through the Isles in 1098 by which King Magnus Barelegs of Norway claimed the Kingship of the Isles. When, however, he came to Iona he gave peace and quarter to all men. He had St Columba's Church locked up and forbade anyone from entering it. There was a concentration of early stone grave-markers around this chapel, including those supposed to commemorate early abbots of Iona. They are now displayed in the Abbey Museum.

In excavations undertaken by Professor Charles Thomas in 1957 the remains were identified of a small sub-circular hut with stone footings and, probably, walls of wattle, subsequently burnt. In the interior there was a rough bench of natural rock along one side, and in front of it an arrangement of slabs that may well have been the remains of another seat or the base of a desk or table. The location of this discovery was the rocky knoll to the west of the abbey church (Fig. 6), known as Tòrr an Aba (Gaelic, 'hill of the abbot'). It appeared likely to the excavators that they had found evidence for St Columba's cell. Adomnàn describes on two occasions how Columba climbed a little hill to enjoy the view over his monastery. The hill is not necessarily Tòrr an Aba, and more to the point, Adomnàn does not actually specifically say that the saint's wooden hut, where he did his writing, was there. He says it was a 'raised wooden hut', which could be interpreted in several ways. It does not mean with any certainty that it was on raised ground.

Nevertheless, radiocarbon determinations have now been obtained on charcoal from the walls of the hut on Tòrr an Aba dating it securely to the years 540 to 650. The careful way the foundations of the hut were filled in with beach pebbles, perhaps soon after its destruction, might suggest that the site was being marked as one of significance, and it now has a medieval cross-base set upon it, indicating it was a place of veneration, at least at a later date.

Excavations, still to be fully published, found evidence for other early timber buildings and structures in the general area between and to the south of the medieval abbey complex and Tòrr an Aba. It is believed likely that all of the earliest monastic structures would have been substantially of wood, with stone architecture not making an appearance prior to the 8th century. In 1979 John Barber excavated just north of Reilig Odhráin two concentric arcs of large post-holes that might have belonged to a large round house with a diameter of about 20m. The suggested date for this is between the early 7th and the 11th centuries. The excavator drew attention to Adomnàn's story of how St Columba intervened to save the life of a monk who fell from the top of the round house in the monastery of Durrow in Ireland – the great house which was then under construction. The saint had a vision of the accident while copying a book and sent an angel to catch the monk. Perhaps both at Iona and Durrow there were large round houses that served as communal sleeping places for the monks.

There was also evidence for metalworking and the manufacture of glass beads. Water-logged deposits in the vallum ('ditch 1'), where it was excavated just to the northeast of St Oran's Chapel, produced waste material from leatherworking (especially shoes), turned wooden bowls and much evidence for their manufacture. Animal bones indicated a farming economy that relied heavily on raising cattle, with fewer sheep and pigs. Horse bones showed signs of butchery, perhaps indicating that eating horse meat was not totally prohibited in earliest times in the monastery. Red and roe deer, wild fowl and grey seals also formed part of the diet. Evidence from other archaeological work at Iona indicates the consumption of hake, cod and shellfish.

The large collection of stone sculpture – crosses, grave-markers and other commemorative monuments – is the most tangible link with the early monastery. They vary in size and form from smallish boulders to large rectangular slabs, upstanding stones and free-standing crosses ornamented on all their faces. There are over 100 pieces that date prior to the 12th century. Although close dating is not easy for most of them, expert opinion would assign many to the years from the foundation of the monastery to the early 9th century. Many of the best and most interesting pieces are now displayed in the Abbey Museum. There are several slabs with crosses of different designs. The simplest have incised designs; others are carved in low relief. Many of them would have served as grave-markers.

A few of the slabs have Latin or Irish inscriptions identifying the person commemorated, and in some cases specifically asking for prayers for the repose of their souls. One describes itself as the 'stone of Echodi' and may have marked the burial place of King Eochaid Buide, king of Kintyre from 609 until his death in 631 (Fig. 8). He was a son of King Áedán of the Corcu Reti (the kin

Figure 8. 'The Stone of Echodi' (no. 22), displayed in the Abbey Museum; a grave-marker with a 'Chi-rho' monogram, thought to commemorate a 7th-century king

group which later split into the Cenél nGabrain and the Cenél Comgaill). Adomnán tells how St Columba prophesised that he would succeed his father as king, instead of three elder brothers who would all die in battle. Eochaid had been called to the saint's presence and demonstrated that he was the chosen one of God by rushing directly into his arms. Two other slabs carved with ringed crosses, from the paving in front of St Columba's Shrine-chapel, have Irish inscriptions seeking prayers for 9th-century abbots, Loingsechán and Flann mac Maíle-dúin (Fig. 9).

Adomnán describes how a cross was set up, fixed in a millstone at the roadside, where St Columba took a rest in the very last days

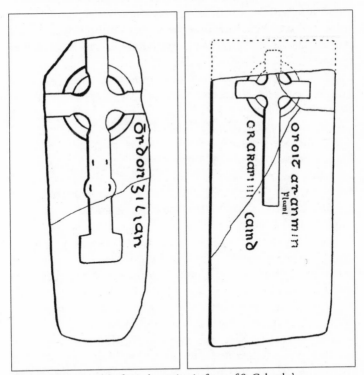

Figure 9. Two cross-slabs from the paving in front of St Columba's Shrine-chapel with inscriptions seeking prayers for 9th-century abbots, Loingsechán and Flann mac Maíle-dúin (Allen and Anderson 1903, vol. 2, figs 416, 415). They are displayed in the Abbey Museum (nos 47, 46)

of his life, and there is other evidence, including the cross-base on Tòrr an Aba, for millstones being reused in this way. Several of the surviving monuments would have been intended to mark places where events took place. They might also have marked boundaries or places where pilgrims, clerics and others were encouraged to stop and pray. The so-called 'high crosses' of Iona, large pieces of free-standing monumental sculpture dating from the late 8th to the 10th century, would certainly have served the latter function. It has been supposed that many early monuments, especially larger crosses, were carved in wood. None such survive, but it is certainly the case that three of the Iona high crosses, St Oran's, St John's and St Martin's (Plate 14), have constructional features more typical of woodworking than stone, suggesting that they are a translation from one medium into the other. These features include the mortice and tenon joints holding arms and shafts together and the composite base of St John's Cross.

St John's Cross is of particular importance, not just as an outstanding piece of sculpture, but because it appears to be the origin of one of the most enduring and iconic cross designs, the ringed cross, associated with the church in Scotland and Ireland and Celtic Art in general. The ring around the head of St John's Cross was added soon after it was first erected in the 8th century, primarily as an attempt to strengthen and repair the original composite structure (Fig. 10). The result was visually attractive and the idea caught on. Soon other free-standing crosses like the one at Kildalton in Islay were carved with rings, even though it is of monolithic construction, and ringed-cross designs are to be found engraved and carved on slabs. The idea of ringed crosses spread rapidly to Ireland as well where several free-standing high crosses are of that form.

Other treasures that belonged on Iona are now dispersed elsewhere. They include the *Cathach*, a manuscript of about 600 which is believed to have been the work of Columba himself. It is now in the Royal Irish Academy in Dublin. Most famous of all is the *Book of Kells*, an outstanding gospel book illuminated in insular style, now in Trinity College, Dublin. Few scholars doubt that it was produced in Iona in the 8th century and only taken to Kells with other treasures after the devastating Viking raids against Iona.

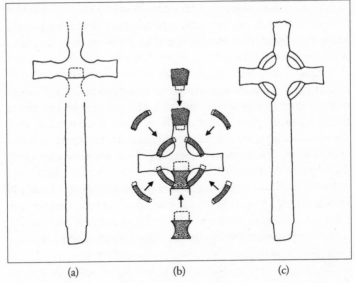

Figure 10. St John's Cross (no. 82), diagram showing, (a) its original ringless design and, (c) its modified form as the first ringed cross by the addition of, (b) four quadrants of a ring, a separate lower arm and top piece for the cross-head (based on RCAHMS 1982). The surviving pieces of the cross are exhibited in the Abbey Museum. A replica is positioned where the original stood, to the west of the abbey church

At issue, however, is to what extent it was a completed work when it crossed over to Ireland and to what extent it was worked upon at Kells.

SCANDINAVIAN RAIDERS AND SETTLERS

Iona's wealth and status unfortunately attracted unwelcome attention. The first recorded Viking raid on it occurred in 795 and others followed in 802 and 806. In 806 the whole community of monks, 68 in all, were murdered, and in 825 the abbot, Blathmac, was martyred there. Iona survived as an important monastic centre but was superseded as the main centre of the Columban *parochia* of churches by Kells in Ireland, founded in 807. The church at

Dunkeld in Scotland, also founded in the early 9th century, became the centre of the Columban church in Scotland, and the treasures of Iona that survived the Viking looting were dispersed to these two centres.

Viking raids on the Western Isles and elsewhere in Britain and Ireland from the 790s were primarily about looting. These pagan pirates from Scandinavia had clinker-built longships, technically of a high standard. They had the skill and confidence to undertake long sea voyages under sail. They also rowed them far up rivers or carried them over land from one stretch of water to another. A Frankish source records that in 847 these Northmen gained control of the islands all round Ireland. This should probably be understood to include the Hebrides where place-name and archaeological evidence suggests settlement by these newcomers. A recent study of the place-names of Islay by Alan Macniven, paying particular attention to the prevalence and distribution of names of Norse origin, has led him to conclude that that island was subjected to something akin to ethnic cleansing by these invaders. Similar traumas were no doubt visited on other neighbouring islands.

In the case of Mull, the evidence for Scandinavian impact is certainly discernible through a study of place-names. There are names that clearly have a Norse origin, like Aros ('river mouth'), Assapol ('farm of the rocky ridge'), Carsaig ('brushwood bay'), Scarisdale ('Skari's dale') and Sunipol ('Suni's farm'). The Mull place-names of Norse origin appear fewer in number than those in other neighbouring islands like Islay and Tiree. It is possible this picture may change with more scholarship. Some farm names containing the element 'penny' reflect a system dating back to Scandinavian times when large units of land were assessed at a penny for purposes of taxation. The names themselves, like Penmore ('the big pennyland') and Pennycross ('the pennyland of the cross'), are Gaelic in origin.

A particularly interesting place-name of Norse origin is Gruline, situated on a narrow neck of land between the head of Loch Bà and the sea at Loch na Keal. The name has been interpreted as meaning the assembly place (*thing*) in stony ground. *Thing* places are found throughout the Scandinavian world, and Gruline, centrally placed in Mull, would have been an appropriate one for the whole island. There is a crannog at the head of Loch Bà, apparently occupied in the mid 16th century and possibly much earlier, and amongst the adjacent prehistoric monuments is a cairn on top of a prominent knoll known as Càrn Bàn (Plate 16). Mounds are a feature of other early assembly sites. While there can be little doubt that the cairn is a Bronze Age funerary monument, the similarity of this situation – a natural mound crowned by a cairn – may also be compared with Cnoc Seannda at Finlaggan in Islay, where it is supposed inauguration ceremonies for kings and lords of the Isles took place.

The archaeological evidence for settlement by the Norse is also rather limited. One or more oval Viking brooches are said to have been recovered from Mull, possibly indicating a high-status female burial, but there is no clear evidence of pagan burials with grave goods and the remains of boats, as found elsewhere in the Hebrides, and the houses of any early settlers have still to be identified and excavated. Similarly, with the notable exceptions of Iona and Baliscate (5.1), it is difficult to identify churches and other Christian monuments in Mull prior to the 12th century. Paganism amongst Scandinavian settlers is unlikely to have lingered much longer than the 10th century. A cross-shaft of that date displayed in the Abbey Museum has a long ship with central mast full of armed warriors. Above is a smith with his tools and to the right an animal identifiable as an otter (Fig. 11). The smith was presumably Regan, who forged Sigurd's sword. The otter is Otr in disguise. It was compensation for his death that provided the gold hoard and ring eventually acquired by Sigurd. These representations are hardly appropriate, it might be thought, for a type of monument which otherwise would have been deemed as Christian.

The question remains for Mull and Iona, to what extent the lack of evidence for Scandinavian settlement reflects an underlying reality or the lack of research in modern times at identifying its presence. The folk of Mull would have become part of a hybrid Norse/Gaelic society in the 9th and 10th centuries, linked with a great network of Scandinavian communities, on a major sea route stretching from Dublin to Norway and beyond. Their inhabitants owed no allegiance to the kings of the Scots. Lip-service, at least, would have been paid from time to time to the ultimate authority

Figure 11. A cross-shaft (no. 95) of the 10th century with a longship with central mast full of armed warriors. Above is a smith with his tools and to the right an otter. It is exhibited in the Abbey Museum

of the kings of Norway, but more local leadership would have been provided by 'lawmen'. Lawmen were men well versed in legal matters and were the spokesmen at local assemblies.

Irish annals relating to the late 10th century provide some evidence of political control in the Hebrides, probably including Mull and Iona. In 980 Amlaíb Cúarán (Olaf Sihtricsson), previously king of Scandinavian York and Dublin, retired to Iona. He probably also controlled many of the Hebrides. He was succeeded by Gofraid mac Arailt, a notable warrior in the Irish Sea region, described as king of the islands of the Gaill (the Hebrides). It is possible that an attack by 'Danish' raiders on Iona at Christmas 986, in which the abbot and other churchmen were killed, was part of a wider campaign to establish his kingship, one which came to an end three years later when he died at the hands of the men of Dál Riata. Gofraid mac Arailt was succeeded as King of the Isles by his son Ragnall, who was probably a client of King Brian Bóruma of Munster by the time of his death in 1004 or 1005. Other sources suggest that the powerful Norse earls of Orkney were by this time extending their authority in to the Hebrides. Their local man in the late 10th century was 'Earl Gilli', based in Coll, or perhaps more probably, Colonsay. There is disagreement amongst place-name experts as to which island is meant by the name which appears in early sources as Colosus. There is also some evidence for the kings of Alba (Scotland) taking an interest in the west in the early 11th century, including, perhaps, a military campaign in the Isles.

Two coin hoards have been discovered. One deposited about 986 near Iona Abbey consisted of over 360 silver coins, mostly Anglo-Saxon, along with a silver ingot, a piece of gold rod and a fragmentary finger ring. It is possible it was buried to escape being taken by the 'Danish' raiders who landed in 986. The other was deposited about 1000 in Inch Kenneth and consisted of 24 Anglo-Saxon, Danish, Hiberno-Danish and foreign coins, along with a fragment of silver wire chain.

5. The Kingdom and Lordship of the Isles: The Medieval Period

THE KINGDOM OF THE ISLES

The Kingdom of the Isles consisted of the Isle of Man and the islands off the west coast of Scotland, including the islands of Arran, Bute and the Cumbraes in the Firth of Clyde, prior to their capture by the Scots at unknown dates, certainly by 1204 in the case of Bute. Even parts of the mainland, including Kintyre, the Rhinns of Galloway and Glenelg, were at times under the sway of kings of the Isles, as well as the important Scandinavian town of Dublin in Ireland.

The origins of the Kingdom of the Isles extend back, as we have just seen, to the 10th century, but its earlier history, prior to 1079, is poorly documented. In that year Godred Crovan, possibly either a son or nephew of Ímar mac Arailt who ruled Dublin from 1038 to 1046, captured the Isle of Man and established a dynasty of kings that ruled in Man and the Isles until 1265. The Kingdom of the Isles has been seen as Scandinavian, and indeed it was part of a wider Scandinavian world. Much of the population was descended from 9th-century settlers from Norway and its kings (at least of Godred Crovan's line) were of Norwegian stock. The Kingdom of the Isles was briefly annexed by King Magnus Barelegs of Norway in 1098. The saga account of his expedition through the Isles provides the colourful detail that the people of Mull ran to exhaustion, but in Iona he gave peace and quarter to all men. He had Columba's church – St Columba's Shrine-chapel? (Plate 11) – opened but refused to go in, and then forbade that anyone else should do so. There was no follow-up after his death in 1103 by his successors as kings of Norway to retain the Kingdom of the Isles or maintain royal overlordship over it. The latter only came about in 1152/3 because Godred, son of King Olaf of the Isles, went to Norway to seek support from King Ingi. The price of Norwegian overlordship was a feudal relief of ten gold marks on the accession of every Norwegian king. Norwegian royal expeditionary forces were sent to the Isles in 1230 and 1263 and kings, bishops and nobles from the Isles are recorded as having made visits to the Norwegian court.

The Kingdom of the Isles was small in geographic extent and in terms of population, perhaps at most about 50,000. Its natural resources were also rather limited, although there is evidence for the mining of lead in Man and Islay and for cattle rearing, both activities providing income in more recent times. It has been surmised that a major source of wealth for the kingdom was the provision of mercenary services to kings and lords in other parts of the British Isles, and also piracy. Clinker-built longships, now provided with stern-mounted rudders, provided fast and efficient transport for large bodies of warriors.

Early documentary sources for the kingdom focus on internal dissensions and civil wars, especially those which involved Somerled, a prince with his power base in Argyll, and his descendants (Gen. Table I, p. 221). Some later historians have interpreted these in terms of a struggle between the Scandinavian kings descended from Godred Crovan and a resurgent Gaelic society led by Somerled. This is undoubtedly an oversimplification of complex issues and events, but there was a re-emergence of Gaelic by the 11th century, replacing Norse as the dominant language within the kingdom, perhaps no earlier than the 13th century. It then remained the language of Mull and Iona until it was gradually replaced by English from the 19th century.

The kingdom was usurped in 1156 by Somerled. After his death in 1164 in battle near Renfrew, several of his descendants, known collectively as the MacSorleys, appear with the title 'king' and this has been interpreted to mean that there were two rival dynasties ruling different parts of the kingdom, with the descendants of Godred Crovan holding Man and Lewis and the MacSorleys most or all of the other islands.

The sources, however, do not make it clear to what extent the MacSorleys were over-mighty or rebellious subjects of kings of the Godred Crovan dynasty or kings of a separate kingdom within the Isles. The situation is complicated by the fact that Somerled and his descendants owed allegiance to the kings of Scots for mainland territories. The failure of the Norwegian invasion in 1263 and the subsequent Treaty of Perth in 1266, by which Norway ceded Man and the Hebrides to Scotland, meant that the Isles became part of that latter country and henceforth were treated as marginal when viewed from royal administrative bases in the east Lowlands. There was little political sympathy for their culture and language, and most Isles' lords and chiefs did not find it easy to, or chose not to, integrate with mainstream Scottish life. The limited evidence, historical and archaeological, for Argyll and the islands in the later 13th century suggests that the Scots were slow or unable to impose their authority on their new territories and fully integrate them into the Kingdom of Scotland. The Isle of Man was effectively annexed by England from 1333. The Hebrides, from about the same time until 1493, were formed into a lordship of the Isles.

THE LORDSHIP OF THE ISLES

The Lords of the Isles, the MacDonalds, with their main base of power in Islay, were by the mid 14th century the most powerful kindred descended from Somerled. They were granted lands, including Mull, which had previously been MacDougall territory but were forfeited by them as a result of their support of the English cause in the Wars of Independence. Through marriage to Amy, sister of Ranald, the head of the MacRuairi kindred about 1337, and the subsequent murder of Ranald by the Earl of Ross in 1346, John I Lord of the Isles also acquired the extensive island and mainland territories of the MacRuairis. MacDonald lordship thus extended over all the Hebrides and large areas of the western mainland. In the 15th century they came into possession of the vast earldom of Ross, and a branch of the family held significant estates in Antrim in Ireland. Their power and patronage extended throughout the Highlands and further afield in Ireland. John I was succeeded as lord by his son Donald, his grandson Alexander, and his great grandson John II. Their lordship was underpinned by the continued militarisation of the Isles and control of the western seas.

The MacDonalds did aspire to kingship and the re-creation of a kingdom of the Isles, but their take on these was probably significantly different from the kings and kingdom prior to 1266. In any case, the story of the MacDonalds is normally seen as one of a recalcitrant or rebellious clan that had to be dominated and civilised by central authority. In 1493 John II Lord of the Isles was forfeited, and this marked the end of the Lordship. It had been brought about by MacDonald intransigence, internal squabbling and considerable pressure exerted by the bellicose King James IV.

MULL FAMILIES IN MEDIEVAL TIMES

It is difficult to identify any Mull family with a presence in the island prior to the 12th century. Mull was the home of three important clans – the MacDougalls, MacKinnons and Macleans, all of whom are discussed below. There were, of course, also several other kindreds who left less of a mark on local or national history, like the MacFadyens, who are said to have been evicted from Lochbuy to make way for the Macleans, and the MacGillivrays, long associated with Pennyghael. The MacQuarries, or Clan Guaire, held the island of Ulva and the adjacent part of Mull by 1461, and probably a lot earlier, down to the 1770s. They are descended from Guaire, son of Cormac, son of Airbertach who flourished in the later 12th century, possibly in Knapdale on the Argyll mainland. Angus Og, the MacDonald leader at the time of King Robert Bruce in the early 14th century, is said to have made the then chief of the MacQuarries a thane. Major-General Lachlan Macquarie, Governor of New South Wales from 1810 to 1821, whose mausoleum is at Gruline (6.41) was of this family.

An English visitor (William Sacheverell) to Iona in 1688 noted that the majority of the villagers there seemed to be called Mac-en-Oysters. Martin Martin, a few years later, described them as the Clan vic n'oster. They claimed descent from a door-keeper (Latin, *ostiarius*) of the monastery appointed by Columba himself. They died out in the 18th century.

Other families of importance included those with hereditary skills and responsibilities like the poets and seannachies of the Macleans of Duart, the Ó Muirgheasains (Morisons) in the 17th century and earlier, and the Rankins (Clann Duiligh), already a well-established family of pipers by the late 17th century. There was a harper who held Fanmore on the shore of Loch Tuath from Maclean of Duart, by virtue of his office, at the time the Duart estates were acquired by the Earl of Argyll. He was apparently from a family of harpers in Caliach in Mornish.

Angus Og, the leader of the MacDonalds, married Áine, a daughter of the chief of the Ó Catháns of Keenaght in Ireland, some time in the late 13th century. A retinue of men, including the ancestors of several Highland families, came with her to Scotland. Prominent amongst these was a medical kindred, many of whom were to adopt the surname Macbeth or Beaton. The family were first settled in Islay but branches spread elsewhere including one which settled in the 16th century at Pennycross in Brolass. In 1572 Hector Maclean of Duart granted Gille-Anndrais ('Andrew MacDonel vik inoldif') the lands of Pennycross and the supreme and principal office of surgeon within all his territories. His descendants continued to practise as medical experts and to hold Pennycross as late as the 1760s. It was probably his son, Malcolm, who was the 'Dr Beaton, the famous physician of Mull' who had a remarkable escape in 1588 when the Spanish Armada ship anchored in Tobermory Bay blew up. He is said to have been sitting on the ship's upper deck but was blown clear by the force of the explosion.

There was another Beaton family of medical experts based at Dervaig in the north of Mull. They seem to have been of long standing by the 16th century and a descendant, James Beaton, was still practising in Mull in the 1770s. Several Gaelic manuscripts survive that belonged to both Mull branches of the family, many of them in the National Library of Scotland, and there is a cross at Pennycross associated with the Beatons of Pennycross (Plate 17).

THE MACDOUGALLS

The MacDougalls took their name from Dugald, (the eldest?) son of Somerled (Gen. Table 1). About 1155 an Isles' chief, Thorfin son of Ottar, dissatisfied with the tyranny of King Godred, persuaded Somerled to put forward Dugald, perhaps then under age, as king in place of Godred. Dugald was taken on a progress through the Isles to gain their allegiance, but when King Godred became aware of this he gathered a fleet to deal with this usurper. He was opposed by a fleet commanded by Somerled. After a sea battle, which is said to have taken place on the night of Epiphany (8 January) 1156, Godred and Somerled agreed to divide the kingdom between them. Nothing more is heard of Dugald until much later, and two years afterwards Somerled attacked Godred in the Isle of Man and forced him into exile in Norway. He only returned to regain his kingdom in 1165 after Somerled's death.

The MacSorleys continued to hold large parts of the kingdom. It is believed that Dugald's share included Mull and the neighbouring islands of Coll and Tiree, and that he also possessed the large mainland territory of Lorn. It was probably Dugald who was largely responsible for having a new diocese of Argyll created in the 1180s with the seat of the bishop in the island of Lismore. The bishops' authority extended over all of Dugald's mainland territories, but not Mull and Iona, which were included in the Diocese of the Isles established more than a hundred years earlier. Moreover, the Bishops of the Isles came under the metropolitan authority of the Archbishops of Nidaros (Trondheim) in Norway from 1153.

In 1230 King Hakon IV of Norway sent an expedition to the Isles, probably with the dual intention of opposing increased interference in his sphere of interest by the Scots and to sort out internal problems in the Isles caused by fighting between the MacSorleys and the Manx-based kings descended from Godred Crovan. The leader chosen for this expedition was Uspak, possibly a son of Dugald, who may have been intended to take the Kingship of the Isles himself. When Uspak rendezvoused with his supposed brothers, Duncan and Dugald Screech, and another relative called Somerled, somewhere on the Sound of Islay, there was a falling out. Somerled was killed and Dugald taken prisoner. Uspak apparently restored some sort of peace by letting Duncan escape and taking Dugald into his protection. He then moved on to besiege and capture Rothesay Castle, built by the Scottish Stewart family in the Isle of Bute, previously part of the Kingdom of the Isles, but otherwise the expedition did not achieve its aims, and Uspak fell ill and died. It was in either 1230 or the following year that Duncan founded a religious house at Ardchattan on Loch Etive in mainland Argyll for Valliscaulian monks. Significant parts of it are still upstanding, now in the care of Historic Environment Scotland.

The MacDougalls remained a power in the Isles, and in 1248 Ewen, son of Duncan, was picked to be king by King Hakon of Norway in Bergen, in preference to his distant relative Dugald (MacRuairi). The extent of his regal power is not clear. Possibly it was only to cover those parts of the kingdom possessed by the MacSorleys, including the Mull and Islay groups of islands, and was recognition by Hakon that the kings descended from Godred Crovan had failed to provide effective rule throughout the Hebrides.

Meanwhile, when King Alexander II of Scotland discovered that Ewen, one of the barons of his realm, had been raised to kingship by Hakon, he reacted in fury, leading an army over to Argyll in 1249 to bring Ewen to heel. Although Alexander became ill and died on the island of Kerrara off Oban, and the Scottish expedition had to be abandoned, Ewen was still forced into resigning his kingship, which was soon taken up by his rival Dugald MacRuairi. Ewen, however, was in the Isle of Man in 1250, apparently trying unsuccessfully to have his kingship of the Isles recognised. In 1253 he and Dugald joined King Hakon's expedition against Denmark and in 1255, thanks to the intervention of King Henry III of England, he was restored to his lands in Argyll.

In 1263 Ewen was again put under enormous pressure because of his allegiances to two competing kings. During his invasion in that year King Hakon called for the support of King Magnus of Man and the MacSorley chiefs – Angus (MacDonald) of Islay, King Dugald and Ewen himself. Only Ewen refused, on the basis that he held more of the Scots king than he did of the Norwegian. He asked Hakon to dispose of the dominion he had given him. How this, and the subsequent acquisition of the Isles by the Scots in 1266, affected the MacDougall hold in Mull, if at all, is not known. Ewen died about 1268 and was succeeded by his son Alexander, who was clearly prepared to embrace the new political order. In 1275 he was one of the commanders of a Scottish force sent to suppress an uprising in the Isle of Man and in 1293, when King John (Balliol) established three new sheriffdoms in the west, he was appointed sheriff of one of them, probably including the Mull and Islay groups of islands.

Alexander also appears twice in the records because of his interest in trade. In 1275 King Alexander III wrote on his behalf to Edward I of England seeking release of his ship and men detained at Bristol, and in 1292 he was given a licence by Edward I to trade in Ireland. His lordship of Lorn paid a red mantle, probably of wool, to the king every year in return for holding the land, and it may have been such textiles as well as cattle and animal products that he had to trade for imports of wine, manufactured goods and luxury food.

The main power base of the MacDougalls in the 13th century was probably Dunstaffnage Castle in mainland Argyll, near present-day Oban. They also held the island fortresses of Cairn na Burgh More, Cairn na Burgh Beg (also known collectively as Cairnburgh Castle) and Dun Chonnuill. Alexander MacDougall probably erected the castle of Achanduin in the island of Lismore about 1300. There is considerable uncertainty, however, about where they were based in Mull. The two obvious candidates are the castles of Aros (Plate 18) and Duart (Plate 19, Fig. 12), both on the Sound of Mull. The impressive hall-house at Aros is later in date than the

Figure 12. Duart Castle (MacGibbon and Ross 1887–92, vol. 3)

enclosure castle at Duart and, it might be surmised, was erected as a new lordly residence at a time when Duart was no longer available or suitable for such a purpose, for instance because it had been confiscated or had a garrison installed in it by the Scots sometime in the years between 1263 and 1293. If both castles were Mac-Dougall strongholds it is difficult to offer any other explanation as to why there was a need for both of them so close together, both overlooking the same stretch of water.

There is evidence of a falling-out between the MacDougalls and the MacDonalds despite, or because of, a marriage between the chief of the MacDonalds, Alexander Og, and Alexander MacDougall's daughter Juliana, prior to 1291. The married couple had to try and seek redress from King John when Juliana's father failed to hand over dower lands in Lismore, and when that failed, go over the Scottish's king head to Edward I of England in 1295. In 1297 Alexander Og, then in English service, complained to the English king that Alexander MacDougall had devastated his lands and killed his people, and two years later there are records of yet more slaughter of the MacDonalds by the MacDougalls.

In the independence struggle that saw Robert Bruce crowned as King of Scots in 1306, the MacDonalds changed sides to support the new king and the MacDougalls switched their allegiance to the English, largely because Bruce had murdered John Comyn, a MacDougall ally and kinsman. The MacDougalls were thus notable losers as Bruce consolidated his position and defeated the English. Alexander MacDougall's son John (succeeded 1310) almost prevented Bruce's escape westward in 1306 when he opposed his small force at Dalrigh in Argyll, but in 1308 Bruce turned the tables on John, securing a major victory over the MacDougalls at Ben Cruachan, and the surrender of Dunstaffnage Castle. John, however, escaped and continued in English service along with at least two of his sons. On more than one occasion he was appointed an admiral of English fleets and recaptured the Isle of Man for the English in 1315. He died on pilgrimage to Canterbury in the following year. A grandson of John MacDougall, John *Gallda* ('the foreigner'), re-established the family in Argyll in the 1350s with very much reduced power and influence, but they had lost their Mull lands forever.

THE MACKINNONS

The Clan Finguine were a powerful kindred in early times. They held Mishnish in Mull, where they had a castle at Dun Ara (Fig. 13), as well as other lands in Tiree and Skye. An agreement in 1354 between John I Lord of the Isles and John Gallda MacDougall contains the condition that the former will never give custody of the castle of Cairnburgh to any member of Clan Finguine, which surely hints at some power struggle between the MacKinnons and MacDougalls in earlier times. In Mull they lost ground to the Macleans in the 14th and 15th centuries. Later tradition identifies the MacKinnon as marshall of the army of the Lord of the Isles, but if the Mackinnon chiefs were the military strongmen in the Lordship they were superseded by the Macleans. A curious tale in a 17th-century MacDonald history has 'MacFinnon' as master of the household of the MacDonald insult the sons of Gillean (the early Macleans), who then stabbed him. The reputation of the MacKinnons was also blackened by the life and doings of Abbot Finguine MacKinnon of Iona, a younger brother of the MacKinnon chief. He was known as the 'Green Abbot' of Iona, from *c.*

Figure 13. Dun Ara Castle

1357 to *c*. 1408. He was complained of to Rome for his scandalous living with a concubine, to whose children he gave many of the abbey's possessions. He is also said to have been behind the rebellion of John Mor MacDonald against his elder brother, Donald Lord of the Isles, for which the MacKinnon chief was executed. Despite this, the Green Abbot's son, also called Finguine, became prior of the abbey and John MacKinnon, son of a later chief, was abbot in the later 15th century. His effigy is in the choir of Iona Abbey (Fig. 56).

Finguine, the eponym of the clan, was the brother of Guaire, commemorated in the surname of the MacQuarries. They apparently flourished in the 13th century, and Finguine's ancestors are supposed to have spread westwards from Knapdale into Mull about 1160, at the same time as Somerled and his descendants were consolidating their position in the Kingdom of the Isles. There is a fine warrior effigy at Iona that records the names of several MacKinnon chiefs (Fig. 14). It was commissioned for, or by, Gille-Brigde (Brice) MacKinnon, who may have fought at Bannockburn in 1314. It shows him holding an upright spear, presumably shortened to fit neatly on the slab, and with a sword tucked in his belt. He is clad in an aketon – a quilted, protective coat covered in hide or leather. The sleeves have elbow bands to help provide more flexibility to the arms. On his head he wears a basinet, a simple iron helmet, with a mail coif or aventail covering his neck and shoulders. His hands are protected with metal gauntlets and straps round his ankles probably indicate he is wearing spurs. His legs and feet are possibly also protected by armour. On his left arm he is holding a shield decorated with a heraldic device of a galley with a lion and an otter and a salmon below.

This image of a warrior can be related to an Act of Parliament of 1318 concerning arming in time of war. This act may be supposed to result from King Robert I's experience of warfare, and be designed to produce the warriors with the type of kit that had led to his remarkable military successes. All men with goods worth £10, that is, those of reasonable prosperity, were to have an aketon, basinet, gloves of plate, a spear and a sword, or else a habergeon (mail coat), a hat of iron and gloves of plate. Gille-Brigde is demonstrating that he was such a warrior, and it is worth recalling that the

Figure 14. Warrior effigy commissioned for, or by, Gille-Brigde (Brice) MacKinnon, who may have fought at Bannockburn in 1314 (Brydall 1898). It is displayed in the Abbey Museum (no. 207)

core of King Robert's army at the battle of Loudoun Hill in 1307, where he won his first significant victory, consisted of Islesmen and Irish contingents. Gille-Brigde's shield, however, may not reflect reality, but merely be an artistic device to show off his heraldry.

The chief of the MacKinnons is listed as one of the four 'thanes', leaders of lesser rank than lords and leaders of the main MacDonald kindreds, who sat in the Council of the Isles that advised the Lord of the Isles and governed on his behalf. They were also said to have been responsible for seeing that weights and measures were adjusted.

THE MACLEANS (CLANN GILL-EATHAIN)

Mull is the heartland of Clan Gillean – the Macleans – one of the most distinguished clans of medieval times (Gen. Table 2, p. 222). They may have originated as one of the hereditary learned families of the Gaelic world. The clan eponym, Gille-eoin, seems to have flourished about the later 12th or earlier 13th century. His descendants' rise to power was aided by advantageous marriages, the first by his grandson Gille-Coluim to a daughter of the native earls of Carrick in the 13th century. Later clan tradition identifies the early Macleans as supporters of the MacDougalls but contemporary documentation indicates that the sons of Gille-Coluim were supporters of Robert Bruce, providing at least one ship for his service in 1326. Possibly they already had lands in Knapdale and Kintyre, and there may have been a marriage alliance between Gille-Coluim's son John and one of the MacDonalds, key Bruce supporters.

The exact circumstances of the Macleans' arrival in Mull are difficult to disentangle from later traditions, some frankly unlikely, and a general lack of authoritative early sources. The key documents are three charters by Donald Lord of the Isles to Lachlan Lubanach (Gaelic, 'wily'), son of John, son of Gille-Coluim, all dated 12 July 1390. The lands, rights and offices given are very extensive, amounting, it would seem, to a considerable part of the heritage in the Isles of the MacDougalls, not just in Mull but also in Jura, Tiree and elsewhere, the keeping and constable-ship of the castles of Cairn na Burgh More and Cairn na Burgh Beg in the Treshnish Isles (5.13) and of Dun Chonnuill Castle in the Garvellachs, the offices of fragramannach and armannach in the island of Iona (meaning that they would be stewards of the lands there), and the position of steward in the household of the Lord of the

Isles. Duart Castle in Mull (Plate 19) was the prime piece of property and it was from it that Lachlan and his descendants were to take their territorial designation. Although these grants were very generous, and must demonstrate Donald's high opinion of Lachlan, it might appear surprising that Lachlan had to wait so long to be rewarded in this way. After all, by 1390 he had been married to Mary, Donald's sister, for some 23 years. These grants are only known from royal confirmations of 1495, but the one giving Duart Castle and most of the Mull lands includes the statement that all other rights were included as granted by Donald's father (John I Lord of the Isles, died *c.* 1387). It is, therefore, probable that this grant at least updates a previous one made by John I. There is a tradition that the wedding between Lachlan and Mary took place at Knockantivore on the bank of Loch Bà. The Macleans of Duart were to remain loyal supporters of the Lords of the Isles and retained their status as the leading branch of Clan Gillean.

Lachlan's brother, Hector Reaganach, was the founder of one of the other main branches, the Macleans (or Maclaines) of Lochbuie. He is said to have been given 80-mark lands by the Lord of the Isles. (In medieval Scotland, the value of lands was assessed in terms of marks, a mark being two-thirds of a pound, as a basis of paying dues, rents, taxes, etc.) Certainly, by the 1490s the family held extensive lands of the Lord of the Isles, including in Jura and Morvern, but particularly in Mull, including lands in Torosay Parish, Ardmeanach and around Loch Buie and Loch Spelve. Their main residence was Moy Castle (Fig. 15) at the head of Loch Buie, possibly erected by Hector Reaganach. It was superseded by (Old) Lochbuie House in the mid 18th century. The Lochbuie family long retained a significant relic of medieval times in the form of a large, circular, silver-gilt brooch, decorated with small bosses, and filigree work. Ten turrets set with river pearls surround a central capsule set with a large rock crystal. It is West Highland work of about 1500 and may have been a badge of office. It is now in the British Museum in London. A less elaborate silver medieval brooch, decorated with niello, animals and flowers, and a repeated black letter inscription – *ihcn* (an abbreviation for Jesus of Nazareth) – was found at Kengharair in Mull (Fig. 16).

Figure 15. (Right) Moy
Castle (MacGibbon and
Ross 1887–92, vol. 3)

Figure 16. (Below) Silver
brooch of about 1500,
decorated with niello,
animals and flowers, and
a repeated black letter
inscription – *ihcn* (an
abbreviation for Jesus of
Nazareth) – found at
Kengharair in Mull
(from *Proc Soc Antiq Scot*
28, 1893–94)

Another important branch of Clan Gillean was the Macleans
of Coll, descended from Lachlan, a younger son of Lachlan
Lubanach of Duart. Their main residence was Breacachadh Castle
on the island of Coll, but they also held the land of Quinish in
Mull. The history of Mull from the late 14th century onwards is
one largely about the Macleans, not that they always acted as a
cohesive clan or did not have major interests elsewhere in the
islands and on the mainland of Scotland.

'Red Hector of the Battles', Lachlan Lubanach's son and heir, is remembered as one of the heroes of the battle of Harlaw in 1411, when an army from the Lordship of the Isles squared up to a royal army under the Earl of Mar near Inverurie in Aberdeenshire. Hector is said to have engaged one of the enemy leaders, Sir Alexander Irvine of Drum, in single combat, killing him but dying in the process. The battle has traditionally been seen as an epic, bloody clash between the Lowlands and the Highlands with the latter seen off, since the forces of the Lordship left Mar in control of the battlefield. The Lords of the Isles, however, achieved their objective of retaining control of the earldom of Ross.

As the Lordship of the Isles disintegrated in the late 15th century the Macleans remained loyal to John II Lord of the Isles in opposition to Angus Og and other leaders of Clan Donald. There was a naval engagement between the two sides – 'the battle of Bloody Bay' – fought near Tobermory, Mull, perhaps in 1484. John II and his supporters came off worse, Hector Odhar Maclean of Duart being captured.

In the 16th century the Macleans of Duart emerged as one of the most powerful clans in the West Highlands and Islands, sometimes in rebellion against the Crown, sometimes courted by monarchs in both Edinburgh and London, keen for their support locally and also in Ireland, where the Macleans were one of the main contractors able to provide fighting men for the wars. Hector Odhar was one of the main backers of Donald Dubh in his attempt to claim the Lordship of the Isles. Donald Dubh was the son of Angus Og and had been kept in custody since his father's death by the Earl of Argyll, who, if Donald was legitimate, was his grandfather. King James IV sent ships to bombard the Maclean stronghold of Cairnburgh Castle. Duart was forfeited as a traitor and John Maclean of Lochbuy was amongst those chiefs summoned to answer for his treasonable activities. In 1505, as a result of further royal expeditions into the west, the rebellion began to peter out. Duart, Lochbuy, and many of the other chief backers of Donald Dubh submitted, although the rebellion was not finally over until the following year and the recapture of Donald Dubh.

The main branches of the Macleans did not always act together as a unified clan. In 1531 there was serious feuding between the

Macleans of Lochbuy and the Macleans of Duart that pulled in Clan Donald South, the Campbells and others. In 1533 Alan, son of Hector Maclean of Duart, received a remission for the killing of John, son of John Maclean of Lochbuy.

In 1533 Hector Mor, chief of the Macleans of Duart, along with Clan Donald South plundered the Isle of Man. An English warship, the *Mary Willoughby*, was captured and Hector Mor got credit for gifting her to King James V. In the summer of 1540 the king, with his chief men, sailed around Scotland in a well-armed fleet and visited the main Western Isles, including Mull, and rounded up the main chiefs in those parts. Thus James Mac-Donald, the chief of Clan Donald South, ended up in prison and a royal garrison was installed in his castle of Dunyvaig in Islay. Hector Mor may have got off relatively lightly.

As the century progressed, there were increasing signs of enmity between the Macleans and the MacDonalds. Much of it related to disputes over lands in Islay, and resulted in considerable violence between Angus MacDonald of Dunyvaig and Lachlan Mor Maclean of Duart. Their feud was to dominate events in the West Highlands in the second half of the 16th century. It reached a dramatic turning point in 1586 when Lachlan imprisoned Angus while on a good-will visit to Duart. He only secured his release on promising to hand over the Islay lands that Lachlan claimed. When the latter went to Islay to take possession of them he in turn was imprisoned by Angus, despite being his guest, and several of his men were murdered.

News of these events reached the Earl of Argyll, who was instrumental in securing the release of Lachlan. That, however, was by no means the end of the hostilities, for Lachlan soon returned to Islay while Angus was in Ireland, and burned a great part of it. Inevitably Angus then invaded Mull and Tiree, and Lachlan went on to waste the MacDonald lands in Kintyre. Hostilities spread to the lands of MacDonald and Maclean allies in the other islands. One of the most remarkable elements in this sorry story was the pressing of a force of 100 Spanish hagbutters (soldiers armed with long guns) and pieces of artillery into service by Lachlan to burn the islands of Canna, Rum, Eigg and Muck and besiege the house of Ardnamur-chan (Mingary Castle). The Spaniards were from one of the ships of the Spanish Armada, the *San Juan de Sicilia*, a large merchant ship from Ragusa (Dubrovnik in Croatia) which sought shelter in Tobermory Bay in September 1588. She blew up in mysterious circumstances a few weeks later prior to being ready to sail, leaving few tangible signs of her stay on the seabed of Tobermory Bay, despite several efforts over the years to locate salvageable material. The cessation of hostilities was only brought about after King James VI summoned Angus and Lachlan to Edinburgh in 1591. Despite assurances, they were both imprisoned in Edinburgh Castle, but released soon afterwards on paying remissions. In the years that followed Lachlan was more successful than Angus in winning support for his cause, particularly from the increasingly powerful Campbells. In 1594 the chief of Clan Campbell, Archibald, Earl of Argyll, was tasked by King James VI with leading an army against the Earl of Huntly, and although it met defeat in battle at Glenlivet a significant role was played by Lachlan and his clan in supporting Argyll. Meanwhile Angus was being threatened with the confiscation of many of his lands by an increasingly exasperated monarch.

The king was not the only one to be infuriated by Angus, whose son, Sir James, had been held as a hostage in Edinburgh for his father's good behaviour since 1591. The king allowed him to go west in 1598. This resulted in him pursuing a course of action that would put him at the head of Clan Donald South in place of his father. Having burned Angus out of the house of Askomil in Kintyre and imprisoned him in irons, Sir James crossed to Islay to oppose the occupation of the Rhinns by Lachlan Maclean. Although Lachlan was actually Sir James' father-in-law, James may never have forgiven him for using him as a human shield when a child in 1586 and Lachlan was resisting being taken by Sir James' father. The forces of the two men met at Traigh Gruineart at the head of Loch Gruineart on 5 August 1598, and the Macleans were decisively beaten. Lachlan lost his life, and it is said that 80 of the chief men of his kin and 200 common soldiers also died, out of a force that was 600 strong.

King James may not have been unhappy to have Lachlan Maclean eliminated. There was no condemnation of Sir James for his death. Although the Macleans were not to make good their claims to Islay lands, the MacDonalds were also to be considerable losers, being deprived of their lands in Kintyre and Jura in 1607 and of Islay in 1614. The real winners were to be the Campbells, who gained both.

MULL AND IONA IN MEDIEVAL TIMES

After the 1493 forfeiture of the Lordship of the Isles an effort was made by King James IV to collect rents from Mull and other islands. The total 'extent' of Mull along with Ulva, Gometra, Inch Kenneth and Iona was 350 marks (£233 6s 8d). The lands which had been given or mortified to the Church in the past are identified in a rental of 1509, along with those estates held or rented by Maclean of Lochbuie, MacQuarrie and MacKinnon. Maclean of Duart was still forfeit and Cairnburgh Castle was being kept for the Crown by the Earl of Argyll. The estate of Aros, which had been retained by the Lord of the Isles, can also be identified. Within these estates, the farms held by leading tenants typically had an extent of 16 shillings and 8 pence (1¼ marks), the equivalent of a pennyland in a previous taxation system, imposed in Norse times, probably about 1000. In Iona and the Ross of Mull, however, each pennyland was valued at 6 shillings and 8 pence (½ mark), perhaps because the conversion from one system to another in the lands held by the Church was made at an earlier time.

A later royal rental of 1541 shows that rents were largely paid in kind in marts (cows), (oat)meal and cheese. A rental of the Ross of Mull in 1588 adds coal and lime, both of which do occur, though there is no evidence of them being mined or quarried. In 1549, Donald Monro, Archdeacon of the Isles, wrote a description of all the islands off the west coast of Scotland. He notes that although Mull was overall 'roch' (rough) and very hilly there was still a fair amount of fertile ground. There were woods and many deer, and salmon in the rivers, especially the River Forsa. Herring abounded in the waters round the coast. Iona was said to be good land for growing corn and grazing, and there was good (sea) fishing. He lists all the other islands adjacent to Mull, including the larger ones like Ulva and Gometra, and small islands like Soa and Eilean a' Chalmain, many of them occupied or used seasonally for grazing, fishing, etc.

Little is as yet known about medieval farming in Mull and Iona. Ordnance Survey maps and aerial photographs show networks of small irregular fields enclosed by turf dykes in some areas that have not been ploughed or enclosed in recent times. Good examples of this are at Cillchriosd in Mornish, to the east of the dun (3.13) on the bank of the Allt Cill Chriosd and to the south of the fort (3.1) at Cillchriosd, and also on the Torloisk estate extending along the northern shore of Loch Tuath between the road ((B8073) and the moors. The lands of Fanmore and Ballygown are included. Some of these field systems could originate in prehistoric times. It is likely that they represent a pattern of land use which continued into the 17th century.

In the Treshnish Islands Monro notes the two fortified rocky islands of Cairn na Burgh More and Cairn na Burgh Beg (5.13), both held by Maclean of Duart. Both islands are difficult of access, and although separated by a narrow, swift-flowing channel of the sea, both must have been intended to form one fortress. There are no remains on either obviously earlier than the ruined chapel (15th century?) on Cairn na Burgh More. Nevertheless, it seems reasonable to assume that as a fortress they date back to the time of the Kingdom of the Isles. For the Macleans of Duart they may have been a useful bolt-hole, but they could have originally been intended for monitoring sea traffic and levying customs. They were possibly one or two of the castles demanded by King Alexander II of Scotland from King Ewen (MacDougall) in 1249.

There were also, according to Monro, three castles – Duart (5.15), Aros (5.12) and Lochbuy (Moy – 5.20). He does not mention the MacKinnon stronghold of Dun Ara (5.16), possibly either because it was not then occupied or because it did not conform to his definition of a castle. He also fails to mention Dùn Bàn (5.17), a tidal island site in the narrow sound between Ulva and Gometra (NGR NM 384 416), apparently a seat of the MacQuarries, perhaps known as Glackingdaline Castle. It was connected to Ulva by a causeway and has the remains of a large drystone building, about 5.5m by 11.5m, with opposed entrances on its long sides.

Monro does, however, say there were two island dwellings in Mull. These can be identified as Caisteal Eòghainn a' Chinn Bhig in Loch Sguabain (5.14) and a crannog (artificial island) in Loch

Bà (NGR NM 554 389). Mull belonged partly to the Macleans of Duart, partly to the Macleans of Lochbuie and partly to the Mac-Kinnons. In earlier times some of the island had belonged to Clan Donald, and Monro also tells us that although Aros Castle was then in the possession of Maclean of Duart, it had previously belonged to the Lords of the Isles. After the forfeiture of John II Lord of the Isles in 1493 it had passed to the Crown and may well have been occupied soon afterwards, along with its lands, by the Macleans. Hector Maclean of Duart had his tenancy recognised by Mary of Guise after she became governor of Scotland in 1554.

The houses and homes of lower-status people have so far mostly eluded identification. There are several candidates, however, that merit further study, including the foundations of sub-rectangular houses beside Dun Ara Castle and others adjacent to Dùn na Muirgheidh (3.9). At Baliscate near Tobermory (5.1) a 12th-century kiln barn has been partially excavated. It appears to have consisted of a long building with rounded ends, its walls of turf and stone. The kiln inside had a bowl dug in the ground and lined with stone, heated by hot air drawn along a flue. It was used for drying grain.

Aros Castle, along with Finlaggan (an island dwelling) in Islay and Ardtornish Castle in Morvern, appear to have been the main centres in the Lordship occupied by the Lords of the Isles. As earls of Ross they also took up residence in Inverness and Dingwall. It may be supposed that with their household and a large retinue they progressed from one to the other, perhaps in a reasonably consistent pattern from year to year, largely by boat. Sailing up and down the Great Glen to Inverness would have required relatively few portages. Aros, Finlaggan and Ardtornish all have large feasting halls in common, and excavations at Finlaggan have demonstrated the presence of extensive kitchens. Traditional Highland lordship involved the conspicuous consumption of produce, the rents in kind paid by tenants to regional centres like Aros Castle.

By the 14th century there was a clear divide in Scottish society between the Highlands and Lowlands, and the Lords played a conspicuous role as leaders and patrons of Gaelic culture. They had their own hereditary doctors, poets and harpers, sponsored the erection of churches and the work of local sculptors. Finlaggan was the centre of power for the Lordship and is in many ways unique.

There are no comparable places elsewhere in the lands of the Lordship, and as a centre of power it is most unlike the great castles and burghs favoured by powerful lords elsewhere in Europe. It appears to be the result of a conscious policy to create a Celtic style of lordship, similar to that exercised by native lords in Ireland. It was at Finlaggan that the Council of the Isles met. This was a body composed of leaders of Clan Donald, other major clan chiefs and representatives from the different islands, along with leading churchmen. It was tasked with providing government and judicial decisions for the Lordship. Finlaggan was also the place where new Lords of the Isles underwent inauguration ceremonies, not unlike those for creating kings in Ireland, or kings of the Scots at Scone.

Society in Mull and the rest of the Hebrides was heavily militarised in the Medieval Period. Each island, in a system that was probably devised in the time of the Kingdom of the Isles, was required to support a contingent of warriors, men who were not required to work the land but who were to be ready to go and fight elsewhere whenever required. There were long periods of poor climate when, in any case, it would have been difficult to sustain these men on locally produced resources of food. This method for maintaining a professional force survived the demise of the Lordship of the Isles at the end of the 15th century, and one of the main sources of information for it is a report prepared by an Edinburgh merchant, John Cunningham, in 1596, for the English government, on a mission he had undertaken to sound out Lachlan Maclean of Duart on whether he might support the English administration in Ireland. Maclean was then one of the main potential contractors of fighting men for the wars in Ireland. Cunningham's report lists the quotas of fighting men that were raised by each of the Hebrides along with Arran and Bute, a total of 7,071. Mull alone was required to provide 900 men, Ulva a further 60, Gometra 16 and Inch Kenneth 16. Iona provided no men at all, perhaps because of an ancient exemption as a holy place.

We have already noted the fine representation of a 14th-century warrior, Gille-Brigde MacKinnon, on his grave-slab at Iona (Fig. 14). Other effigies there and at Kilninian show warriors with similar protective clothing and swords but without spears, which may have fallen out of fashion in the 14th century in favour of axes.

Documentary sources also suggest that many of these Isles' warriors fought with bows and arrows, though, by and large, neither axes nor bows are represented on their grave monuments. Instead they are normally shown fastening on their sword belts, one hand grasping the scabbard and the other tugging on the end of the belt that has been passed through its buckle (Fig. 17). This pose appears to be unique to this part of Europe, and may be a deliberate piece of

Figure 17. Effigy of a warrior (no. 210) wearing an aketon with a pose typical of West Highland sculpture, fastening on his sword belt, early 16th century (Graham 1850)

symbolism indicating group membership, in this case of a warrior caste. Effigies of warriors elsewhere in Britain and Europe, if not showing the hands together in prayer, tend to show the sword in the act of being drawn. Some effigies and grave-slabs of the 16th century show two-handed swords of a particular type used by Highlanders. They have drooping quillons with quatrefoil terminals.

None of these effigies are any later in date than the mid 16th century. By 1596, when Lachlan Maclean of Duart was negotiating with the English to provide men for the wars in Ireland, he could offer from his own resources 1,500 bowmen along with 500 'fyremen' (men provided with firearms), presumably mostly from Mull. At least some of the bowmen also had two-handed swords which they could use as occasion demanded, and some were also provided with armour of mail. No deal was actually struck but the documentation gives an interesting insight into local military resources at the end of the 16th century.

It is clear from Maclean's offer of 1596 that he had the ships to transport these men to Ireland. In some cases there was a feudal obligation to maintain ships, like the ship of 22 oars that Angus Og (Master of the Isles) required Hector Maclean of Duart to keep when he gave him a charter of the land of 'Lerebalenele' (Torloisk, as it was later renamed) in 1488.

Ships, described as galleys and birlings, were key to the West Highland way of life in medieval times and underpinned the power of the Kingdom of the Isles, the Lords of the Isles and other west coast lords and clan chiefs down to the early 17th century. Considerable numbers of these ships could be amassed in fleets for major campaigns, like the 160 Somerled is said to have sailed up the Clyde in 1164 and the 180 Donald Dubh, the pretender to the Lordship of the Isles, sailed to Ireland in 1545.

There are several fine representations of medieval warships on grave-slabs and crosses at Iona and elsewhere, though it has to be understood that these are not accurately scaled models (Fig. 18). It appears that the carvers have deliberately given their ships more upright stems and sterns than they had in reality, in order to give them more presence and make them a good fit to the narrow upright panels available for their representation on grave-slabs and

Figure 18. Cross-shaft (no. 214), commissioned by Lachlan MacKinnon and his son John, Abbot of Iona, in 1489 (Stuart 1867). It is displayed in the Abbey Museum

cross-shafts. These ships are descendants of the Viking longships that first plied these waters in the late 8th century. They are shown in West Highland sculpture as clinker-built ships with high prows and sterns, a mast with a square sail, often furled, several oar ports a side and a rudder at the stern. A report to the Scottish Privy Council in 1615 on ships in the Western Isles indicates that there were then galleys with between 18 and 24 oars (that is between 9 and 12 oars a side), and birlings with between 12 and 18 oars. There were also smaller boats with eight oars. The report also says that each oar in these ships was pulled by three men, and hence we can deduce that a galley of 20 oars would have had 60 rowers and a birling of 12 oars would have had 36 rowers. The prime function of West Highland galleys and birlings was to carry troops for fighting on land. Those with three men to an oar, envisaged in the Privy Council report, may have evolved to carry the maximum number of warriors speedily on relatively short sea-crossings. In the latter part of the 16th century they had to be fast enough to avoid, or even outrun, patrols of English ships guarding the approaches to Ireland. With their shallow draft they were ideal for beaching, being manoeuvred in amongst rocks, and taken up rivers. Their size and lightness relative to crew numbers meant that they could easily be lifted out of the water and, indeed, transported over land from one stretch of water to another.

The system by which warriors and ships were maintained in the Isles for service in Ireland came to an end at the beginning of the 17th century with a notable shift in the political map of the British Isles consequent upon James VI of Scotland becoming king of England and Ireland. The flight of the Earl of Tyrone and other Ulster leaders in 1607 removed the main buyers of the services of Isles mercenaries, and Isles chiefs were under severe pressure from stronger and more intrusive government in Edinburgh, which resulted in the Statutes of Iona (of which more below).

THE MEDIEVAL CHURCH

Archdeacon Donald Monro says there were seven parish churches in Mull in 1549. These included the five parishes of Torosay, with its church at Killean (5.7), Kilninian (6.8), Kilfinichen (5.6), Kilvickeon (5.8) and Inch Kenneth (5.3). There are the remains of four other substantial medieval churches at Cill an Ailein (5.2), Pennygown (5.11), Kilcolmkill (5.5, Kilmore, Dervaig) and Laggan (5.9, Caibeal Mheamhair). Which of these might have been considered as parish churches is not known for sure. Iona formed an eighth parish with its church, St Ronan's, adjacent to the nunnery.

The number and extent of parishes in these islands has

undoubtedly changed over the years, but a system with eight parishes could well have been created in the late 12th century, perhaps replacing an earlier arrangement with more, smaller churches. St Ronan's has been found through excavation to have replaced a smaller church of earlier date with clay-bonded walls, and at Baliscate near Tobermory (5.1) the small 14th-century chapel appears to have replaced an earlier church. Baliscate Chapel in its final form may have remained in use as a chapel of ease, a place for worship for those who found it too far or inconvenient to make the journey to the church at Pennygown, Cill an Ailein or Killean. There are other small rectangular churches in enclosed burial grounds in Mull at Cillchriosd and Crackaig (4.2). It is possible that these date prior to the late 12th century or were in use in later times as chapels of ease.

The parish church of Iona came to be held by the Abbey of Iona, as did four of the churches of Mull. Inch Kenneth was held by the Nunnery of Iona, but Cill an Ailein, Pennygown and Laggan are not mentioned, either because they were not appropriated, or because they were considered to be dependencies of Torosay and Kilvickeon. The appropriation of parish churches to religious houses was a usual phenomenon throughout medieval Scotland. It meant that these houses had to take responsibility for supplying clerics, often poorly paid vicars, to officiate locally, but could appropriate the teinds (tithes) for their own use.

Overseeing the local clergy and their churches from the early 12th century, and probably earlier, were the Bishops of the Isles (sometimes called Bishops of Man, Sodor or the Sudreys), whose cathedral was erected on St Patrick's Isle at Peel, Isle of Man, about 1230. These bishops were under the authority of the archbishops of Nidaros (Trondheim) from 1153. With the annexation of the Isle of Man by England, effectively in 1333, the clergy in the rest of the Isles were reluctant to remain under the authority of bishops based in Man. A separate Scottish Diocese of the Isles therefore was created about that time, apparently with its cathedral at Snizort in Skye. In 1472 the Bishopric of the Isles came under the authority of the new Archbishopric of St Andrews. From 1498 Iona Abbey effectively became the cathedral of the Isles, with the bishops also having the status of commendators or abbots of Iona.

Columba's monastery on Iona weathered all sorts of political, military and economic difficulties over the years, including the removal of its prized treasures and relics of its founder, and its demotion from chief Columban monastery in favour of Kells and then Derry, both in Ireland. However, it remained an important centre of pilgrimage. In 1164 an unsuccessful attempt was made by the clergy of Iona, by the counsel of Somerled, to persuade Flaith-bertach Ua-Brolchain, head of the Columban Church, based in Derry, to take the abbacy of Iona. Somerled was killed in battle later that year, and sometime afterwards, certainly prior to 1203, his son Ranald, who like his father took the title King of the Isles, founded an abbey on Iona. This was a new foundation intended to replace and supersede the Columban foundation, a reformed house of Benedictine monks. It is not known where its earliest monks came from, or their nationality, but it can be assumed that it was Ranald's intention to introduce new, European ways into a religious community that was possibly by his time in decline, if not moribund. Ranald was also responsible for founding an abbey of Cistercian monks at Saddell in Kintyre and a priory ('The Nunnery') of Augustinian Canonesses on Iona (Plate 13). His sister, Bethoc, was the first prioress.

It appears that the Columban Church, which maintained a separate presence on Iona after Ranald's foundation of the abbey, may have been unhappy with his initiatives. That may explain why in 1203 the abbey was taken directly under the protection of the Pope. The following year there was a raid on Iona by Irish clergy, including the head of the Columban Church, the Abbot of Derry, and it is claimed that they destroyed the new monastery, which was made without any law and in violation of the rights of the community of Iona. The Abbot of Derry, Amalgaid Ua-Fergail, was then chosen as Abbot of Iona by 'Foreigners and Gaels'. This may have been a compromise solution to resolve the dispute between the old church and the Benedictines.

The Benedictine abbey never achieved great wealth and such documentation as there is for it indicates a house excused from taking part in or contributing to national or international events for reasons of poverty or distance. In 1247 the Pope awarded the abbots episcopal privileges, including the wearing of a mitre. The

MacKinnons appear to have monopolised the position of abbot and control of the abbey in the 14th and 15th centuries, but Finguine MacKinnon, the 'Green Abbot', may have been deposed about 1408 for his misdemeanours, including diverting the revenues of the abbey to pay for the support of his concubine and children. He was also accused of allowing the abbey to become ruinous. Although there was not to be another MacKinnon abbot until about 1467, in the intervening years there was ongoing struggle by the MacKinnons to maintain their influence, with petitions going to the Pope and the king over the refusal of Abbot Dominic, appointed in 1421, to even have a MacKinnon as a monk. To Abbot Dominic, son of Gille-Coinnich, probably from Kintyre, should go the credit for reshaping and building the abbey in the form we know today (albeit largely reconstructed in the late 19th and 20th century). His effigy is in the choir of the abbey church (Fig. 55).

In the 16th century control of the bishopric and abbacy was largely contested between Clan Campbell and the Macleans. At the time of the Reformation struggle, in the middle of the 16th century, the powerful head of Clan Campbell, Archibald, 5th Earl of Argyll, was one of the most prominent supporters of the Protestant cause. He secured the bishopric and abbacy for a member of his own household, John Carswell, also a committed Protestant, who translated the *Book of Common Order*, the liturgy of the Reformed Church, into Gaelic. The fate of the last monks of Iona is not clear. One source says that the monastery was destroyed in 1560 and the monks driven away. In 1588 Hector, son and apparent heir of Lachlan Maclean of Duart, received a charter under the Great Seal of the abbey lands. In addition to almost all of Iona and several properties throughout the Isles and the west of Scotland, it included all of the Ross of Mull, several others in Brolass, and yet more in the north of the island. These were rich pickings, despite an augmentation of the rents due to the Crown.

The end for the religious life of the nunnery is also unclear. A functioning community of nuns may have remained until the middle of the 16th century, but in 1574 the nunnery's lands were granted by the prioress and convent to Hector Maclean of Duart in heritage. They were spread throughout the Isles, and in Mull included the islands of Inch Kenneth and Eorsa, and Gribun.

MEDIEVAL ARCHITECTURE

Wood, turf and stones, either set 'dry' or clay-bonded, were standard building materials for houses from earliest to recent times in Mull and Iona. Straw, turf and bracken were used to cover roofs. There may have beeen some early churches, especially at Iona, of more substantial stone construction, with walls set in lime mortar and windows, doors, etc. with dressed surrounds. St Orans's Chapel at Iona is the earliest surviving example of such a structure, which can be dated on the basis of its architectural detailing and design to the mid 12th century (Plate 12). Use is made of sandstone from Carsaig for quoins, its simple lancet windows, and especially the fine round arched entrance doorway in its west wall, in Romanesque style. It is similar to contemporary work in Ireland. It may have been built by Somerled as a mortuary chapel for himself and his descendants.

The Benedictine abbey church at Iona, as first built about 1200, had an aisle-less choir, transepts with small mural chapels (Fig. 19),

Figure 19. The north transept of the abbey church, work of about 1200 (MacGibbon and Ross 1896–97, vol. 3)

and a nave with aisles only at the east end. The Iona Nunnery Church of about the same date has a simpler plan of just a nave and choir with a north aisle. Both also appear to show Irish influence, although the extensive use of dog-tooth ornament might indicate the presence of masons from mainland Scotland. The masonry walls themselves seem to show the development of a confident, locally based school of masons. As seen in the walls of the nunnery the stonework is set in courses, with blocks and boulders and through courses of pinnings (Plate 13). The effect is colourful, thanks to the contrast between the red Ross of Mull granite, the grey basalt and the Iona Series fine-grained metasediments. The Carsaig sandstone dressings and quoins provide a framework of yellow.

In the course of the 13th century the abbey church was considerably modified and expanded, largely to accommodate an increasing flow of pilgrims who came to venerate St Columba. The creation of a crypt under a greatly extended choir and the intention, never fully realised, to build a greatly enlarged south transept, is reminiscent of changes at Glasgow Cathedral to cater for pilgrims to the shrine there of St Kentigern (Mungo).

After a period of time when it is claimed the abbey buildings were allowed to deteriorate into a ruinous condition, a further ambitious remodelling was undertaken of the abbey church in the time of Abbot Dominic (1421– c. 1465), largely creating the church that we know today (Fig. 20). The work is characterised by pointed arches on cylindrical piers and heavy window tracery, which, as with previous work on Iona, bears comparison with contemporary Irish work. It is therefore not surprising to find that a mason with an Irish name, Donald Ó Brolchán, signed the carving of foliage and animals on one of the capitals, that of the south respond of the east arch of the crossing. He may well have been responsible for all or most of the carving of this phase of work, including figural scenes from the Bible.

None of the other churches in Mull and Iona compares in complexity or richness of detail with these three churches. All were relatively plain, rectangular structures, probably dating originally to the late 12th or 13th century. There is little or nothing in the way of medieval architectural detail to be seen at any of them. Sand-

Figure 20. The choir of the abbey church, looking east (MacGibbon and Ross 1896–97, vol. 3)

stone dressings or other details survive at some, probably mostly stone quarried at Carsaig on the south coast of Mull. The arrangement at St Ronan's of paired lancet windows in the north and south walls, and another in the east gable providing light for the altar, is probably typical. There is also a small cupboard in the east wall, adjacent to the altar. Inch Kenneth is more grand, with two lancet windows in its east gable, as well as windows in the side walls. Here too there is a clear division between nave and chancel represented by a step down, and the door had a pointed arch with an opening of three orders (Fig. 21). Caibeal Mheamhair (5.9) has a relatively simple, chamfered, entrance doorway with a segmental arch, of late medieval date, but the round-headed lancet window, rebated

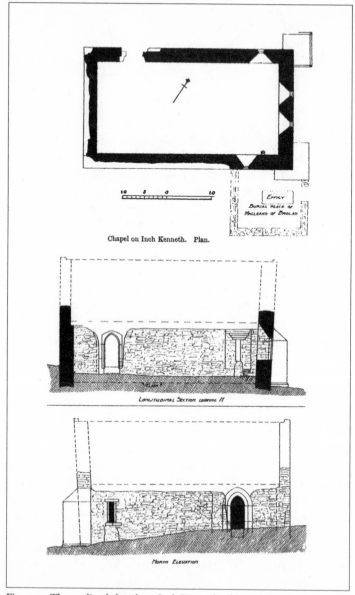

Chapel on Inch Kenneth. Plan.

LONGITUDINAL SECTION LOOKING N

NORTH ELEVATION

Figure 21. The medieval church on Inch Kenneth, plan and elevations
(MacGibbon and Ross 1896–97, vol. 1)

for glass, in the south wall, may be of 12th-century date. Substantial portions of the walls of Kilvickeon (5.8) are still upstanding, but there is nothing to be seen of the medieval church at Kilninian. Here and at the others (except Kilfinichen) there are collections of West Highland monumental sculpture (see below).

The only secular masonry structures of the Medieval Period are a handful of castles. Aros and Dun Ara had defensive walls enclosing irregular summits. Cairnburgh Castle, including Cairn na Burgh More and Cairn na Burgh Beg (5.13), should also be included here, though there is doubt about the dating of its walls of enceinte. At Dun Ara (5.16), a stronghold of the MacKinnons, it appears that the main building was a hall, which by analogy of the plan with that of the great hall of the Lords of the Isles at Finlaggan in Islay, had a separate service area screened off at one end, perhaps with a private room above. Otherwise the main space would have been open to the roof. Interestingly, this was also the plan of the *Tigh an Easbuig* (bishop's house) at Iona (4.3).

Aros Castle (5.12) also contains a large hall, but in this case an impressive structure at first floor level above storage space, in a large rectangular 'hall-house'. It is probably MacDougall work of the 13th century. The inspiration for this first floor hall and others in the West Highlands and Isles, for instance the one at Ardtornish on the other side of the Sound of Mull, probably came from Scandinavia. King Hakon IV of Norway built himself an impressive first-floor hall in Bergen and died in such a hall of the Bishop of Orkney in Kirkwall, on his way home from invading Scotland in 1263.

Duart Castle, perhaps originally of the 13th century, represents a different tradition. It consists of a rectangular enclosure, not dissimilar from the one at Castle Sween in Knapdale, probably the work of a local lord, Suibhne, the ancestor of the MacSweens and McSweeneys. Castle Sween also has an adjacent (hall?) block, which, although the result of a different building phase, may always have been planned and not be much different in date, about the beginning of the 13th century. Similarly, at Duart it may be supposed that the late 14th-century tower-house replaced an earlier hall-block (Fig. 22).

The massive tower-house at Duart no doubt marked the arrival,

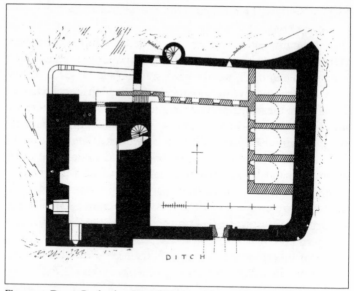

Figure 22. Duart Castle plan (MacGibbon and Ross 1887–92, vol. 3)

the new status, of the Macleans. Tower-houses were typical of Scottish lordly residences from that time through to the 16th century. Duart conforms to the normal pattern with a first-floor hall over a vaulted cellar, and private accommodation at second-floor level and in attic space above. The tower-house of the Lochbuie branch of the Macleans, Moy Castle, is 15th century in date and shows greater complexity in creating chambers and circulating space within the thickness of its walls (Fig. 15). While the tower-house at Duart was only ever the dominant element, the lordly apartments within a larger more complex structure, there is less evidence of other buildings at Moy, only the residual remains of a barmkin (courtyard) wall. While the Moy tower-house would have looked striking enough, standing by the shore at the head of Loch Buie, there can have been few who would not have been more impressed by the scale of Duart Castle and its site on a rocky summit commanding vistas up and down the Sound of Mull. These two castles reflect the relative standing of their owners in medieval times.

WEST HIGHLAND MONUMENTAL SCULPTURE

One of the most enduring legacies of the Lordship of the Isles is its sculpture, grave-slabs and commemorative crosses (Plate 15), to be found in burial grounds the length and breadth of the Lordship and also around Loch Awe and in Cowal. It is all the more remarkable because the stone favoured by the carvers is not a free-stone, but a local chloritic schist, hard to carve and polish, but one which would have sparkled green when freshly worked. One of the quarries where the stone was cut has been identified at Doide on Loch Sween in Knapdale, but there must have been others elsewhere.

This distinctive style of stone carving originates in the 13th century. The crosses are very much a local phenomenon, harking back to Celtic crosses of earlier times. The grave-slabs, with effigies, or crosses and symbols of status, especially swords, are a local variant of funeral art to be found elsewhere in the British Isles. Some slabs with long narrow panels of foliage and scrollwork show Scandinavian influence. The carving tends to be flat, with traditional, conservative use of foliage, leaves and palmette designs. Only the use of interlace seems to be particularly Celtic.

As time went on the sculptors introduced more and more motifs and designs particular to their own cultural environment, making their work a useful source of information on life in the Lordship, with depictions of tools, arms and armour, hunting scenes, and the galleys, not much different from their Viking longship ancestors, which were so important for communications and warfare. Some crosses and slabs have commemorative inscriptions which are an important source of information on people and events. An ongoing research project by the author and a group of geologists has suggested that much of the sculpture may commemorate the professional warriors supported by Isles society.

In a detailed study of this sculpture, undertaken a number of years ago by Kenneth Steer and John Bannerman, it was concluded that there were four schools of carvers working in the 14th and 15th centuries, provisionally placed in Iona, Kintyre, Loch Awe and Loch Sween. In the first half of the 16th century there was a further school associated with Oronsay Priory, as well as a number of independent carvers.

Iona was seen as the place where the tradition started and has the largest collection of medieval monumental sculpture in the Isles and West Highlands, including many of the best examples. There were clearly many carvers and masons working on the abbey and other building projects on Iona in late medieval times and it was therefore natural for Steer and Bannerman to suggest that Iona was the place where many of the monuments were carved. That also chimed with local traditions. There are monuments very similar to ones at Iona in several churches and burial grounds all over the Isles and Argyll which could readily be seen as the work of Iona-based craftsmen. The work of the other schools identified by Steer and Bannerman tends to be more localised, but examples of Loch Awe and Oronsay School monuments are to be found on Iona.

Steer and Bannerman favoured Irish roots for West Highland sculpture, noting that the only known names of carvers have Irish-type surnames, Ó Cuinn and Ó Brolchán. A Mael-Sechlainn Ó Cuinn signed a warrior effigy, probably of about 1500, at Iona (Fig. 23), and he, or another of the same name, signed the great Iona School cross at Oronsay and the rebuilt cloister arcades there, both also about 1500. A fine Loch Sween School slab at Keills in Knapdale also has an inscription recording that it was made by an Ó Cuinn. John Ó Brolchán is recorded on the cross at Ardchattan Priory on the Argyll mainland as its maker in 1500, and he is likely to be related to the Donald Ó Brolchán who signed a capital of a pier in the abbey church of Iona in the 15th century. There should be no surprise that masons and sculptors of Irish origin worked in the West Highlands in the Medieval Period, given the strong links between the Lords of the Isles, Clan Donald and Ireland. None of these works, however, takes us back to the early stages of this sculptural tradition, and no group of Irish sculpture has as yet been convincingly identified as a likely model for West Highland sculpture.

There are, however, several problems with the Steer and Bannerman thesis. The most obvious one is their assumption that there was an Iona School based on Iona. The chloritic schist used to carve most of these slabs and crosses does not occur on Iona, and so we would have to assume that blank slabs were imported to the island, and then exported when carved. It would seem more

Figure 23. Effigy of a warrior, about 1500, by Mael-Sechlainn Ó Cuinn (Drummond 1881). It is displayed in the Abbey Museum (no. 211)

logical that the bulk of the carving of monuments was done in workshops at or near the places where the rock was quarried. Perhaps final finishing was often done after the monuments were shipped, and there is evidence that designs and inscriptions were altered and added at a later date. There is no evidence that carvers worked in anything so formal as schools. It is easier to imagine that there were several workshops throughout the region operated by masters with their apprentices, and that these workshops could undertake commissions to make monuments, and ship and install them where required, including Iona. The distribution of some groups of monuments strongly supports this interpretation.

Much more research and analysis is required to come up with a comprehensive understanding of the whole phenomenon of West Highland sculpture. Here we sketch in some observations which we hope will provide a basis for a better appreciation of the medieval monuments of Mull and Iona. The individual numbers provided for these monuments are those given by the Royal Commission on Ancient and Historical Monuments of Scotland in their Inventories of Argyll. Many of the monuments not specifically mentioned in the groupings below are probably the work of yet other workshops and craftsmen.

Sandstone slabs with long-shafted crosses

Some of the earliest medieval grave-slabs at Iona, dating to the 13th century, are carved in sandstone from Carsaig in Brolass, on the south coast of Mull. They are now all very worn but some had long-shafted crosses with foliated cross-heads and Calvary steps. One (no. 117), less than a metre long and so perhaps for a child, is still in Reilig Odhráin.

Early slabs with plant scrolls

Other potentially early slabs include those with plant-scroll decoration covering the full width of the slab. One (no. 167), with an interlace cross at the top, is set in the floor of St Oran's Chapel (Fig. 24). Some of these slabs at Iona and elsewhere in Argyll and the Isles bear a distinct similarity to grave-slabs in Scandinavia, for example in the cathedral in Trondheim and the 'liljesten' slabs in Sweden. They reflect the influence of that part of the world well into the Medieval Period. Since the slabs in Scandinavia are dated to the 12th century, it may be that our understanding of the dating of the Scottish material should be reviewed.

Figure 24. Grave-slab (no. 167) with plant-scroll decoration covering the full width of the slab, set in the floor of St Oran's Chapel

Iona School class II slabs

Stylistically, gravestones identified by Steer and Bannerman as their Iona School class II, derive from these plant-scroll decorated slabs. They are to be found on Iona and the Argyll mainland. Good examples include nos 173, 176 and 123, displayed in the west cloister walk of Iona Abbey, and no. 129 in the north cloister walk (Fig. 25). Of the 30 known, 15 are on Iona, one is on the Garvellach Islands, two are at the cathedral of Argyll on the Island of Lismore,

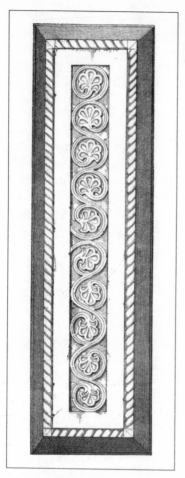

Figure 25. An Iona School class II slab (no. 129) with long narrow panel with foliate decoration (Graham 1850). It is exhibited in the north cloister walk

one at Keills, five at Kilmory in Knapdale, three at Kilfinan in Cowal, three at Kilmartin and one at Kilbride in Lorn. This distribution suggests that they originate in Lorn or Knapdale and ones on Iona mark the burial there of leading members of the MacDougalls, Campbells and other mainland clans.

They bear no comparison to other monuments elsewhere in the British Isles. They are often relatively thick, their edges normally bevelled and carved with roll and other mouldings, including dog-tooth and nail-head ornament. The surface of the slabs is normally carved with a long, thin panel of foliate decoration placed centrally. In some, perhaps later examples, the panel is to one side to allow room for a sword. There is rarely any ostensibly Christian symbolism, and where a sword is represented, it is invariably of an early type that could be of 13th-century date or earlier. One of the effigies of an abbot or bishop (no. 200) displayed in the nave of Iona Abbey Church can be included in this group on the basis of the complex mouldings, including cable-moulding and nail-head, that surround it. Steer and Bannerman considered that the presence on some slabs of dog-tooth was an indication of a late date since there was a revival of such 13th-century detailing in Scotland in the late 15th and 16th centuries. They do not seem to have considered that this might be another indicator of an early date for these monuments. We believe that a date range in the 13th and 14th centuries is more likely. None of them has inscriptions.

The Loch Awe School

This large group identified by Steer and Bannerman, mostly in mainland Argyll, needs much further research which will almost certainly lead to the conclusion that it includes work by different workshops over a long period of time. There are a few examples at Iona, possibly including the two warrior effigies, nos 208 and 209, displayed in the Abbey Museum (though Steer and Bannerman attributed them to their Iona School). Grave-slab no. 182, set in the floor of the choir of the abbey church, is a typical but broken and worn example of Loch Awe School work, dating to the 14th or 15th century (Fig. 26). It is mostly covered with a design of intertwined plant stems, and has a small niche containing an image of a West Highland warrior. Its position in the church suggests it must mark the burial place of an important member of a mainland Argyll family, perhaps a Campbell.

Iona School Class I

Steer and Bannerman's Iona School class I slabs are another easily recognisable group well represented at Iona. They have a central long-shafted cross, normally with a foliate head and semi-circular

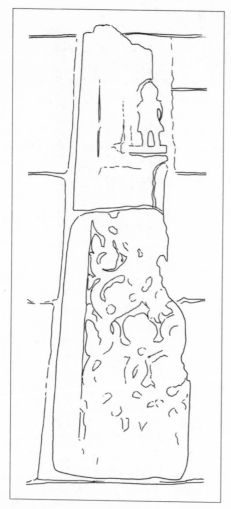

Figure 26. Grave-slab (no. 182), 14th or 15th century, from the area of Loch Awe, set in the floor of the abbey choir. Its design includes a small image of a warrior

base, flanked by other motifs, including swords and foliage scroll. They mostly have bevelled edges and one or more perimeter roll mouldings. Good examples at Iona include nos 118 and 122, displayed in the west cloister walk of the abbey, and no. 119 in the north cloister walk (Fig. 27). These slabs are obviously a local variant of a widespread medieval type of Christian grave-marker with dominant cross design. It may be suggested, however, that

Figure 27. Slab (no. 119) with a long-shafted cross with floriate head and semi-circular base, flanked by foliage scroll. Note the two pairs of shears on a recessed panel at the very bottom. Iona School class I work, late 13th or 14th century (Graham 1850)

the main source of inspiration, and perhaps craftsmen, came initially across the Firth of Clyde from Ayrshire, where there are monuments of this general type at Ardrossan, Ayr and Kilbirnie.

Of the 16 surviving Iona School class I slabs, five are on Iona, three at Kilmory in Knapdale, one at Lochaline in Morvern and the rest on Islay – two of them at Finlaggan, one at Kilarrow and four at Kildalton. None of them have inscriptions or are otherwise identified. They are all dated to the 14th and 15th centuries by Steer and Bannerman, but it may be suggested that an earlier date range from the late 13th through the 14th century is more probable, taking into consideration what is known about the date of broadly comparable pieces elsewhere. The distribution suggests that they originate in Islay. The Iona slabs could commemorate leading members of Clan Donald.

Sculpture with swirling leaves

A large and widespread group of sculpture characterised by designs with swirling leaves may also have come from workshops in Islay and Kintyre, where many of the monuments are located. There are a variety of foliage scrollwork designs used by the carvers of this group but many of them are S-scrolls and guilloches containing swirling groups of leaves. Grave-slabs typically have a foliated cross-head, a sword placed centrally, flanked by foliage scroll. Where there is no sword the full width of the slab is sometimes occupied by foliage scroll, sometimes asymmetrical in design. Leaves identified as oak, as well as acorns, are a particular feature of this group. This group was obviously produced over a long period of time, and includes outstanding works like the late 14th-century cross at Kilchoman in Islay, which commemorates Beaton doctors, and the large cross of the late 15th century at Oronsay Priory by Mael-Sechlainn Ó Cuinn.

At Iona this group of monuments is represented by a grave-slab, no. 157, displayed in St Oran's Chapel, and three others, nos 153, 154 and 163 (Fig. 28), in the abbey cloisters. There is also the warrior effigy no. 211, signed by Mael-Sechlainn Ó Cuinn, in the Abbey Museum, and the slab of Prior Macgillescoil in the nave of the abbey church.

Sculpture with small leaves

Maclean's Cross (Plate 15), on the roadside between the Iona Nunnery and Abbey, has distinctive foliage decoration, some of it very untidy, characterised by small leaves set in four-strand intertwining foliage. Five other grave-slabs at Iona, nos 138, 144, 147, 155

Figure 28. The key characteristic of this slab (no. 163) is the pattern of scrollwork with swirling leaves, late 14th and 15th century (Stuart 1867)

(Fig. 61) and 156, all displayed in the abbey cloisters, show similar characteristics. One of the ecclesiastical effigies, no. 201, of either an abbot or a bishop, in the nave of the abbey church, also has similar foliage ornamentation around the head of its niche. Apart from these monuments at Iona, so far only one other very similar work has been identified elsewhere – a cross at Kilmory in Knapdale, which on the basis of its inscription may be dated to the late 15th century.

Sculpture with paired half-palmettes

Another large and widespread group of sculpture well represented at Iona, Inch Kenneth and elsewhere in Mull has designs with paired, intertwined, up-turned half-palmettes. Typically, the full width of the central portion of the slab, sometimes more, is covered with four intertwining strands. Some the strands develop at the top into pairs of opposed, rampant animals. In others, though none at Iona, there is a sword positioned centrally between two bands of scrollwork with up-turned half-palmettes. Where there is a cross-head it is often of interlace. Some have inscription labels, scenes or galleys. Some of those at Iona have edges and margins with mouldings, extravagantly so in the case of no. 150 in the south cloister walk of the abbey (Fig. 29), perhaps suggesting that some of the group were produced in a workshop or by carvers who had originally made Iona School class II slabs. They may mostly date to the 15th or early 16th century. The inscription on no. 150 can be taken to refer to Angus Og, the leader of Clan Donald at Bannockburn, but have been commissioned as a commemorative piece long after his death. No. 151, also displayed in the south cloister walk, was made for Malcolm, chief of the MacLeods of Lewis, who died some time between 1515 and 1524. There is also a slab (no. 8) on Inch Kenneth and two (nos 2 and 3) at Kilninian in Mull.

The effigy of Abbot MacKinnon and related pieces

This group, mostly on Iona, includes some of the most accomplished pieces of West Highland sculpture anywhere – grave-slabs, crosses and at least one full-size effigy – all united by the quality of their design and execution and details of ornamentation and their inscriptions. It is not clear at this stage whether more than one workshop was involved, how many different masters, or even where they were based. The effigy, no. 203, of Abbot John MacKinnon, in the choir of Iona Abbey Church, was commissioned in the late 15th century and carved out of chlorite schist. It is the most accomplished West Highland effigy by far (Figs 30, 56). The earlier effigy, no. 202 (Fig. 55), alongside it in the choir, supposedly of Abbot Dominic, clearly provided inspiration. It may be the work of a

Figure 29. The design on this slab (no. 150) of intertwining half-palmettes is typical of a number of works of West Highland sculpture, probably dating to the 15th century. It commemorates Angus Og MacDonald (Graham 1850). It is exhibited in the south cloister walk

Lowland sculptor. The detailed treatment of the ornamentation on Abbot John's vestments and the calligraphy of the inscription marks it out as a work of calibre produced by a West Highland carver.

At Iona the group includes a cross (Fig. 18) dated 1489, also commemorating Abbot John, and his father Lachlan, chief of the MacKinnons. Only the shaft survives, now displayed in the Abbey Museum. It has a fine representation of a galley and plant-scroll

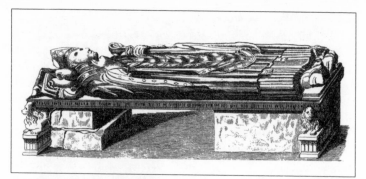

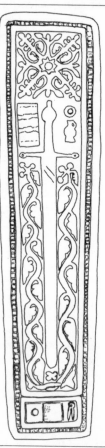

decoration. Exhibited in the nave of the abbey church is a slab (Fig. 31), typically divided into panels, in this case four with foliated cross designs. Its inscription indicates it was made to commemorate four priors of Iona from one clan, probably Campbells, some or all of whom survived into the 16th century. The cross-shaft in the church at Pennygown also belongs to this group. It has a fine representation of a galley on one side and a Madonna and Child on the other.

The inscriptions on this group span the changeover from Lombardic capitals to black letter, and are mostly on marginal inscription bands. Words are often separated by stops that take the form of squares, lozenges, flower heads, etc., and these motifs appear elsewhere in the decorative repertoire of the carvers. The blank portions of some of the inscription bands are concave. The information provided by the inscriptions indicates a date range around the late 15th and early 16th centuries.

Slabs with paired undulating foliage scrolls

A number of West Highland grave-slabs have paired undulating foliage scrolls, often on either side of a sword. There are a variety of leaf forms, including leaves with fruits. Many of them, perhaps misleadingly, have been identified by Steer and Bannerman as products of a school based at Oronsay Priory in the 16th century. Some feature claymores, the distinctive two-handed swords used by Highlanders at that time. Two slabs at Iona (nos 192 and 193) are not on public display, but there are also two at Kilninian (Fig. 32).

Figure 30. (Opposite top) The effigy (no. 203) of Abbot John MacKinnon, died about 1498, in the abbey choir (Pennant 1774)

Figure 31. (Opposite left) Slab divided into four panels (no. 179) and an inscription indicating that it commemorates four Iona priors of the same clan. Early 16th century (Stuart 1867)

Figure 32. (Opposite right) Grave-slab (no. 4) at Kilninian Parish Church (6.8) with paired undulating foliage scrolls on either side of a claymore, 16th century. The hilt is flanked by a casket and a flagon along with a bowl. In a panel beneath the sword there is a pair of shears, a comb and a mirror

6. Improving Ways:
The Early Modern Period

MULL PEOPLE

Maclean chiefs and gentlemen remained the main power in Mull and Iona from medieval times until well after 1674, but in that year there was a significant event that was to introduce far-reaching changes – the acquisition, not without a struggle, of the lands of the Macleans of Duart by Archibald, 9th Earl of Argyll. Argyll, however, held most of the cards, including political power, legal rights and money. He had bought up all the debts of the young Sir Allan of Duart, and in 1673 obtained a decreet of removal against the many Macleans who had failed to pay their rents. This resulted in expeditions to Mull in the following two years to try and bring the Macleans to heel. Resistance carried on for several years, with secure possession of the Duart lands by Argyll only being achieved in 1679. Campbell tacksmen (leaseholders) or lairds and tenants were brought in and installed in many of the best properties. There were 152 tenants on the Argyll lands in Mull in 1742–43, over half of whom were Campbells, including 15 out of 18 tacksmen, each holding on average three farms. Twenty other large tenants held farms as single tenants while the remaining land, amounting to about a quarter of the whole, consisted of joint farms held by 114 small tenants. The influx of Campbell tacksmen and tenants led to a period, extending well into the 18th century, of clan rivalry and resentment of Campbell lordship. Macleans almost inevitably supported the Jacobite uprisings while the Campbells were adherents of the Hanoverian succession.

The Macleans of Duart thus became exiles. The Macleans of Lochbuie were survivors. They held on to their ancestral Mull lands until the early 20th century. The Macleans of Coll sold their Mull lands in 1857. Other Maclean families of importance included the Macleans of Torloisk and Macleans of Brolass.

Torloisk belonged to Allan ('Ailean nan Sop'), a younger son of Lachlan Cattanach of Duart, active in the second quarter of the 16th century, and then to his son Hector. Torloisk was then acquired by Lachlan Og, younger son of Sir Lachlan Mor of Duart, with whose descendants it remained. Torloisk was not part of the Duart estates acquired by the earls of Argyll. The first laird of Brolass, in the south of Mull, to the east of the Ross, was Donald, a son of Hector Og Maclean of Duart. He was still active in the mid 17th century. Allan, the 4th laird of Brolass, succeeded Sir Hector Maclean of Duart to the baronetcy of Morvern. The lands of Brolass had been held as a wadset (mortgage) from the Argyll family, but Sir Allan managed to prise them from the 5th duke after a long legal action in 1783. They then passed to another branch of the Macleans.

The MacKinnons supported the Jacobite uprisings of 1715 and 1745 and, as a result, lost their Mishnish estate. It was regained briefly but sold in 1774 to a Campbell gentleman. The MacQuarries continued to hold Ulva and the MacGillivrays Pennyghael for most of the 18th century.

Most of the inhabitants of these islands continued to live on the land in the Early Modern Period, being directly dependent on the raising of crops and animals for their living. The main landholders, like the Macleans and Campbells, rented many of their farms to single tenants, and also tacksmen, often relatives or clansmen. Tacksmen were leaseholders, often gentlemen who did no farming on their own behalf but who held more than one property, which they sublet to tenants of their own. Tacksmen also often fostered the children of their chiefs, an honour that was much sought after. In a strongly militarised society they were an important element, providing local leadership and helping to maintain clan cohesion. The dukes of Argyll in the 18th century were not the only landowners who saw that they could improve on the flow of rent money directly into their own coffers and gain more leverage in encouraging improved methods of farming by squeezing out the tacksman class and renting their land directly to their own tenants. Although tacksmen, so-called, remained as tenants on the Argyll estates in Mull throughout the period, after 1737 lands were offered on short-term leases to the highest bidders and they were not normally allowed to sublet to tenants of their own.

Throughout the period many farms were let jointly to groups of tenants. The census of the Mull lands of the Duke of Argyll undertaken in 1779 indicate that at that time there were still 20 out of 66 farms held jointly by between two and nine tenants. In an overview of the state of agriculture in the Hebrides published in 1811 Macdonald (see Further Reading) characterised the natives of Mull as generally poorer and behind the times when compared with islanders elsewhere, including Islay, Colonsay and Gigha. Farmland was unenclosed, there were no plantations, and drainage had scarcely been tackled.

In the name of efficiency and to encourage improved farming methods, landowners increasingly preferred to do away with joint tenancy farms. Another approach adopted in the 1790s by the Duke of Argyll was to encourage joint tenants to divide their farms into separate possessions, each to build his house on his own lot. One of the farms cited as a good example of this being achieved was Caliach in Mishnish in the northwest of Mull.

Caliach had been one of the farms that had supported the minister of Kilninian until 1788, but was taken back specifically for the accommodation of small tenants. In 1801 the Duke's chamberlain could report that it was already divided, a great deal had been done, several good houses built, and the breed of cattle much improved. As a result, the tenants were to be rewarded with quantities of free lime. The divisions of Caliach, and indeed the neighbouring lands of Arrine, which may by then have been included in Caliach, are evident on maps and satellite images in the form of long straight turf dykes. Dispersed house groups are also visible. The rough grazing or outfield of the township, including Cnoc Udmail and Bruach na Sean-pheighinne, seems to have been sliced up and included in the lots of each tenant. The original plan may have been for six lots very approximately of about 40 hectares each. In 1779 Arrine had a population of 52, of which six were tenants, while Caliach had a population of 35. None of them were described as tenants, but four were listed as millers, and one, Charles McNeil, as 'residenter'.

Until the beginning of the 19th century the majority of the population on Iona had lived in the village, including the tenants of the two townships into which the island had been divided – the East End and the West End. In 1779 there was a population of 249, of which 32 are described as tenants. In 1802 the Duke required the small tenants to divide these farms and build their houses on their own lots, 30 in number. Most of these lots can still be traced today as rectangular enclosures surrounded by dykes or fences. Several of them have a narrow front on the sea either to the south or north of the abbey ruins. They are mostly smaller than about 200m by 500m (10 ha). The southern end of the island along with the moorland extending across the island to the west of the abbey was retained as common grazings.

Common grazings may have survived well into the 19th century on other farms, like Kilpatrick in Brolass (not to be confused with Kilpatrick beside Duart Castle). It was adjacent to the Duke of Argyll's lands in the Ross of Mull, stretching from the shore of Loch na Corrobha (Loch Scridain) southwards, between the Allt Loch Arm on the west and the Allt Ruadh on the east, taking in an area of about 170 hectares. Much of the land is moorland plateau, and the farm was regarded as the worst in Brolass. In 1779 there were only 20 inhabitants, none of them listed as tenants. Three parallel plots of land had been enclosed by dykes, bounded on the south by a head dyke. Each of these plots was very approximately 250m wide by up to 1000m in length (25 ha). The outfield or moorland to the south shows no sign of having been divided in this way and may have been retained as common grazing by the tenants. There was, however, a temptation for landlords, if not here then elsewhere, to take away the rights of access for small tenants to such moorland and consolidate it in larger farms given over to grazing cattle or sheep.

The archaeological evidence suggests that Caliach, Iona and Kilpatrick represent different models for the way landowners dealt with joint tenancy farms in the 18th and 19th centuries. At Caliach tenants were encouraged to show initiative, to continue a mixed farming economy of growing crops and raising animals, by a closer relationship with their land and less dependency on others. On Iona, the individual plots and access to grazing for a relatively large population were intended to supplement other ways of making a living. At Kilpatrick the inhabitants (including tenants?) would only have been able to make a living provided they had access to grazing. It would probably have been difficult for them to survive solely on what they could grow or raise on the three enclosed plots. There was no long-term future for them.

The small tenants in Caliach and on Iona were what might be called crofters since, as their name suggests, they enjoyed a share of the croft land (infield) as well as limited access to grazing. In 1799 Alexander Maclean of Coll created Dervaig (6.30), a village with 26 houses for crofters. Limited access was provided to hill grazing but the plots attached to their houses were too small to grow enough food to sustain a family. This was a deliberate move, here and elsewhere, to encourage diversification by finding other ways to make a living by fishing, industry or hiring services to others.

Apart from tacksmen, tenants, crofters and their families, there were many other types and grades of residents. Servants were unmarried and lived with their masters, either tacksmen or tenants. Married male servants were known as workmen and provided their labour in return for a share of the crops they themselves grew. Cotters in general paid for their place by their labour, but also included widows and paupers. Meallers (mailers) were to be found on farms belonging to tacksmen. They were married farm servants who, like workmen, contributed their labour in return for a share of their crops. A few bowmen were also to be found on tacksmen's farms. These were sub-tenants who were lent their implements, seed and animals in return for providing a large share of the produce annually to their master. There were also millers, particularly on the farms in the Ross of Mull where grain was grown. The mills in question would have been small, simple 'Norse' mills with a horizontally operated wheel or paddles. Herdsmen, grass-keepers or chasers were necessary to prevent animals straying, since few farms had march dykes. There were also a handful of tradesmen, merchants, innkeepers and schoolmasters. The 1779 census of the Duke of Argyll's Mull lands shows a total population of 996 on 66 farms, an average of about 45 on each.

There is an interesting description of the inhabitants of Mull, more specifically their dress, made by an English gentleman, William Sacheverell, when he visited in 1688 on a mission to raise relics from the Armada wreck at Tobermory. His account is worth quoting in full:

> The usual outward habit of both sexes is the plaid; the women's much finer, the colours more lively, and the squares larger than the men's, and put me in mind of the ancient Picts. This serves them for a veil, and covers both head and body. The men wear theirs after another manner; especially when designed for ornament, it is loose and flowing, like the mantles our painters give their heroes. Their thighs are bare, with brawny muscles. Nature has drawn all her strokes bold and masterly. What is covered is only adapted to necessity: a thin brogue on the foot, a short buskin of various colours on the leg, tied above the calf with a striped pair of garters. What should be concealed is hid with a large shot-pouch, on each side of which hangs a pistol and a dagger; as if they found it necessary to keep those parts well guarded. A round target on their backs, a blue bonnet on their heads, in one hand a broad sword, and a musket in the other, perhaps no nation goes better armed.

Sacheverell's visit coincided with the uprising in favour of King James VII/II, supported by the people of Mull, and, it may be thought, gives a misleading picture of the extent to which the men went around armed. That both men and women were generally dressed in tartan plaids at that time is confirmed by other evidence. The general adoption of this distinctive attire, what we now regard as the mainstay of Highland costume prior to the invention of the kilt in the 18th century, probably dates back to the 16th century. Highland dress and the carrying of weapons in the Highland regions including Mull were both proscribed for many years after the failure of the Jacobite Uprising in 1745. It is not known if the ban on tartan was always rigidly enforced in places like Mull prior to it being lifted in 1782. Two years later when a party of visitors, including the French geologist Faujas St Fond visited Staffa, he was struck by how the locals wore Highland dress, including old Duncan Campbell, tacksman of Aros, wrapped in a plaid, and two young men wearing blue bonnets and tartan plaids, waistcoats and jackets, who acted as guides on the way from Aros to Torloisk. St Fond also describes how the women wore a bodice or vest and a petticoat of woollen tartan, chequered with red, green and brown stripes shaded with blue.

Nevertheless, it does not appear that the wearing of such dress remained general amongst the population at large for much longer. Highland dress for men, now with the kilt as the main garment, was adapted as military uniform and as dress attire for weddings, balls and the like. The clothing adopted by the locals in the 19th century conformed to standards and styles general throughout the rest of the country, although much of it was spun and woven from local wool and flax until later in the century.

REFORMATION AND COUNTER-REFORMATION

A key sign of new times was the change in religion – the establishment of a Protestant Church in place of the old, 'Papist', Catholic Church, thirled to Rome. The key date is normally considered to have been August 1560, when a parliament abolished the Latin mass and the papal supremacy, and authorised a *Confession of Faith* for a new reformed worship. The changeover was neither quick nor smooth as far as Mull and Iona are concerned. Support of the Protestant cause from the late 1550s by Archibald, 5th Earl of Argyll and James MacDonald of Dunyvaig (Islay) was not obviously matched by leading Macleans and others in Mull. In the 1570s and 1580s, however, Lachlan Maclean of Duart was successfully taking over extensive church lands in Mull and Iona from the Protestant Bishop of the Isles, who attempted to fend off his encroachments by a mixture of legal actions and attempts to buy his support. Lachlan was even appointed the bishop's bailie.

The bishop in question, John Carswell, was a keen reformer and Gaelic scholar who owed his advancement to his patron, the powerful Earl of Argyll. Bishops remained as leaders of the Reformed Church until episcopacy was temporarily abolished from 1638 to 1662, and then finally in the Church of Scotland from 1689.

One other bishop should be mentioned here for the significant role he played in local and national politics. Andrew Knox, a protégé of King James VI/I, was elevated to the bishopric of the Isles in 1605. He was appointed in 1608 to aid Lord Ochiltree in curbing the power of island chiefs and getting them to pay their rents into the royal coffers. Several of them, including Hector Maclean of Duart, were captured at Aros in Mull by trickery, by being invited on board ship to hear a sermon by the bishop, and were taken off to imprisonment in the Lowlands.

Knox is credited with persuading the king not to dispossess them but to go for a policy of conciliation. This resulted in the meeting on Iona in the following year at which Knox persuaded the chiefs, including those imprisoned the previous year, to agree to the so-called Statutes of Iona. These required obedience to the Protestant Church and several changes designed to curb the power of the chiefs and, in Lowland terms, to civilise them. Thus the size of their households was to be limited and those living freely on the poor inhabitants were to be sent away. The use of firearms was banned. These measures were clearly designed to undermine the system by which forces of warriors had been maintained to fight in the wars in Ireland and elsewhere. Drastic restrictions were placed on the drinking of wine and aquavite (whisky) and the eldest sons (or daughters if there were no sons) of gentlemen and better-off tenants were to be sent to the Lowlands to be educated in speaking, reading and writing English. Inns were to be established for the use of travellers, and bards were to be banished. The statutes do seem to have been instrumental in introducing significant changes in Isles society.

We do not have detailed knowledge of how the Reformation affected religious provision in the diocese of the Isles on a day-to-day basis. Many Catholic incumbents may have remained in place long after 1560, making few concessions to the reformed worship. Others may have abandoned their charges. Fingon MacMullen, recorded as chaplain of St Mary's Chapel, Tobermory in 1539, was by 1573 Vicar of Iona for the Reformed Church. There were clearly difficulties for a considerable time, however, in finding men with sufficient education and the right reformed views to be parish ministers. With three in 1626, Mull was much better provided for than many other islands.

Little is known about how the actual church buildings themselves faired in the aftermath of the Reformation. In 1622 the lairds of Lochbuie and Coll appeared before the Privy Council in Edinburgh and promised to repair the parish churches within their territories. The churches in question are not specified but could have included Pennygown, Kilmore and Laggan. These and other medieval churches may have remained in use for worship into the 18th or 19th centuries. In 1635 King Charles I authorised payment to be made to Neil Campbell, Bishop of the Isles, for repairing the cathedral church (the abbey church), but this initiative came to an end with his deposition soon afterwards.

Significant efforts were made by the Catholic Church to regain the Isles for the Church of Rome, not without a remarkable amount of success in some areas. Redmond O'Gallagher, Catholic Bishop of Derry, had apparently visited Mull and Kintyre in 1590 as part of a programme to encourage a Spanish-funded Catholic rebellion. From 1619 to 1637 Irish Franciscans mounted several missions in the Isles. Cornelius Ward and Paul O'Neill came to Mull and Ulva in 1624, and among their converts was Maclean of Lochbuie. Maclean of Duart was so hostile to the mission that on a visit to the island in 1625 Ward had to flee to avoid capture. In the same year another missionary, Patrick Hegarty, had much more success in gaining converts in the Ross of Mull. He also converted Duart's brother, Gillean, but made little headway on Iona. He claimed the masses he said there were the first heard on that island since the Reformation. Hegarty and his companions boasted by 1633 to have gained 10,000 for the Catholic faith in the Hebrides, a figure which their own superiors considered an exaggeration. Nevertheless, they had clearly had considerable success, although in the case of Mull, not long lasting.

FIGHTING FOR THE STEWART CAUSE

Despite the demise of the system of maintaining warriors in the Hebrides, the martial traditions of the islanders continued to manifest themselves throughout the 17th century and, indeed, much later. Despite a 17th-century effigy of a warrior wearing an aketon on Inch Kenneth, these probably largely disappeared from battlefields in that century to be replaced by plaids – large woollen blankets that increasingly came to be woven with tartan patterns. They were multi-purpose, usable as cloaks and bedding, and adaptable into tents and bags.

A significant number of men from Mull and Iona were involved in the Civil Wars of the mid 17th century, mostly fighting in support of the Royalist cause against the Covenanters and the Cromwellian forces. Local men also took part in large numbers in the Jacobite uprisings of 1689–90, 1715 and 1745–46 in favour of the deposed King James VII/II and his descendants. In 1631 Lachlan Maclean of Duart had been made a baronet (of Morvern) by King Charles I, and from then on he and his descendants showed a dogged determination to support the House of Stewart, even though they lost their lands as a result.

In 1647 the Committee of Estates (the Covenanting regime) sent an army under the command of the experienced General David Leslie and the Marquis of Argyll to root out supporters of King Charles I in the west, many of whom, including men from Mull, had taken part in the campaigns of the Marquis of Montrose. After taking the castles of Dunaverty in Kintyre and Dunyvaig in Islay, Leslie and Argyll moved on to Mull. There Sir Lachlan Maclean of Duart gave up Duart Castle without much of a fight. Cairnburgh Castle in the Treshnish Islands was also taken. Cairn na Burgh More has a late medieval chapel within its defences and also a rectangular building of two storeys, about 16m by 6m overall. It has been identified as a barracks block in origin, probably dating to the 16th century.

Although far from Mull, one military exploit that must have left a particularly deep impression was the Battle of Inverkeithing on 20 July 1651, where an experienced Cromwellian army managed to break out from a bridgehead it had recently established at the Ferry Hills by Inverkeithing by crossing by boat from the south side of the Firth of Forth. It was faced by Scottish forces now united in support of the young Charles II because of the execution of Charles I by the English three years earlier. A strong detachment was sent to deal with the incursion at Inverkeithing. Some of the hardest fighting involved a foot regiment, apparently largely composed of men from Mull, under the command of the young chief of Duart, Sir Hector Maclean. Clan tradition claims that not

only was Hector killed in the fighting but only 35 out of his regiment of about 800 men survived. The figures may be exaggerated
but it was certainly a black day for Mull, and a major turning point
in the civil wars, opening up the control of all of Scotland to
Cromwellian forces.

This, and the defeat of the main Scottish army by Cromwell at
Worcester on 3 September 1651, did not quite extinguish Royalist
efforts in Scotland to keep the cause of the Stewarts alive. Thus in
September 1653 a flotilla of six Cromwellian ships anchored off
Duart Castle, intent on converting it into a government
stronghold. Three of the ships were lost in a violent storm, including a small warship called the *Swan*. It is apparently the wreck of
this ship that was rediscovered in 1979 and has since been excavated. It lies just off the coast, immediately to the north of Duart
Castle, and can be visited by experienced divers (6.33).

In the civil wars of the 17th century the Macleans of Duart had
mostly been on the opposing side to the Campbell earls and
Marquis of Argyll and animosity between the two clans continued
into the period after the Restoration of the monarchy, being greatly
exacerbated by the acquisition of the Duart lands by the Campbells.
It is not surprising that in changed political circumstances a few
years later in 1685, Argyll failed to secure any support in Mull when
he launched his rebellion against the new king James VII/II. Despite
Argyll's complete failure and execution, the Campbell fortunes rose
again. The new earl, Archibald 10th (later 1st Duke of Argyll), led
an army 2,000-strong to Mull in October 1690 to pacify it in the
wake of the Jacobite uprising of the previous years in which Sir John
Maclean of Duart had led the men of Mull to the mainland to
support King James VII/II's commander in Scotland, Viscount
Dundee. Duart Castle continued to hold out until 1692 for Sir John,
who meanwhile had fled to Cairnburgh Castle. On 9 October 1690,
a Royal Navy warship, HMS *Dartmouth*, sent to the Hebrides to
daunt the Jacobites, sank in a violent storm when she was anchored
in Scallastle Bay on the Sound of Mull. She was driven onto rocks
at Eilean Rubha an Ridire with the loss of most of her crew. Local
tradition claims the malign influence of local witches in her wreck-
ing. Her wreck (6.34) was rediscovered and excavated in the 1970s.

The men of Mull, commanded again by Sir John Maclean of

PLATE 1. The barrow at Suie (Suidhe) with an arrangement of slabs on its eastern edge, possibly the remains of a chamber (2.12).

PLATE 2. A Bronze Age kerb cairn at Kilninian (2.8).

PLATE 3. A standing stone at Ardnacross, one of a row of three, with a denuded kerb cairn in the foreground (2.15).

PLATE 4. A Bronze Age stone row near Dervaig, two stones still standing, another three fallen (2.18).

PLATE 5. The Iron Age fort, Cillchriosd, beside the road to Sunipol (3.1).

PLATE 6. Dùn Aoidhean, an impressively sited dun on the island of Erraid, overlooking the tidal sound adjacent to Mull (3.22).

PLATE 7. The dun, Dùn Bhuirg, Ardmeanach, now crowned by a monument to a girl who drowned nearby in 1896 (3.23).

PLATE 8. The entrance of the broch, An Sean Chaisteal, overlooking the Sound of Mull at Ardnacross (3.29).

PLATE 9. The broch, Dùn nan Gall, on the shore of Loch Tuath (3.30).

PLATE 10. The restored medieval abbey of Iona.

PLATE 11. Iona, the reconstructed St Columba's Shrine-chapel, probably dating to the mid 8th century (4.3).

PLATE 12. Iona, St Oran's Chapel, a 12th-century funerary chapel erected by Somerled or his son Ranald.

PLATE 13. Iona Nunnery, founded by Ranald, son of Somerled, prior to his death in 1207. The work is mostly early 13th century.

PLATE 14. Iona, St Martin's Cross, a monolithic 'high cross' dating to the mid or late 8th century.

PLATE 15. (Left) Iona, Maclean's Cross, a 15th-century commemorative cross on the route from the nunnery to the abbey.

PLATE 16. (Below) Càrn Bàn, a natural hillock at Gruline, crowned by a Bronze Age cairn; possibly a *Thing* site or assembly place in Viking times (2.7).

PLATE 17. Pennycross, the *Crois an Ollaimh*, commemorating Beaton physicians (5.10).

PLATE 18. Aros Castle, the 13th-century hall-house (5.12).

PLATE 19. Duart Castle, the heavily restored medieval castle of the Macleans (5.15).

PLATE 20. Locbuie House, the late 18th-century residence of the Maclaines of Lochbuy (6.5).

PLATE 21. Ardalanish, the Baptist's Cave, occupied by a schoolmaster and his family in the 1840s (2.14).

PLATE 22. Iona Parish Church, a 'Parliamentary kirk' of 1828 (6.29).

PLATE 23. Crackaig Township, Treshnish, ruined houses of the 18th century (6.15).

PLATE 24. Inivea Township, Calgary Bay, ruined houses of the 18th century (6.18).

PLATE 25. Killean, a sheep fank built in the ruins of the township (6.19).

PLATE 26. Suidhe, the ruins of a township near Bunessan (6.25).

PLATE 27. Bunessan, corn mill (6.37).

PLATE 28. Gruline, the mausoleum of Major-General Lachlan Macquarie (1762–1824) (6.41).

PLATE 29. Tormore, granite quarries, in the Ross of Mull (7.5).

Duart, supported the Jacobite Uprising of 1715, fighting at Sheriffmuir as a clan unit. A list survives from 1716 of the men of Mull and neighbouring islands, listing the arms they were required to surrender. From it we learn that of 976 in Mull, Ulva, Gometra and Iona, 160 admitted to have taken part in the rebellion. They did not include Conduiligh MacRacing (Rankin), resident at Kilbrennan, Torloisk, head of that piping family, but his son Hector confessed to having supported the Jacobite cause. The arms that were handed in included guns, swords, targes and dirks. Many Mull men also turned out in 1745 in support of Prince Charles Edward Stewart.

HOUSES

The Englishman William Sacheverell noted in 1688 that the house on Iona of 'Lady Macleod' (*recte* Maclean), where he was entertained by the Laird of Brolass (Donald 3rd of Brolass) was 'a neat little cabin; it was the first boarded house I has seen in these parts, and had been formerly prettily furnished; it had three good rooms belonging to it'. This wooden house was clearly exceptional. Practically nothing is known of the residences of other lairds and tacksmen prior to the 18th century. Many no doubt continued to live in houses either dating back to medieval times, or ones little different in style – simple halls with earth floors and thatched roofs. The Laird of Ulva's house (at Bracadale, Ulva) had earth floors when visited by Johnson and Boswell in 1773. The remodelling of Duart Castle in 1673 with a three-storey northeast range with kitchens, offices and accommodation, forming a wing to the southeast range with its first-floor hall dating to the mid 16th century, was exceptional in creating a noble house that would have been admired in the Lowlands (5.15). Sir Allan Maclean of Duart had little chance to enjoy it prior to the loss of his estates to the Campbells in 1674.

The Macleans of Lochbuie only abandoned Moy Castle as their main residence in 1752, when John Maclean 17th of Lochbuie erected a small two-storey house nearby. It remained their residence until 1793. This was where Boswell and Johnson were entertained in 1773, and it still survives, much altered, behind the present Lochbuie House built by Murdoch 19th of Lochbuie some time about the later 1780s and early 1790s (Plate 20). While Boswell considered the earlier house poor, this one can be characterised as spacious and handsome, though a relatively plain three-storey main block with two-storey wings, a Georgian standard and style that many landowners across the country aspired to.

In the course of the 18th century other lairds and tacksmen aspired to build two-storey, lime-mortared stone houses with slate roofs. An early example is Erray near Tobermory (6.2), built in the early 18th century for the Laird of MacKinnon. Others, like Old Gruline House (6.4, now called Macquarie House), Pennygown and Kilfinichen (Killiemore), date to later in the century. Substantial two-storey stone houses became the norm for the more important tenant farmers in the 19th century. The creation of the town of Tobermory from the late 1780s brought comfortable Lowland-style urban housing to the island (Fig. 33).

In 1688 the Englishman William Sacheverell described staying in a Mull changehouse (inn) – a place that had neither bed, victuals, nor drink. He was obliged to have his servants cut ferns for bedding. Substantial, modern inns appeared in the 18th century including Craignure, still in use, and the Grass Point Ferryhouse. Nevertheless, the only 'public house' in Iona in 1798 for a visitor, a medical doctor, Thomas Garnett, to stay in turned out to be a 'wretched hut' with 'a floor of liquid mire, and open to the roof,

Figure 33. Tobermory in 1813 (Daniell 1820)

except where two or three boards had been put over to prevent the rain from falling on the beds'. Apart from the 'light infantry' in the beds themselves, the visitors had to put up with an assortment of chickens, pigs, cats, a lamb and a dog.

There is a useful contemporary description of houses for the lower class of tenants on the estates of the Duke of Argyll, given by John Smith, minster of Campbeltown in 1798. Although he describes them as 'dark, damp and cold', his description appears to be describing an ideal version:

Their houses are generally low, narrow, dark, damp and cold. The walls are built sometimes with dry stones, and sometimes with clay or mud for mortar: couples are set about 6 feet asunder; ribs are laid on these couples; poles or brushwood across these ribs; divot, or thin turf, covers these poles; and then the whole is covered with a cot of thatch. The thatch, which commonly consists of straw, sprots or rushes, is laid on loosely, and fastened by ropes of the same materials, or of heath; except in Kintyre, where the straw is fastened by driving in the one end into the roof with a thatcher's tool, as in the low country. A few roofs are covered with ferns, and fewer still with heather.

The tenant at his entry receives, and at his departure pays, whatever repairs the houses need for being put in a habitable or tenantable condition, according to the estimate of stated and sworn appraisers in every parish...

A dwelling-house, 30 feet by 16, within walls, and 10 high in the sides, above the level of the threshold, which ought to be always at least a foot higher than the ground without, in order to make the floor dry and comfortable. These dimensions will admit of a kitchen in one end, and a family room in the other. They will also admit of excellent garrets (having 3 feet of the side walls) for keeping and sleeping places, with a stair in the middle, opposite to the main door. Each of these garrets will, if requisite, admit of 2 beds on either side, as will also each of the ends below; and there will be a small cellar under the stair, and a closet at the top of it; all which will give any ordinary family abundance of accommodation.

Dwelling houses in Mull, like those in the townships of Crack-aig, Inivea and Suidhe, were presumably the sort of houses Smith had in mind (Plates 23, 24, 26), though he appears to have greatly exaggerated the wall heights, or at least given ten feet as an ideal. The division between kitchen and family room was presumably formed by a wooden partition. He does not mention fireplaces and chimneys but the need for a vent to improve air circulation. What he would have had in mind was a hanging lum, a wood-lined vent through the roof, positioned above an open fire. The stair to sleeping accommodation was no doubt in most cases a mere ladder giving access only to space in which to lie down. It also has to be stressed that most houses were not so commodious or well appointed as the above description outlines, like the 'mean and wretched hovels' occupied by cottagers and tradesmen.

Smith also describes an appropriate suite of 'offices' for a lower-class tenant, including an apartment to serve as a milk-house in summer and a potato-house in winter, a barn with a loft for storing grain, and a byre. His preferred arrangement was that these should be built in a line as an extension of the dwelling house, but in Mull it appears that they were normally built as separate units. Small enclosures or gardens adjacent to houses were either for growing vegetables or use as stackyards.

The township of Inivea is known to have been a joint tenancy farm in the 18th century, let to four tenants in 1739 and cleared in 1832. The ruins there include four substantial dwelling houses of the type just described. Others are to be seen at Crackaig and Glac Gugairidh, both cleared in 1867.

It was a different class of Mull house that caught the attention of Dr Garnett in 1798, ones which he thought much worse than those on the mainland (Fig. 34). They were built of field stones or 'earth' (turf) with earth floors and roofs covered with thatch or turf. They were usually divided into two rooms, one for the family to live in with an open fire in the middle over which was an iron pot, suspended from the roof. Sometimes there was a hole in the roof for the escape of smoke. Windows (one per house) were only about a foot square and closed either by glass or a wooden shutter; doors might be of wooden boards or wickerwork; beds were of heather. The other room would have been for animals. Such was the stan-

Figure 34. A Mull cottage (Garnett 1800, vol. 1)

dard of living enjoyed by cotters, workmen, tradesmen and others.

An archaeologist, James Miln, visiting Iona in 1868, not only describes a cottage in which he sheltered as having a central fireplace, consisting of a stone slab on which a few pieces of turf were burning, but recounts how the lady of the house used it for making 'small vases' of clay dug from her garden. They were shaped by hand, placed on the fire and filled with milk. After this had boiled for some time they were hard enough for use. This tradition of handmaking 'croggans' had also survived in other islands including Tiree and Lewis.

In Mull and Iona traditional houses and cottages tend to have hipped roofs with the supporting couples resting directly on the wall heads. Turf walls would not have been load-bearing, and so in houses made of that material the roofs must have been supported on crucks from ground level. The stone-walled mill at Ormaig in Ulva (6.43), dating to the late 18th or beginning of the 19th century, had a roof given extra solidity by support on cruck-couples set in the wall thickness from about half a metre above floor level, and this may have been a usual means in Mull for supporting roofs. A few houses, like one at Crackaig and others at Suidhe, have one gable end. Hybrid forms like this were particularly common in the Ross of Mull.

In the later 19th century fireplaces in end walls with chimneys became usual. Such an arrangement can be seen in the restored 'Sheila's cottage' in Ulva, which serves as a museum. It also has furniture and furnishings typical of the 19th century.

CHURCHES

The medieval churches of these islands, as elsewhere, were taken over for worship by the Reformed Church in the aftermath of the Reformation. As times changed, ministers and congregations found themselves having to make do with increasingly ruinous buildings, in many cases not conveniently sited for centres of population. It took until 1755 before there were any purpose-built churches for Protestant worship. In that year a simple oblong building with a bell-cot on its west gable was erected at Kilninian (6.8), possibly on the site of the medieval parish church, and another church, since replaced but perhaps similar, was built as Kilmore Parish Church at Dervaig, to replace the nearby medieval church of Kilcolmkill. A church was built in Salen in 1777 and another about the same time at Kinlochspelve (both replaced). The parish church of Torosay was erected at Craignure in 1783 and is still in use.

Further much-needed church provision was supplied in 1828 by the Parliamentary Commissioners appointed to build additional places of worship in the Highlands and Islands. 'Parliamentary kirks' were erected on Iona (Plate 22) and Ulva, and at Kinlochspelve, Tobermory and Salen. Kinlochspelve has now been converted into a house and the other two on Mull have since been replaced. These churches were built to a standardised plan by the great engineer Thomas Telford. Generous manses were also provided for the ministers.

FARMING

In the Early Modern Period, the land on Mull farms was divided into infield, outfield and rough pasture, and joint tenants distributed arable land amongst themselves by a system known as runrig. When and how this system first made its appearance in Mull is not known. It dates back to medieval times elsewhere in Britain, but it is possible that its introduction to this island may only have been in the 16th century. The arable land of some farms may still have consisted of clumps of small enclosed fields as late as the arrival of Campbell tacksmen and tenants in the Maclean of Duart lands in the late 17th century.

The infield or croft land consisted of the best land, normally around the actual settlement, land that was manured and intensively cropped. In pre-improvement agriculture it was divided into rigs – long, thin, raised beds, separated by furrows. They are normally orientated so that water can drain off down the furrows. Rigs on some farms were created and maintained by ploughing. Traditional ploughs were heavy and clumsy, mostly of wood apart from an iron share that broke the ground. They were pulled by a team of oxen. At the end of the 18th century they were beginning to be replaced in Mull by more efficient two-horse ploughs. Many rigs, often called lazy-beds, were made by turning over the turf with spades, and mounding it up, especially for growing potatoes. These rigs, either individually or in groups, were normally unenclosed. The rigs of the different tenants on a farm were intermixed, and reallocated by joint agreement every so often, perhaps every three years. The evidence for these unenclosed rigs can be seen in many places in Mull, for instance adjacent to (north and east) the township of Inivea (6.18), alongside the track between Tiroran and Burg, in Ardmeanach, and in the fields around the chapel, Caibeal Mheamhair, at Laggan.

Beyond the infield was the outfield, green or better quality pasture, parts of which were cropped from time to time, perhaps after an application of manure. It was separated from the rough pasture or moor by the head dyke. Good examples of head dykes include one running approximately north/south between the fort and dun at Dùn Haunn on the Treshnish coastal walk (3.7, 3.25). The contrast between the green pasture to the west and rough ground and cliffs to the east is striking. Other head dykes can be seen running approximately NSW–ENE to the north of the deserted township of Tìr Fhearagain (Tireragan) in the Ross of Mull (6.28) and bounding the south end of the three crofts into which the farm of Kilpatrick (in Brolass), to the northeast of Bunessan, was subdivided. This dyke runs approximately east–west at a height above sea level of between 140m and 150m. An earlier head dyke runs parallel to this, within the crofts to the north, between a height of 90m and 100m above sea level.

In the cool, damp climate prevalent in these islands it was essential that grain should be dried prior to being ground. This was done in small kilns, which in medieval times may generally have been housed inside barns, as at Baliscate (5.1). Another kiln barn of unknown, but probably later date, has recently been surveyed at Aird in Mornish. In post-medieval times many kilns were in the open, adjacent to settlements. The one at Achnahaird (6.10) may be typical. Another at the deserted township of Lephin near Glengorm Castle was partially excavated by Mull Museum staff a number of years ago, revealing a small stone-lined bowl and part of the flue. A wasteful and dangerous alternative to kiln drying was graddaning, the burning of the ears of corn on the stock, and immediately thrashing out the flames. This was a technique that was discouraged by landowners as it went hand in hand with the use of querns, hand mills, which deprived them of the multures due from having grain ground by professional millers in their mills.

Prior to the late 18th century these mills, sometimes known as horizontal, black, click or Norse mills, were small and simple structures. Their millstones were turned by being directly connected by a spindle to a horizontal arrangement of awes or feathers (paddles) placed in running water. None survive in Mull or Iona in any state of completion and traces of them are difficult to locate. One has recently been identified at Salachry in Ardmeanach (6.22). The site of one of unknown date has been excavated on the Sruth a' Mhuilinn, Iona (4.3). Another was possibly located on the burn flowing through the settlement at Inivea (6.18), and the remains of a third have been identified at Glac Dhubh, Torloisk (NGR NM 431 441). The evidence for this structure consists of 'two rectangular remnants' on the verge of streams immediately below a waterfall. It is situated at the top of a track heading onto the moors from Ballygown, beyond the remains of three houses. In the 1790s three out of eight corn mills in the parish of Kilninian were still mills of this type and perhaps this was one of them. They were apparently still prevalent in the parish of Torosay (southeast Mull) in the early 1830s. In the later 18th and 19th centuries estate owners had more sophisticated mills with upright wheels constructed, like the one at Bunessan (Plate 27).

In the summer months many of the inhabitants of the farms, especially the women and children, decamped with their animals to the moors to avail themselves of the pasture there and to keep the animals well away from damaging the growing crops. This trans-humance also had considerable social significance, presenting different opportunities for interaction, particularly amongst the younger folk. Township communities based themselves at tradi-tional shieling sites where milk was turned into butter and cheese and stored for taking back to the main settlements or winter towns for sustenance and payment of rents. Shielings are the temporary shelters occupied on the moors, made of branches covered with turf or stone, refurbished or rebuilt every year. Sometimes shielings have the appearance of having been erected on mounds, actually the collapsed remains of earlier structures. The individual shieling houses were often circular or oval, with an internal space of only about 2.4m to 4m in diameter. According to the *New Statistical Account* for Ulva published in 1845, the habit of going to the shiel-ings had survived on that island until about 40 years previously. Four shieling huts have recently been surveyed at Blar Na Fola near Baliscate (6.13), and others are noted in the gazetteer. Those at Airigh a' Bhreac Laoigh on the farm of Kilpatrick in the Ross of Mull are sited not far outside the head dyke (6.12). Dykes separat-ing the infield from the outfield, around gardens, and increasingly used to subdivide farms and create separate crofts, were invariably until the late 18th century of turf, sometimes with an admixture of stone. Drystone dykes are essentially a phenomenon of the late 18th and 19th centuries, built by specialist dykers.

Access to peat, cut and dried for use as fuel, was an essential element in the farming economy. Plentiful supplies were not too difficult to find in most areas of Mull and could be managed on a farm by farm basis. It was a different matter for the inhabitants of Iona, who had to cut their peat in Mull.

The inhabitants of these islands traditionally grew bear (a coarse variety of barley) and oats for their own consumption. Potatoes were introduced as a crop in the middle of the 18th century and rapidly took hold. By the end of the 18th century they were the main food for the poorer people for three quarters of the year. More than one late 18th-century and early 19th-century commentator noted that Mull did not grow enough food for its inhabitants, and grain, especially oatmeal, had to be imported. This was because there was too much concentration on the raising of cattle and sheep, activities which provided money, not least to pay rents. Agriculturally productive land was limited but the Rev. Dr John Walker, who reported on the Hebrides for the Commission for Annexed Estates in 1764, thought that a lot more ground could be given over to arable production. He could see land where crops had previously been grown but which was now overgrown with heather. Flax was also grown, but most of the linen worn by the inhabitants had to be imported. The production of natural hay was practised to a limited extent.

By 1764, 2,000 of the native breed of black cattle were being exported from Mull annually along with 500 native horses (Highland ponies). The cattle were young animals destined for sale at mainland markets and fattening on Lowland or English farms before being slaughtered for meat. This business undoubtedly had its roots in medieval times. Maclean of Duart was one of the West Highland chiefs who successfully petitioned the Scottish Privy Council in 1609 to rescind a recent proclamation forbidding the purchase of cattle and horses in the Isles. On the one hand this proposed restriction in trade would have hurt them economically, and, on the other, it would have seriously affected their ability to pay their rents to the Crown.

The raising of cattle and horses was a relatively lucrative business for the larger tenants, tacksmen and the drovers who bought the beasts and transported them to buyers and markets in the mainland. Increasingly in the 18th century the letting of farms to single tenants who would concentrate on raising beasts was preferred by landlords to farms with joint tenants concentrating on growing food for their own consumption. The enclosure of these farms meant that there was little need for herdsmen and others to stop the beasts from straying.

In Mull there was a fair for cattle and horses at Druim Tighe Mhic Ghille Chatain, Tenga (6.39), held each August as late as the early 19th century. This was evidently the one described by John Ramsay of Ochtertyre as the most considerable fair in the West Highlands. He describes how it was held on the side of a high hill, four or five miles from any houses. It lasted for a week and attracted great numbers from the Isles and further afield, including pedlars from the Lowlands and Ireland, and members of the gentry. Those who came from afar were obliged to eat and sleep in tents or temporary huts. There are the remains there of over 50 small rectangular, turf structures which represent the remains of these shelters. Others are to be found at Torness, where the market may only have been for horses (6.45). By 1843 the fair ground had been shifted to Bailemeonach (Fishnish) on the Sound of Mull, where there was a stone-built pier for mooring the boats that took animals and passengers over to Lochaline in Morvern. There were two fairs there annually for black cattle and one for horses.

One of the main drovers in the later 18th century was John Stewart, tacksman of Achdashenaig (an earlier name for Glen Aros). Others came from the mainland. Cattle from the neighbouring islands of Coll and Tiree were also ferried via Mull. They were landed at Kintra in the Ross of Mull and driven overland to the ferry at Auchnacraig (Grass Point) at the southeast tip of the island whence the crossing was made to Kerrera and Oban. The Gregorson family were tacksmen of Auchnacraig and ran the inn and ferry there. They also raised a considerable number of cattle on farms in Mull and Morvern, which they held from the Duke of Argyll. In earlier times it is probable that Scottish burghs, including Dumbarton, Stirling and Perth, were important destinations for the cattle, but in the earlier 19th century Falkirk rose to prominence as the main fair and redistribution centre.

The travel writer Thomas Pennant noted in 1772 that Iona supported about 180 cattle and 500 sheep. It is probable that this relatively high number of sheep reflected a local interest in cloth production. In Mull the advantages of giving land over to sheep rearing only became apparent to landowners from the late 18th century, and unfortunately this new development in land management was very much to be at the expense of the sitting tenants. Already by 1792 the 5th Duke of Argyll was wanting to encourage 'new settlers' (that is sheep-masters) to make offers for his farms. Sheep, including introduced black-faced and Cheviot breeds, could thrive on the open moors, on large runs created from clearing and amalgamating existing farms. Large herds could be looked after by one or two shepherds and there was limited need for buildings or equipment. Most obviously, large pens or fanks were required for rounding up and sorting out the animals (Plate 25). At some, for instance Pennyghael (6.21), shearing stools, low banks of turf and/or stone, have been identified. It was claimed that by 1802 most of Mull had been given over to sheep farming.

As the 18th century progressed there were increasing signs of population pressure. In 1764 the number of people in Mull, Ulva, Gometra, Inch Kenneth and Iona was about 5,500. By 1821 it had just about doubled. With limited options for many to grow or catch their own food, or be gainfully employed by others, many increasingly turned to other options. For some that was joining the army or navy. For others it was seasonal work in the more prosperous Lowlands. A new life in the West Indies and North America was attracting some in the second half of the 18th century.

There had never been security of tenure for anybody in these islands, or indeed elsewhere in Scotland. Clan solidarity and the need for chiefs to raise fighting forces had been factors that led to a preference for sitting tenants when leases and tacks were up for renewal. Being seen and acting as clan chiefs became less attractive options for landlords as the 18th century progressed. Making money from their assets became paramount. More and more pressure was heaped on tenants to introduce changes and improvements that would increase productivity and rents. The main moneymakers in local farming, raising cattle, horses and sheep, did not require a large work force. Would-be small tenants found it more and more difficult to obtain holdings, especially since they were required to engage in competitive bidding with others equally desperate. It was very easy for landowners and their agents to shift the majority of the people on their lands – cotters who did not pay them any rent and had no rights.

The long-standing landowners, including the Duke of Argyll and the Macleans of Lochbuie, were certainly responsible for clearing tenants from their lands, as indeed were new men who have often attracted more opprobrium. Opprobrium for oppression on the Argyll estates, including significant rent rises, tended to attach to the Duke's local agent, John Campbell, the 'Factor Mor', rather than the Duke himself. Significant changes in landownership in the early 19th century brought in landowners primarily interested in making money from their estates with no feeling of clan solidarity with those already occupying their lands, potentially in the way of sheep or deer. In the 1830s Hugh MacAskill cleared much of Mornish in the northwest of Mull.

LOCAL INDUSTRIES

There were local alternatives to subsistence farming; some, like fishing and kelp manufacture, greatly encouraged by landlords such as the dukes of Argyll. The 5th Duke was Governor of the British Fisheries Society, which aimed to encourage that industry by the establishment of fishing villages, hence the foundation of Tobermory in 1788 (6.32). There was soon a custom house and post office, a population of about 300, including merchants, a boat builder and a cooper, a smith, a wright, tailors and innkeepers. There was a pier and a large store of salt for supplying boats involved in the herring fishery. Tobermory was to thrive as the main local centre, but it never took off as a fishing port. In the late 1780s and early 1790s the Duke was also encouraging the establishment of fishing communities at Creich and Kintra (6.31) in the Ross of Mull, but these were not long-lasting successes either. Hector Maclean of Torloisk encouraged the development of a local linen industry in the 1750s, establishing a spinning school which attracted pupils from Mull and beyond, but this venture does not seem to have survived for more than a few years. Nor was the Duke's attempt in the 1790s to establish a spinning school in Iona so that the womenfolk could learn to produce linen yarn as a source of income any more successful.

Another Iona venture that failed to take off about this time was the marble quarry at the southeast end of the island. The marble was (re)discovered in 1789 and workmen were brought to the island to quarry it (7.4). Some marble was exported, but it was to be another hundred years or so before there was a successful industry. Ross of Mull granite was quarried at Camas Tuath (North Bay, NGR NM 352 242) on the north coast of the Ross of Mull in the 1830s and 1840s for building the lighthouses on Skerryvore and at Ardnamurchan, and extensive evidence of other quarrying activity can be seen at Tormore (Plate 29), just to the north of Fionnphort. Ross of Mull granite was used in prestigious building projects throughout Britain and even as far away as New York.

The kelp industry was much more promising. There were plentiful supplies of this seaweed around the coasts of Mull. It was gathered, dried and burned from the late 18th century to make alkali for making soap and glass. This work provided a living for many in the Western Isles and considerable income for landowners until the second decade of the 19th century, when the market was flooded with much cheaper alkali of Spanish origin. At the height of the boom some 430 tons were being exported from Mull annually.

There were still natural woods in Mull in the 18th century that could be exploited for charcoal production by ironworks on the Argyll mainland. As early as 1756 the Lorn Furnace at Bonawe acquired an eight-year lease of the woods of Lochbuie. Not encouraged, but a significant earner for some in the 18th and earlier 19th century, was the manufacture and smuggling of whisky. Along with a copper still head with three outlets, from Glen Clova, displayed in the Mull Museum in Tobermory, is a list of 18 known or rumoured sites of whisky production, including the Whisky Cave at Crackaig (6.38). The only legal distillery operating on a commercial scale was founded at Ledaig (Tobermory) in 1798 by John Sinclair (6.44). Much of the whisky, of course, was for local consumption. Martin Martin noted at the end of the 17th century how 'the natives [of Mull] are accustomed to take a large dose of aqua-vitae [whisky] as a corrective, when the season is very moist'. He added that they chewed 'charmel root' (the root of heath pea) to 'in some measure prevent drunkenness'.

ROADS

Across Mull there was a network of routes for humans and animals. Wheeled transport was almost unknown prior to the 19th century, at least partly because the roads were not suitable. Boswell noted how his travelling companion, Dr Johnson, was cheered by their first sight of cart tracks for a very long time when they landed on Inch Kenneth in 1773. 'It gave us a pleasure similar to that which a traveller feels, when, whilst wandering on what he fears is a desert island, he perceives the print of human feet.' It was probably as much for the convenience of shifting animals as enabling humans

Figure 35. The bridge at Aros in 1813 (Daniell 1820)

to pass dry-shod that bridges made an appearance on some of the main river crossings from the late 18th century. The route from Aros to the ferry at Grass Point was key, and hence the bridges at the mouth of the Aros River (Fig. 35) and at Auchnacraig at the head of Loch Don.

George Langlands' map of 1801 shows substantial routeways from Tobermory down the east coast to the ferry at Grass Point, and from the head of Loch Don to Lochbuie. There was also a road from Fidden, at the tip of the Ross of Mull, round through Bunessan to Ardtun. Otherwise Langland only shows tracks. Many of these were the precursors of the present day road system established in the course of the 19th century, but it is notable that there was no route all the way through Glen More, the one taken nowadays by so many tourists and pilgrims on their way from the mainland ferries to Iona. There were, however, tracks connecting many of the settlements on the southside of the Ross of Mull, townships on Ulva and in Treshnish. Other tracks went from Pennygown on the Sound of Mull through Glen Forsa and by a series of lochs on the Lussa River to Lochbuie, and from the head of Loch Scridain via Mam Clachaig (7.7) and Loch Bà to the head of Loch na Keal.

TOURISM

Tourism was to lift off in the early 19th century as one of the main-stays of the local economy. The influx of curious visitors was greatly aided by the development of steamships, which were plying the waters around Mull and Iona by the 1820s, almost as soon as they were invented. Iona, since the days of St Columba, had drawn pilgrims, and latterly those interested in antiquities. Iona was one of the main attractions for the literati Samuel Johnston and James Boswell, when they ventured into the Highlands and Islands in 1773. The young Scotsman, Boswell, was worried that his elderly English companion would fail to be impressed by the place, or think the visit not worth the trouble of going. Johnson's actual response was to muse that 'That man is little to be envied, whose patriotism would not gain force upon the plain of Marathon, or whose piety would not grow warmer among the ruins of Iona'.

The geological wonders of Staffa were also attracting interna-tional attention by the later 18th century. The naturalist Sir Joseph Banks was the first to draw attention to the island in a detailed description published by Thomas Pennant in 1774. When he saw the main sea-cave he wondered 'compared to this what are the cathedrals or places built by men?' Quite so, but what really caught the imagination of his readers was the identification of this natural phenomenon as the cave of 'Fhinn MacCoul, whom the translator of Ossian's works has called Fingal'. This is a reference to James Macpherson's Ossianic Cycle of poems, then attracting worldwide interest and scepticism. Macpherson claimed his work was based on old Gaelic sources which he never produced, although chal-lenged to do so. Nevetheless his fame and estimation as a poet were enough to secure his burial in Westminster Abbey.

The combination of spectacular rock formations and legendary Celtic hero was to prove irresistible as a tourist draw. Indeed, it still is. Another influential visitor was the German composer Felix Mendelssohn. He made a tour in Scotland in 1829, stayed in Tober-mory in a house set back from the Main Street, and went on to view Staffa. His enduringly popular 'Hebrides Overture', the idea for which came during his trip, captures the flow of the sea and the magnificence of Fingal's Cave.

7. Modern Times:
Mid 19th Century to the Present Day

The islands that emerged in the second half of the 19th century as part of the Modern World were a very small part, for many seemingly remote, of a very large, politically and economically dominant British Empire. The 1905 clock tower on the seafront of Tobermory commemorating Henrietta Bird must have helped raise awareness of this wider world (6.32). Many were to experience life overseas as emigrants as evictions left them very limited options to carry on making a living in these islands. The pace of evictions was to increase considerably in the mid 19th century as a result of the failure of the potato crops and consequent famine.

Potatoes grew well and easily in the poor soils of Mull, and were a vital mainstay of the local diet, until disaster struck in 1846 with the arrival of the blight, a fungus (*Phytophthora infestans*) that had already rotted crops in Ireland and elsewhere in Britain and Europe. This was not the first famine to affect Mull, nor the worst in terms of its toll of death, but it is well documented and the social and population changes that resulted totally transformed the island.

The blight was not easily eradicated and affected crops well into the 1850s. The years from 1849 to 1851 were particularly bad, with 80% or more of the potato crop failing. The lack of food and poor diet generally amongst the islanders led to outbreaks of dysentery, typhus and influenza, all of which had a devastating effect, carrying many off to their death. While local men of standing made efforts to get government assistance to alleviate starvation, it was clear that removing hungry mouths from the land would be a useful solution from the point of view of landowners. Francis William Clark cleared Ulva in the 1840s and tenants were forced from Dervaig by James Forsyth in 1857. Sheriff Court records indicate 1,277 summonses of removal for residents in Mull between 1846 and 1852.

The potato famine and clearances in the mid 19th century were a major turning point in shaping the landscape and reducing population, which fell from 10,612 recorded in the 1821 census to just over 5,000 in 1871. The move to commercial stock raising, cattle and sheep was now completed, with farms soon totally in the hands of new farmers, many of them incomers to the island. Tobermory became overrun with paupers, many awaiting the means and opportunity to head overseas. In 1861–62 a poorhouse was erected to the west of Tobermory to accommodate up to 130 paupers, male and female, from Mull, Ardnamurchan, Morvern and the neighbouring islands of Coll and Tiree. It remained in operation until 1923 and has since been demolished.

There were considerable changes too to landownership. One was the return of the Macleans to Duart Castle after a period of exile stretching back to the late 17th century. In 1910 Sir Fitzroy Maclean, chief of the Macleans of Duart, regained his ancestral seat through purchase from the then owner, Walter Murray Guthrie. Duart Castle was then in ruins but has since been restored as a fitting clan centre and one of the main heritage assets in Mull.

To some extent a by-product of a perception that the Church of Scotland was on the side of landowners was the arrival and popularity in these islands of other Protestant Christian sects. The Baptists had a meeting house in Bunessan as early as 1823 and later had a church there as well as in Tobermory. The Free Church, formed in 1843, had a church at Lochdon by 1852 and another in Tobermory by 1877. The Scottish Episcopal Church, however, appeared largely because of support from landowning members. St Columba's at Gruline, built in 1873, was followed three years later by St Kilda's at Lochbuie.

The marble quarry in Iona was to have a final flurry of commercial success in the years from 1907 to 1918 (7.4) and the quarrying of granite at Tormore continued into the early 20th century (7.5). In recent times, however, life in Mull and Iona has been largely sustained by tourism, fishing, farming and forestry. The Burg Estate was gifted to the National Trust for Scotland in 1936 (6.14). It was not well endowed with money, was difficult to access and had few obvious heritage attractions with the exception of Macculloch's Fossil Tree. The main house, occupied by the tenant, Duncan MacGillivray and his sister Chrissie, consisted of two rooms and a kitchen, constructed in the early 1920s of corrugated iron. There was no running water or electricity. The Trust decided to leave Burg in the MacGillivrays' hands and treat it as an experiment for farming techniques which might be applicable on other island farms, particularly methods for the suppression or eradication of bracken. The MacGillivrays had 20 or so head of cattle, including half a dozen milk cows, a flock of 200 sheep and some hens. They grew crops of hay, potatoes and oats. Wild rabbits were plentiful, the taking and sale of which provided a significant income stream. This experimental phase came to an end in 1948, but the MacGillivrays stayed on at Burg, Chrissie until her death at age 91 in 1989, a well-known and respected lady, always keen to entertain those who passed on their way to the fossil tree.

Forestry has proved more successful as an industry, a way of managing the land. The Forestry Commission has a string of major forests extending the length of the island from Ardmore at the northeast point down to Scallastle on the Sound of Mull. The Commission is very aware of its social responsibilities and the need to encourage tourism, providing access to sites of archaeological interest on its estate, like the chapel at Cill an Ailein in Glen Aros (5.2), and working with other organisations to facilitate the spotting of golden eagles and the reintroduced white-tailed eagles. In recent years other forests at Langamull and West Ardhu in the northwest of Mull and the Tiroran Forest in Ardmeanach have been the subject of community buy-outs. The latter forest includes the deserted settlement of Knockroy (6.20).

The whisky distillery in Tobermory, originally opened in 1798, has had a chequered history over the years with long periods of closure (6.44). It closed in 1930, largely due to the fall in demand caused by prohibition in the United States. It reopened in 1972 thanks to a resurgence in interest in whisky. Some of its production is for blended whiskies but it also produces single malts labelled as Tobermory and also Ledaig. There is a visitor centre at the distillery.

Having reached a low of about 2,150 in 1961 the population is again on the increase, perhaps about 3,000 today. Many properties have been acquired by outsiders as holiday homes, and others have come for work or to retire. The 2001 census indicates that 33% of the population were not even born in Scotland. Nevertheless, there is still a core of the population with roots in the past. Traditions and old ways of life are remembered thanks to bodies like the Mull Museum in Tobermory and the work of ethnographers. There is a rich seam of stories about witches, fairies, mermaids and water-horses, still to be adequately mined. Real figures from the past, like Ailein nan Sop (Alan of the Straw) and Eoghann a' chinn bhig (Hugh of the little head), both 16th-century Macleans, feature in tales, while the legend of the Spanish princess in her large ship coming to seek out Maclean of Duart would seem to have been suggested, at least in part, by the arrival of the ship from the Spanish Armada in Tobermory Bay.

Music, song and poetry, strongly rooted in the past, remain a significant part of local life, and in some cases have had a remarkable international reach. Such is the case with a hymn, written by Mary MacDonald, who lived at Ardtun in the Ross of Mull in the 19th century. It was translated into English in 1888 as 'Child in the manger', sung all round the world at Christmas-time to a popular tune known as 'Bunessan'. There is a monument to Mary (7.2) by the side of the A849 about a mile and a half to the east of Bunessan. Another similar monument at Ardura (7.1) commemorates the 19th-century Gaelic poet and writer, Dugald MacPhail.

Not specifically local in flavour are the artistic endeavours supported by Comar, an umbrella organisation overseeing the Mull Theatre and An Tobar. The theatre, which has Mull roots as far back as 1963, is now located at Druimfin near Tobermory. It has been billed as the world's smallest professional theatre and sends productions all over Scotland. An Tobar, based in a Victorian school building in Tobermory, is a heritage hub with workshops, studios, recording facilities and performance space.

Gaelic remained the main language of the locals until World War II (1939–45), and although only 10% of the working age population could speak or understand it by 2001, thanks to schooling and a revival of interest in this fine language, there is real hope that it has a future in these islands.

As in previous centuries, the people of Mull and Iona made a large contribution to war efforts in the 20th century. War memorials commemorating the ultimate sacrifice made by many in the two world wars of the 20th century are to be found on Iona, at Creich Church near Fionnphort, at Bunessan, Loch Buie, and at the parish churches at Kilmore (7.3, Dervaig), Salen, Craignure and Tobermory. During the Second World War, Tobermory became a major naval training base for anti-submarine warfare, under the command of 'The Terror of Tobermory', Vice-Admiral Sir Gilbert Stephenson, with his flagship, HMS *Western Isles*. From the summer of 1940 all navy escort ships intended for Atlantic convoy duty were required to undertake training at Tobermory before being allowed to deploy. During the Battle of the Atlantic, ships manned by Tobermory sailors were responsible for sinking at least 130 enemy U-boats and shooting down over 40 enemy aircraft. Hundreds of thousands of British, Commonwealth and allied service personnel spent some time here. This was a major turning point in opening up the island to outside influences.

The RAF also had a Second World War presence in Mull, with one of their chain of early warning radar (Chain Home Low) stations being located at Carsaig on the south coast. Carsaig was also where much of the 1945 British classic romantic film *I Know Where I'm Going!*, by Michael Powell and Emeric Pressburger, was filmed. Moy Castle featured as the ancestral home of the film's hero, Torquil MacNeil, the Laird of Kiloran.

A considerable boost to tourism was provided by the opening of the railway to Oban in 1880, linking with large mainland centres of population. The pier at Craignure for handling the main influx of ferry traffic from Oban dates to 1964 and has made Mull and Iona very accessible for private cars and tour buses, many of which head for Iona as a day trip from the mainland. From 1983 to 2011 a narrow-gauge railway line, about 2km in length, was in operation from the ferry terminal at Craignure to Torosay Castle (6.7). Its closure was seen as potentially a major setback, one that has not materialised. Mull and Iona remain as popular with residents and visitors alike and there is a great deal to enjoy.

PART II

Gazetteer of Selected Sites and Monuments

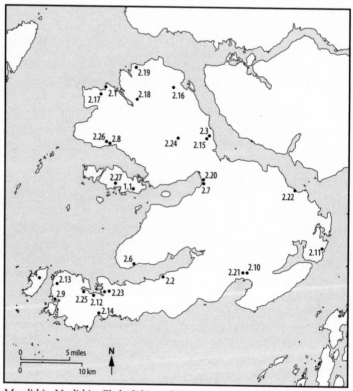

Mesolithic, Neolithic, Chalcolithic and Bronze Age sites

1. Mesolithic Sites

1.1 A' Chrannag, Ulva: occupied cave NM 431 384

A substantial cave in the bottom of a cliff, now often called Livingstone's Cave, after the family that lived nearby from which the famous explorer, David Livingstone, is descended. Indeed, David's grandfather is said to have lived in the cave with his family temporarily, until a house was built for them nearby. Excavations were undertaken in the cave by Clive Bonsall of Edinburgh University in 1989–91. The cave has probably been occupied at various times since the end of the last Ice Age. The remains of a rough wall of stones and boulders across its entrance probably dates to post-medieval times, and a fine brass Highland brooch was found within the cave, probably worn by a local woman in the 17th century. Early evidence for occupation is in the form of middens dating from about 5800 to 3680 BC, sealed under early Neolithic layers including sherds of pottery, and a pit containing burnt bone, shell and carbonised cereal grains. This could be dated to about 3000 BC on the basis of a radiocarbon date. The Mesolithic middens in the cave consisted mostly of shells, especially limpets and periwinkles, and also included mammal bones, fragments of crabs' claws, and flint artefacts. There was also a bone implement identified as a limpet scoop.

2. Neolithic, Chalcolithic and Bronze Age Sites

2.1 Croig Cave: occupied cave

NM 3859 5442

A small cave in a cliff on the northwest coast of Mull. Recent archaeological excavations demonstrated occupation over a span of three millennia, especially in the Bronze Age from about 1720 BC onwards. There are substantial midden deposits, which include shellfish and the bones of a variety of small fish that could have been caught inshore. There were also a number of small hearths. About 950 BC a bronze bracelet and amber bead were deposited in a small pit, and a piece of iron slag along with charcoal suggests smelting or smithing activity about 400 BC.

2.2 Torrans, Brolass: hut circle

NM 480 249

A circular feature defined by a low enclosing bank, about 12m in overall diameter, its entrance in its southeast side. It is adjacent to the ruins of the post-medieval township of Torrans.

BURIAL MONUMENTS

2.3 Ardnacross: cairns

NM 549 489

There are several cairns, including one visible from the road (A848) at NGR NM 549 489, two to the north of the broch, An Sean Chaisteal, at NGR NM 550 500 and NM 550 502, and a fourth on a low ridge to the north of Ardnacross farm at NGR NM 545 496. A group of three kerb cairns is associated with the nearby Ardnacross stone rows (2.15).

2.4 Blàr Buidhe, Iona: cairn

NM 284 243

A small, disturbed cairn, still with two boulders in place, which are likely to be the remains of a kerb. It appears as a grassy mound, situated below the high ground behind the Aosdàna Gallery.

2.5 Bunessan: cairn

NM 390 220

The low spreading remains of a cairn, with several boulders which may be the remains of a kerb. It is adjacent to the Bunessan War Memorial.

2.6 Burg, Ardmeanach: cairns

NM 427 264

Two large cairns by the shore at Port na Croise near the deserted township of Burg (6.14) and the dun of Dùn Bhuirg (3.23). They are both composed of pebbles, are about 13m in diameter, 1.6m in height and 90m apart.

2.7 Gruline: cairns

NM 546 393

These monuments occupy a narrow neck of land between the head of Loch na Keal and Loch Bà. The more prominent of the two is the grass-covered cairn which surmounts a natural conical mound known as Càrn Bàn, situated in a relatively flat field (Plate 16). The possible importance of this site and location in Scandinavian times has been dealt with in the main historic text above. In a plantation a few metres to the east (NGR NM 547 393) are the much robbed remains of another cairn. There are also two standing stones nearby (2.20).

2.8 Kilninian: cairn

NM 394 454

Adjacent to the road (B8073) between Tostary and Kilninian. It is still about 2m high with evidence for a kerb of boulders (Plate 2).

2.9 Knockvologan: cairn

NM 308 203

The site is quite striking, atop a low rise overlooking the neighbouring tidal island of Erraid. It consists of a low grass-covered mound up to 16.5m in diameter. From here the dun on Erraid, Dùn Aoidhean (3.22), can be viewed, and reached at the right state of the tide.

Essential viewing

2.10 Lochbuie: cairn, stone circle and standing stones

NM 614 252
NM 617 251

This group of monuments is located in fields just to the north of Lochbuie House. The cairn is in a clump of trees and has suffered badly from robbing. It, nevertheless, has many of its kerb stones still in place, two additional stones adjacent to the southeast edge serving as a false portal. The stone circle (2.21), over 12m in diameter, has had nine stones, of which one is now missing. There are two outlying stones, and a third, some distance away, to the north of the cairn, at NGR NM 616 254.

2.11 Port Donain: chambered cairn

NM 737 292

This chambered cairn is strikingly situated on a low rise overlooking the raised beach in the small sheltered bay of Port Donain. Further inland, a distance of about 100m across relatively fertile land, is a circular kerb cairn, adjacent to it a slab, which would once have been erect. Access to both involves a walk of less than 2km across fields from the car park for the Grass Point viewpoint. The outline of the chambered cairn can still be traced despite robbing of much of its superstructure. It has a length of about 32m and formerly had a concave façade at its northeast end with a chamber off it. Several stones of the façade and chamber survive *in situ*. There is a cist, presumably secondary, near the other end of the cairn with four side slabs and a capstone.

2.12 Suidhe: barrow

NM 370 218

A substantial, circular grass-covered mound, about 19m by 22m and 1m in height, not far from the deserted township of Suidhe (6.25). The mound appears to be composed of earth rather than stones (hence the description 'barrow' rather than cairn). There are two standing stones adjacent to its northern edge, one of them perforated, and an arrangement of slabs on its eastern edge, which might represent the remains of a chamber (Plate 1). It has, traditionally, been identified as St Columba's seat, hence the name Suidhe, Gaelic for the seat, or resting place.

For other cairns, see:
7.7 Carn Cul Righ Albainn, Mam Clachaig
7.8 Càrn Cùil ri Éirinn, Iona

STANDING STONES, STONE ROWS AND CIRCLES

2.13 Achaban House, Fionnphort: standing stone   NM 313 233

It stands in the garden of Achaban House, a rectangular slab of Ross of Mull granite with pointed top, about 2.4m high.

2.14 Ardalanish Bay: standing stones   NM 378 188

There is a standing stone on the raised beach, adjacent to a rocky outcrop with a cave. About 12m to the southeast of the standing stone is another, lying flat. An attempt has obviously been made to cut a quern or a millstone from it. It is possible that these two stones represent the remains of a short stone row. The cave has been walled off for human occupation. It is known as the Baptist's Cave since it became the home of Donald MacDonald and his family in the early 1840s (Plate 21). Donald was the schoolmaster at Ardchiavaig, dismissed for allowing his school to be used as a meeting place for fellow Baptists.

2.15 Ardnacross: stone rows and cairns   NM 542 491

The most obvious feature of this important ritualistic centre is a standing stone, flanked by two recumbent ones, all three originally forming a row of three, orientated NNE–SSW over a distance of about 11m. There are a further three recumbent slabs nearby, originally forming a row about 15m long with a similar orientation. Between these two rows there is a group of three kerb cairns, the largest, with a diameter of about 5.5m, being the best preserved (Plate 3). This group of monuments is situated on rising ground in a field with views up and down the Sound of Mull. For other nearby cairns, see 2.3.

2.16 Baliscate, Tobermory: stone row

NM 499 541

Three standing stones in a row, the middle one fallen, are sited on a low rise adjacent to a track leading southwestwards from the back of the Mull Pottery just to the south of Tobermory towards the medieval chapel of Baliscate (5.1). Archaeological excavation in 2004 revealed the stub of a fourth stone on the same alignment, just to the north, and adjacent to it a possible cremation burial of the late 8th or 9th century BC.

2.17 Cillchriosd: standing stone

NM 377 534

Some 2.6m high, this standing stone is in a field to the east of Cillchriosd farm.

2.18 Dervaig: stone rows

NM 439 520

There is an alignment of five standing stones, three of them fallen, on rising ground to the east of Dervaig (Plate 4). They are now in a clearing in forestry, in an area of former rig and furrow, accessible from a car park on the road from Tobermory. There is another alignment of four stones, three still standing, deeper in the forest on Maol Mór (NGR NM 435 531). More accessible, and visible from the road, is a third group of three stones at NGR NM 438 516 behind a stone dyke enclosing a cemetery.

2.19 Glengorm, Mishnish: stone row

NM 434 571

A triangular grouping of three standing stones on a terrace overlooked by higher ground. Two of the stones were re-erected in the late 19th or early 20th century and they are now within an oval enclosure of orthostatic stones. They can be reached from Glengorm Castle (6.3). Excavation in 1987–88 showed the stones were originally arranged in a straight line, and led to the discovery of a small pit containing charcoal near the middle stone and cremated bone near the northernmost one. There is said to have been a large mound of stones nearby in the 19th century, possibly a burial cairn.

2.20 Gruline: standing stones NM 545 396

There is a standing stone in the field to the north of the cairn on Càrn Bàn (2.7). Another is buried in woodland across the B8035 at NGR NM 543 397.

2.21 Lochbuie: stone circle and standing stones NM 617 251

See 2.10.

2.22 Scallastle: stone row NM 699 382

Only one of three stones is still upright, in a field beside the road to Scallastle Farmhouse. The adjacent mound is recent clearance.

2.23 Taoslin: standing stone NM 397 223

A rectangular slab of Ross of Mull granite, in a field to the south of the road from Bunessan to Pennyghael. The stone must either have been a glacial erratic or transported by human endeavour from further west in the Ross of Mull.

2.24 Tenga: the Carrachan NM 504 463
(Gaelic, 'standing stones')

There are four upright stones on moorland in a trapezoid arrangement, possibly representing the remains of a stone circle.

2.25 Tirghoil: standing stone NM 353 224

A rectangular slab of Ross of Mull granite, in a field to the north of the road from Bunessan to Fionnphort (Fig. 4).

2.26 Tostary: standing stone NM 391 456

A leaning, rectangular block of basalt, about 1.8m high, just south of the B8073 road.

2.27 Ulva: standing stones NM 402 390

There are two standing stones in pasture about 400m to the west of Cragaig.

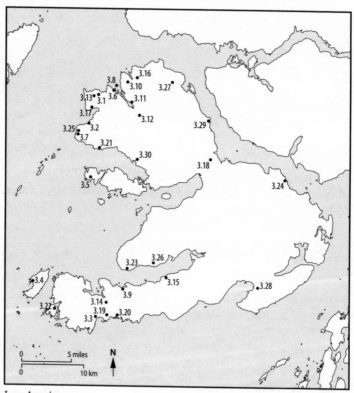

Iron Age sites

3. Iron Age Sites

FORTS

3.1 Cillchriosd: fort   NM 373 536

This fort occupies the level summit of a rocky hillock beside the unclassified road to Sunipol (Plate 5). The remains of a rampart can be traced along its south edge, including an entrance.

3.2 Creag a' Chaisteil, Calgary: fort   NM 358 495

This promontory fort is adjacent to the B8073 on a cliff-top location at the mouth of Calgary Bay. There are the remains of a rubble wall curving around the landward sides with two entrances. Excavations in 1964 revealed evidence of a large hut circle in the interior. It had a beaten earth floor, timber posts and wattle and daub walls.

3.3 Dùn an Fheurain, Ardalanish: fort   NM 370 185

The name is Gaelic for 'the fort of the green grassy field'. The fort itself is sited on top of a rock stack, difficult of access, at the west end of Ardalanish Bay. There is car parking at the nearby Ardalanish Farm and a track leading down to the bay. The fort has a main summit area about 20m by 45m with a substantial enclosing wall, traceable at the southwest end, where there is an outwork at a lower level.

3.4 Dùn Cùl Bhuirg, Iona: fort   NM 264 247

Denuded remains of a stone wall around this rocky summit can be traced around the south, extending to the northeast. Excavations led to the discovery of a small circular round house and evidence for occupation of the site in the early centuries AD.

3.5 Dùn Eiphinn, Gometra: fort NM 358 402

An irregularly shaped, level summit with traces of a perimeter wall and an outwork to the northwest. There are the turf-covered foundations of a post-medieval house in the interior.

3.6 Dùn Guaire: fort NM 399 543

The remains of this small fort ('Godfrey's fort') stand on a low summit adjacent to the north of Croig pier at the mouth of Loch a' Chumhainn, looking across to the island fort of Eilean nan Gobhar. There is a restored drystone house adjacent to it. The walling is reduced to a low stony, grass-covered bank, the entrance from the south.

3.7 Dùn Haunn: fort NM 333 470

Dùn Haunn is Gaelic for the 'fort at the haven'. It crowns the summit of a rocky stack adjacent to the path round the shore of Treshnish, overlooking Port Haunn, a natural haven, and a substantial stretch of raised beach with remains of rigs. There is a dun nearby (3.25).

3.8 Eilean nan Gobhar: fort NM 402 542

This small rocky island at the mouth of Loch a' Chumhainn is crowned by a commemorative obelisk, set within the remains of a small fort.

3.9 Dùn na Muirgheidh: fort NM 412 236

This fort, about 30m by 21m internally, is set on a small rocky promontory at the head of a rock-girt bay at the mouth of Loch Scridain. It is well protected on the landward side by a strong wall across the neck of the promontory, much of which, along with an entrance passage, reduced in width in antiquity, still survives. There are also three outer defensive walls. In the interior of the fort there are the foundations of two houses, probably medieval in date, and there are the foundations of other similar houses just outside the defences. The name means 'fort of the fish spear' in Gaelic, but it was also known as Dùn a' Mhorair, 'fort of the lord'.

3.10 Mingary: fort NM 417 556

This fort is sited on the level summit of a rocky knoll. It is about 30m by 15m within its defensive stone wall. There are the foundations of a more recent house within it.

3.11 Tòrr a' Mhanaich, Dervaig: fort NM 428 519

Situated in woods on the level summit of a spur, the denuded ramparts of this fort are represented by moss-covered stones. The walling does not extend along the southwest side where there is a cliff. It is about 27m by 26m internally. The name is Gaelic for 'Monk's hill'. There is a small cave just to the south of the fort which is said to have been where a monk hid.

3.12 Tòrr Aint, Dervaig: fort NM 442 500

A fort sited on a rocky ridge adjacent to the unclassified road from Dervaig to Aros. An area about 70m by 32m is enclosed by a single stone wall, most in evidence at the northwest end where there is an entrance, and at the opposite southeast end. Adjacent to it are the ruins of a substantial 19th-century township.

DUNS

3.13 Allt Cill Chriosd: dun NM 369 533

At the tail of a rocky ridge on the left bank of the Allt Cill Chriosd, about 18m in overall diameter. The entrance is to the southwest.

3.14 An Caisteal, Bunessan: dun NM 387 214

This small dun occupies a rocky crag near Bunessan. Excavations in 1960 appear to show that the stone defensive wall was thickened. A large stone slab blocking the west-facing entrance passage was believed to have served in place of a wooden door. There was little recovered to provide any firm idea of a date for construction or occupation. The excavator thought that this dun was not likely to have been the home of a local 'petty chieftain' but a lookout point for raiders from the sea, which could be defended by a relatively small garrison.

3.15 An Dùn, Torrans: dun
NM 484 254

This dun occupies the summit of a prominent rocky knoll between the A849 and Loch Scridain. A low stony bank, the remains of its wall, can be traced around the edge of the hill, with an entrance at the east end. The area enclosed is about 30m by 14m.

3.16 An Sean Dùn: dun
NM 431 562

A well-preserved dun (or possibly a broch?), 'the old fort', on a height to the east of Loch Mingary. Its circular enclosing wall is about 3m thick and up to 1m high, enclosing a space about 9m in diameter. There is a small outer enclosure to the east, protecting the entrance. There is evidence for a chamber or stair in the thickness of the dun wall.

3.17 Calgary Pier: dun
NM 367 515

The site of this dun is a rocky outcrop overlooking Calgary Bay near Calgary Pier. The summit is difficult of access and the remains of the dun wall are grass-covered.

3.18 Cnoc na Sroine, Salen: dun
NM 555 433

This large hilltop dun can be approached along a track from Glenaros House. It is oval in shape, about 34m by 26m, its enclosing wall standing several courses high in places, but almost totally tumbled down on the steep northern side. A lower plateau to the south has traces of an enclosing wall, probably contemporary with the dun. The dun entrance, facing southwest, gave access to it.

3.19 Dùn a' Chiabhaig, Uisken: dun
NM 387 189

This dun crowns an oval-shaped knoll, sloping from one end to the other, adjacent to the road from Bunessan to Uisken, a few hundred metres away from the beach car park. The tumbled remains of a circuit wall can be traced round most of the summit. The name is Gaelic for 'fort at the cattlefold bay'.

Figure 36. Dùn a' Geard, Ross of Mull, dun (3.20), with its partially tumbled circuit wall still standing several courses high

3.20 Dùn a' Geard, Ross of Mull: dun   NM 377 452

An impressive dun with stretches of circuit walling standing several courses high (Fig. 36). It crowns a hilltop overlooking the sea, and can be reached with relative ease by a track from the medieval church of Kilvickeon. It is sub-rectangular in plan with opposed entrances. The north-facing one is easier to access and the wall here is massively reinforced with a revetting wall. The walls contain galleries or passages, originally roofed with lintels, some of which are still in place. The name is Gaelic for 'fort of the guard(s)'.

Essential viewing

3.21 Dùn Aisgain: dun   NM 377 452

This is one of the most impressive prehistoric monuments in Mull, overlooking Loch Tuath about 2km to the west of Kilninian Church. Its stone enclosing wall still rises to a height of 2.75m. It has an overall diameter of about 15m, galleries in the thickness of its wall and an entrance to the west, still with some of its lintels in place. It stands on a low rocky summit which is girt by an outer defensive wall, overlooking the ruins of the township of Cruinnleum 6.16).

3.22 Dùn Aoidhean, Erraid: dun   NM 306 202

This dun crowns a rock overlooking the tidal sound separating Erraid from Mull (Plate 6). The remains of its enclosing wall can be traced, especially to the landward side. Here the entrance was also positioned. 'Aoidhean' is probably a personal name.

3.23 Dùn Bhuirg, Ardmeanach, Mull: dun   NM 421 262

This dun is a prominent landmark on a knob of rock on the edge of a sheer drop towards the south (Plate 7). The dun itself, the walls of which still stand to a height of about half a metre, is oval in shape with an entrance to the east and a mural chamber giving access to steps up to a higher level. There are two outer lines of defence, giving the whole site a tiered appearance. The interior of the dun has a monument to a girl, Daisy Cheape (a daughter of the Cheapes of Tiroran), who drowned nearby in 1896. For nearby cairns and the deserted township of Burg see 2.6 and 6.14.

3.24 Dùn Earba: dun   NM 676 401

This dun enclosure is situated adjacent to the car park at Garmony Point. There are only slight traces of its wall. Dùn Earba is Gaelic for 'fort of the roe'.

3.25 Dùn Haunn: dun   NM 334 475

The dun, with substantial outworks, stands on a rocky knoll about half a kilometre to the north of the Dùn Haunn fort (3.7), adjacent to an early field system associated with the township of Haunn. It is not known to what extent the occupation of both overlapped.

3.26 Dùn Scobuill, Ardmeanach: dun   NM 468 274

This dun occupies the level summit of a rocky knoll just to the north of the track leading from the car park at Tiroran towards Burg. It is irregular in shape, its entrance to the west approached by a ramp.

3.27 Dùn Urgadul, Tobermory: dun

NM 494 552

A dun with a pear-shaped plan surrounded by a wall now low and grass-covered. Several facing stones are evident, and an entrance in its broad end, facing east. It is sited on the end of a low ridge adjacent to the minor road to Glengorm Castle on the outskirts of Tobermory, from which it can be reached with difficulty. There is an outer wall across the ridge to the east of the dun.

3.28 Dùnan Mór, Laggan: dun

NM 625 234

This dun occupies a rocky knoll across a field to the southwest of the restored medieval church (5.9). It is roughly rectangular in plan, its walls now reduced to low spreads of stone.

BROCHS

3.29 Ardnacross, An Sean Chaisteal: broch

NM 550499

The grass-covered mound that represents the remains of this broch surmount a knoll by the edge of the shore, overlooking the Sound of Mull. Galleries and chambers in the thickness of its wall are evident as well as the rubble-filled entrance on the landward side, still spanned by two stone lintels (Plate 8). An Sean Chaisteal is Gaelic for 'the old castle'.

Essential viewing

3.30 Dùn nan Gall: broch

NM 432 431

Perhaps tellingly, the name of this broch is Gaelic for 'fort of the strangers'. It is sited at Ballygown on low ground by the edge of Loch Tuath (Plate 9). Although it survives to a substantial height it is mostly lacking its facing stones and its interior is clogged with rubble. Its entrance faces east and galleries and stairs can be traced in the thickness of its wall.

For another site occupied in the Iron Age see:
2.1 Croig Cave

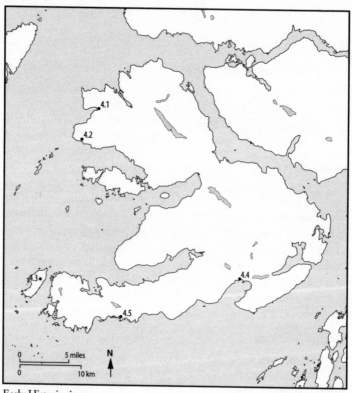

Early Historic sites

4. Early Historic Sites

4.1 Calgary: burial ground   NM 375 511

There are two cross-marked stones of early Christian date reused as grave-markers in this cemetery at the head of Calgary Bay. One has an incised cross design on one face, another in low relief on the back. The other, a small 'pillar-stone', has an incised cross on opposite faces. The rest of the grave monuments are of no earlier date than the 18th century and are contained within a rectangular enclosure of no great age. There are no traces of a chapel although a rising piece of ground within the enclosure could mark the site of one. The old name of the place is Cladh Mhuire, indicating dedication to the Virgin Mary. Calgary is perhaps Norse for 'Kali's garden'. The name was taken to Canada by Mull emigrants and given to a city in Alberta.

4.2 Crackaig: chapel and burial ground   NM 351 459

The foundations of a small drystone chapel, about 5.5m by 8m overall, with entrance in its west wall, are set within an egg-shaped enclosure on a cliff-top terrace below the post-medieval settlement of Crackaig (6.15), with views across to nearby Cairn na Burgh More and Cairn na Burgh Beg in the Treshnish Islands. The positioning of the church door suggests an early date, in Scandinavian times.

4.3 Iona: churches and monuments   NM 285 244

In the following account the main sites and monuments, both of early historic and medieval date, are described in the order in which a visitor, coming from the ferry, is likely to view them. The ecclesiastical monuments on Iona are all grouped together on the east side of the island, in and just to the north of the village. Visitors

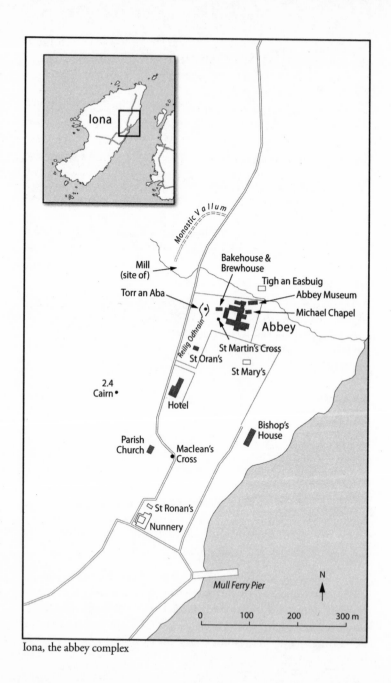

Iona, the abbey complex

are not normally permitted to take vehicles onto Iona but it is an easy walk of a few hundred metres from the ferry jetty at the village to see all the monuments, which are now in the care of Historic Environment Scotland. The nunnery and other ruins, St Oran's Chapel, the burial ground of Reilig Odhráin, the abbey church and cloisters, and the Abbey Museum housed in the restored abbey infirmary, are all accessible during visiting hours. St Ronan's Chapel, presently used as a store for pieces of sculpture and grave-slabs, is not normally open to the public, nor are most of the restored ranges around the abbey cloisters, including the chapter house and refectory, used and occupied by the Iona Community.

Essential viewing

The Nunnery

There are substantial upstanding ruins of the church and the foundations of a cloister garth with a chapter house, all dating to the early 13th century (Figs 37, 38). There are also the upstanding walls

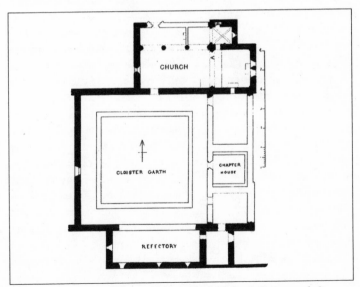

Figure 37. Plan of Iona Nunnery (MacGibbon and Ross, 1896–97, vol. 1)

Figure 38. Iona Nunnery, view from northwest (MacGibbon and Ross, 1896–97, vol. 1)

of a refectory of about 1500. The walls of the church are striking for their large blocks and boulders of red and pink Ross of Mull granite, laid in courses and interspersed with pinnings (Plate 13). Quoins, window dressings, columns, etc., are of yellowish-green sandstone from Carsaig in Mull. The rectangular church consists of a chancel, originally vaulted, and nave with a north aisle of three bays. Adjacent to it is a small aisle chapel, with quadripartite vaulting still in place and a triangular-headed window opening. The windows of the church are otherwise all round-headed and the columns cylindrical. The Carsaig sandstone has not worn well but sculptural detail includes dog-tooth ornament and capitals of scalloped or zoomorphic form. The most interesting surviving feature of the refectory is a sheela-na-gig in the exterior of its south wall (cf the one at Kilvickeon old parish church in the Ross of Mull, 5.8). The erection of this building was part of a larger building scheme about 1500 that led to the creation of a larger cloister garth, the blocking off of the north aisle of the church from the nave, and the insertion of a timber gallery in the west end of the nave. Decorative corbels for supporting the latter are still in place but only decorative fragments of the cloister arcade survive, indicating it had ogee arches supported on paired columns.

Strictly speaking this church was not a nunnery but a priory of Augustinian Canonesses, said to have been founded by Ranald, son of Somerled (died 1207). It was dedicated to St Mary. The first prioress was Bethoc, sister of Ranald. The National Library of Scotland in Edinburgh now has a fine illuminated psalter (MS 10000) produced in England, probably Oxford, about 1180–1220. It is believed to have belonged to Bethoc. A hoard of four silver spoons, three partially gilt and the fourth with inlaid niello, were found along with a decorated gold fillet from a woman's headdress, buried under a stone at the base of the south respond of the chancel arch (Fig. 39). They all date to about 1200, and are now in the National Museum of Scotland. A row of 18 medieval grave-slabs, all very worn, is laid out to the east of the church. The Englishman William Sacheverell, who visited Iona in 1688, noted that the

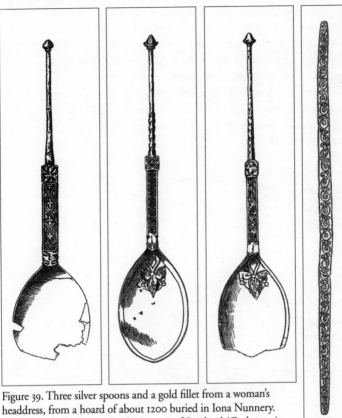

Figure 39. Three silver spoons and a gold fillet from a woman's headdress, from a hoard of about 1200 buried in Iona Nunnery. They are now in the National Museum of Scotland (Curle 1924)

nunnery was the burial place of all the women. In its church he observed a great many grave-slabs, all laid flat except, as far as he could recall, one, evidently that of Prioress Anna Maclean (no. 204), now exhibited in the Abbey Museum.

St Ronan's Church

This ruined medieval church is adjacent to the nunnery. It had its walls completely restored in the late 19th and early 20th century and a discreet glass roof has been inserted. It is a simple rectangular structure, lit by three lancet windows, one in the east gable, the others opposite each other towards the east end. The form of the original door is not known. Quoins and window dressings are of sandstone. St Ronan's was the medieval parish church for Iona, erected in the late 12th or early 13th century. It was possibly ruinous by the 1640s. The Ronan of the dedication is believed to have been an abbot of Kingarth in Bute who died in 737.

Part of a gold fillet of 12th-century date, a piece of gold wire and a gold finger ring (Fig. 40), all now in the National Museum of Scotland, were found in the southeast corner of the church in 1923. Excavations by Jerry O'Sullivan in 1992 in the church interior revealed that the church was a successor to an earlier, smaller one with whitewashed, clay-bonded walls, of unknown date. There were even earlier burials, presumably Christian, aligned east–west. In more recent times, probably after the church had fallen into ruin, it was used as a burial place for women and children.

Figure 40. An early medieval gold finger ring found in St Ronan's Church, now in the National Museum of Scotland (Curle 1924)

Maclean's Cross

This 15th-century cross (Plate 15) stands by the edge of the road about 100m beyond St Ronan's. The name suggests it was commissioned by, or intended to commemorate, a leading Maclean. An alternative explanation is that, together with the early medieval high crosses adjacent to the abbey, it served as a way-marker, or place of prayer, on a pilgrimage route on the island. Other crosses may have marked ecclesiastical or sanctuary boundaries at Iona and elsewhere. Early medieval crosses and cross-slabs at Kilchoman in Islay and Cill Chaitriona in Colonsay are examples of this.

The cross is carved from a thin slab of chlorite schist and still stands in its original base. It has a disk head carved on one side with a crucifixion, and there is a mounted horseman with a spear at the base of the other side along with a now unreadable inscription in Lombardic capitals. Both sides are covered with foliage and interlace work. Late 15th century (sculpture with small leaves).

Essential viewing

Reilig Odhráin and St Oran's Chapel

Reilig Odhráin, the burying place of Oran, is named for a cousin and companion of St Columba. A story known from as early as the 12th century has Oran volunteering to be buried here to consecrate the soil of the island in accordance with Columba's wish. Many of the early and later medieval slabs discussed further below are known to have come from this burial ground, the main one on Iona. It still has many medieval grave-slabs, but few are left now with obviously interesting carving still visible on them. There are also many later grave monuments and Reilig Odhráin is still used, exceptionally, for interments, for instance in 1994 for John Smith, Leader of the Labour Party. It is an enclosed quadrangular space, about 45m to 50m, but may originally have been rather bigger.

Donald Monro, Dean of the Isles, writing in 1549, describes Reilig Odhráin, which had been a sanctuary, as a fair churchyard enclosed with a wall of mortared stone. In it there were three tombs of stone formed like little chapels, each with a Latin inscription, one indicating that it was the burial place of the kings of Scots, another the place of burial of the kings of Ireland and the third the sepulchre of the kings of Norway. Monro goes on to say that this cemetery was also the last resting place of the Lords of the Isles (MacDonalds) with their lineages, two of the Maclean kindreds (presumably Duart and Lochbuy), MacKinnons and MacQuarries as well as many others. It was considered to be the most honourable and ancient place (for holy burial) in Scotland.

Monro's account has been very influential, with much of his information being used by later travellers and historians. The Englishman William Sacheverell, who visited Iona in 1688, added the interesting observation that St Oran's was then the burial place of notable local families, including the MacLeods (apparently an error for Macleans), MacDonalds and MacKinnons. He describes it as the burial place of all the men whereas the nunnery was the burial place of all the women.

Other early travellers have provided identifications or associations for some of the monuments and slabs, but for more detailed information on the tombs of the kings we have to turn to the work of the Rev. Dr John Walker, invited in 1764 by the Commissioners of the Annexed Estates to write a report on the Hebrides. He spent some time in Iona in the summer of that year and he believed he could trace the remains of the three royal tombs described by Monro. The most complete of the three was like a small building facing east, not above 10 feet (3.05m) long and five feet (1.52m) broad inside. Its walls were only about three feet (0.94m) high and its roof corbelled or vaulted. It was very rudely but strongly built, complete apart from at one corner, which had collapsed or been pulled away so that the inside could be viewed. No inscription could be traced upon it. The other two tombs, on either side, were merely overgrown heaps of stones.

The Welsh travel writer Thomas Pennant visited Iona in 1772 during his voyage to the Hebrides (Fig. 6). He notes that of the celebrated royal tombs there were then only slight remains. They were built in a ridged form, arched within. They (or the ridge they were on?) were called Jomaire nan Righ (Gaelic for 'the ridge of the kings'). There was also 'a red unpolished stone; beneath which lies a nameless king of France' (Fig. 41), situated about 70 feet (21.34m) to the south of St Oran's chapel.

Figure 41. Cross-slab (no. 54) of Ross of Mull granite, said to be from the tomb of a king of France in Reilig Odhráin (Graham 1850)

There was clearly a strong tradition that Iona was the burial place of kings. Much of it is clearly fanciful and improbable, like this last identification of a grave-slab of a French king. Nevertheless, there is other documentary evidence that some kings were indeed interred here. The 13th-century Chronicles of the Kings of Man and the Isles record this of Godred, King of the Isles, died 1187, and Uspak/Hakon, King of the Isles, died 1230. A 17th-century MacDonald history (in The Black Book of Clanranald)

claims that Ranald, son of Somerled, King of the Isles, Lord of Argyll and Kintyre, died c. 1210, was also buried on Iona, and although this is a late source it is recounting something that might reasonably have been assumed or inferred.

When writing his account of royal burials at Iona, Dean Monro was aware of earlier chronicle sources, almost certainly including Walter Bower's Scotichronicon, a compilation of the 1440s, from which could have been learned that Iona was a royal island, the burial place and royal seat of the kings of Pictavia and Scotland right up to the time of King Malcolm III in the 11th century. Bower or his sources were clearly aware of the existence of St Oran's Chapel and identified it as the specific location for some royal burials, including the early historic kings Gabran of the Corcu Réti (died 558) and Constantine II of Alba (died 952). St Oran's, however, at least in its present form, only dates from the 12th century.

Iona was certainly not such an important centre for royal burials as claimed by medieval chroniclers but we cannot lightly dismiss Monro's description of three royal tombs. What he may have seen was three small funerary chapels, small, gable-ended buildings like others to be seen elsewhere in the Hebrides at Howmore in South Uist and Skeabost in Skye. But what about the Latin inscriptions recording the burial in them of kings of Scots, Ireland and Norway? There is no good reason to doubt that they were there to be seen and recorded by Monro, but if so, we must doubt that they were of any earlier date than the 14th century, and possibly not even very old at all at the time of Monro's visit.

Just as the chiefs of the MacDonalds boosted their status as great lords or kings with inauguration ceremonies, so in death they would have wished to add to their prestige by interment surrounded by other kings. It would have suited them to embellish the traditions of royal burials and reinforce them with funeral chapels and inscriptions. Another possible sign of this approach is a grave-slab (no. 191) in the abbey cloisters which, on the basis of its form and design, is of the 15th century, but which might possibly commemorate a MacDonald ancestor, Ranald, son of Somerled, King of the Isles, said to have died in 1207 (Fig. 42). The decoration on the slab includes a large sword and a casket, and also

Figure 42. A grave-slab (no. 191) of the 14th or 15th century, possibly commemorating King Ranald, son of Somerled. It is exhibited in the north cloister walk

a cross. Ranald is said in the clan history in The Black Book of Clanranald to have received a cross from Jerusalem (meaning he went on crusade?). An object adjacent to the sword blade may be interpreted as the white staff of kingship with which he would have been presented when inaugurated as king.

Monro was on surer ground in ascribing burials at Iona to the leaders of Isles' society. Such burials were no doubt still taking place in his day. Inscriptions confirm his statement and show that not just local clan chiefs and heads of kindreds chose Iona for their mortal remains.

St Oran's Chapel stands within Reilig Odhráin. It is a small, rectangular chapel, restored and reroofed in 1957, believed to have been erected in the mid or later 12th century either by Somerled or his son Ranald, to be a family funerary chapel (Plate 12). The round-arched doorway in the west wall has two orders, pilasters with cushion caps and voussoirs with saw-tooth chevrons and human or animal heads (Fig. 43). There is also a hood moulding ornamented with pellets. The church is lit by two paired lancet windows towards the east.

Amongst the worn slabs set in the floor is no. 167, an example of an early slab with plant-scroll decoration (13th century?), showing Scandinavian influence (Fig. 24). Another one (no. 161, fig. 44), ornamented with a sword and a staff, is noteworthy. Since these were two of the insignia presented to new Lords of the Isles at their inauguration ceremonies, it might reasonably be supposed

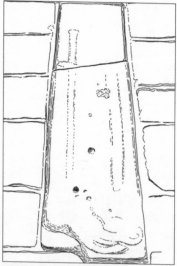

Figure 43. The entrance of St Oran's Chapel (MacGibbon and Ross, 1896–97, vol. 1)

Figure 44. Grave-slab (no. 161), ornamented with a sword and a staff, now very worn, set in the floor of St Oran's Chapel

that this sandstone slab marks the burial place of one of the Lords. There is a triquetra decoration at the foot. Also of note is the tomb recess that has been built into the south wall in the late 15th century, with decorated trefoil arch (Fig. 45). Martin Martin claimed it was a MacKinnon monument but it was surely the intended burial place of either John II Lord of the Isles, or else his son Angus Og.

Four late medieval grave-slabs from the chapel plus a fifth (no. 131) from the nunnery, are mounted on the north wall, from west to east: nos 131 (Fig. 46), 174, 126, 152, 157. Nos 131 and 174 are examples of Iona School class II, possibly work of the 13th or 14th century from mainland Argyll. The rest probably date to the 14th or 15th century. No. 126 has an interlace cross flanked by a sword and single stem with half-palmettes; no. 152, an example of the paired half-palmettes group with a galley at the top; no. 157 a swirling leaves group slab with foliate cross-head and a sword with a belt. It is said to have been made for a Maclean of Gruline.

Figure 45. Tomb recess that has been built into the south wall of St Oran's Chapel in the late 15th century (Graham 1850)

Figure 46. Grave-slab (no. 131), an Iona School class II work, possibly work of the 13th or 14th century from mainland Argyll. It is exhibited in St Oran's Chapel

St Mary's Chapel

In a field to the east of Reilig Odhráin, but outside the area under guardianship, the ruins of this medieval chapel can be seen.

Sràid Nam Marbh (Street of the Dead)

Stretching from St Oran's Chapel to the abbey is this processional road. Although it dates back to the time of the early monastery, its exposed cobbled surface is probably no earlier than the 14th century.

Essential viewing

Tòrr an Aba (Hill of the Abbot)

A small rocky knoll to the west of the abbey church, surmounted by the pedestal for a commemorative cross (Fig. 6). The cross-base itself has been adapted from a millstone. The pedestal partially overlies the foundations of a small hut with stone footings that has been identified by many as Columba's cell, where the saint wrote and received visitors.

Essential viewing

St Martin's Cross

A monolithic 'high cross' carved from epidiorite, with a pierced ring around its arms (Plate 14), stands in situ between Sràid Nam Marbh and the west front of the abbey church. It dates to the mid or late 8th century. It was already known as St Martin's Cross by the end of the 17th century. The lower portion of the east face of the shaft is carved with cruciform arrangements of bosses inter-twined by snakes. Bosses ornamented with interlace fill the upper portion of the shaft and cross-head, along with snakes and animals, probably intended as lions. More lions and bosses and snakes appear on the west front, but here the main designs are figurative with a Virgin and Child flanked by angels in the cross-head. Below this are four rows including scenes which can be identified as Abraham about to sacrifice Isaac and King David with musicians. The blank panel at the foot originally had an inscription. There are slots in the ends of the side arms for attaching extensions, possi-bly of wood or metal.

St John's Cross (replica)

This replica of a high cross is sited near St Martin's Cross, where the original stood. The latter is now housed in the Abbey Museum.

St Matthew's Cross

Near the replica of St John's Cross is the monolithic base for another high cross, known as St Matthew's. Its broken remains are now displayed in the Abbey Museum.

St Columba's Well

There is a prominent, circular well head in front of the west end of the abbey church. The stonework dates to the late 19th century and the well itself may be no earlier than post-medieval.

St Columba's Shrine-chapel

This name is applied to the heavily rebuilt and restored little church (Plate 11) adjacent to the west end of the abbey church, probably dating to the mid 8th century. It was intended to house the precious metal shrine containing St Columba's bones which was made about that time. The projecting antae or buttresses on either side of the entrance door are an early feature. Inside, the modern wooden floor hides two medieval slab-lined graves and post-holes, possibly of an earlier timber church.

Stone basin

Adjacent to the main (west) entrance to the abbey church is a block of granite, carved with a shallow basin. It is incised at one end with a cross. It is said that this was for pilgrims to wash their feet before entering the church. By throwing three handfuls of water it was supposed that St Columba could be invoked to give favourable winds for travel. Hence the name by which it was known locally – 'Cradle of the north wind'.

Essential viewing

The Abbey Church

Now a complete structure, with nave, choir, transepts and central tower (Plate 10, figs 47, 48), in regular use for religious services, this iconic building was long roofless and derelict. It had probably fallen out of regular use for divine worship soon after 1560 and when plans were afoot in the 1630s to restore it as the cathedral for the Isles it appears that the nave was already too ruinous to be part of that scheme. Work on restoring it commenced in 1874 and was completed in 1910. The overall appearance of the building and much of its fabric is of 15th-century date, albeit incorporating work of earlier dates. It is possible to deduce from an architectural analysis of the fabric that the original Benedictine church of about 1200 was also cruciform with a narrower nave and much shorter choir. In the late 13th century there was an ambitious scheme to build a very large south transept, but this is now only evident as a stretch of foundation of its east wall to the south of the choir-aisle.

On entering the church through the west processional door (restored 15th-century work) there is a vista of the whole length of the interior to the large pointed window with flamboyant tracery in the east end of the choir. What at first seems surprising is the way the building is stepped down so that the choir is considerably

Figure 47. Iona Abbey in 1772 with the Michael Chapel in the foreground (Pennant 1774)

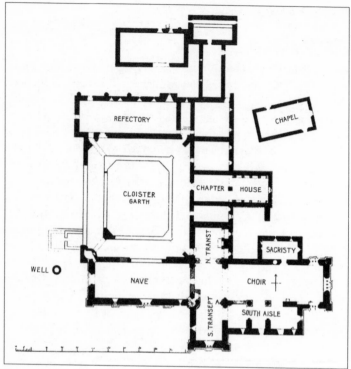

Figure 48. Plan of Iona Abbey prior to rebuilding in the late 19th and early 20th century, and the construction of a west cloister range (MacGibbon and Ross, 1896–97, vol. 3)

lower than the west end of the nave. The wall surfaces have all been stripped back to roughly coursed rubble work with yellow Carsaig sandstone dressings and sculptural detailing. There is an open timber roof in the choir; a wooden ceiling in the nave.

Six medieval grave-slabs of clerics are displayed against the south wall of the nave, from east to west:

205: Brother 'Cristinus' (Gille-Crìst) MacGillescoil, Prior of Iona, whose image in vestments is carved on the slab (Fig. 49). The decoration includes a chalice. Mid 15th century. Nine other similar slabs, all part of the swirling leaves group, with effigies of clerics survive, one of them at Trumpan in Skye, the rest in Islay and Kintyre, where there are other monuments which show similarities

Figure 49. Grave-slab (no. 205), 15th century, of Brother 'Cristinus' (Gille-Críst) MacGillescoil, Prior of Iona, removed from the old parish church at Kilvickeon in the Ross of Mull (Graham 1850). Now exhibited in the nave of the abbey church

in the style of their carving. It is possible that that is where the carver of this slab at Iona worked. It probably, however, does not really belong at Iona. It is first recorded at the old parish church at Kilvickeon in the Ross of Mull in the 19th century and was transferred to Iona in the mistaken belief that since McGillescoil was a prior of the abbey it must have been stolen from there.

201: Effigy of a bishop or abbot with mitre and crosier, formerly in Reilig Odhráin. The overall design is reminiscent of the effigies of senior clergy elsewhere in Britain dating to the 12th and 13th centuries. It is clearly local work, perhaps rather later in date, and made by the same workshop as produced the Maclean Cross or other works with small leaves.

199: Effigy of a bishop or abbot with mitre and crosier and two hooded figures (monks?) below, formerly in Reilig Odhráin (Fig. 50). This is local work, probably of the 12th or 13th century. The figure was apparently identified in earlier times as 'Teague' (Tadhg), King of Ireland.

179: Slab from Reilig Odhráin divided into four panels with foliate cross designs and an inscription indicating that it commemorates four Iona priors of the same clan. The clan in question was probably the Campbells (Fig. 31). It is fine quality work of the early 16th century. The inspiration for many of its design elements comes from the late 15th-century effigy of Abbot John MacKinnon in the choir.

137: Slab formerly in Reilig Odhráin with a typical medieval West Highland design of a sword flanked by foliage scrolls and animals. At the top of the slab, however, there is a scene of a priest and an attendant saying Mass, but unfortunately the accompanying inscription, which would no doubt have identified who the slab commemorated, cannot now be read (Fig. 51). It is likely to have been a cleric. 14th or 15th century.

200: Very worn slab with an effigy of a bishop or abbot with mitre and crosier, formerly in Reilig Odhráin. 13th or 14th century, Iona School class II, possibly from Lorn.

The crossing has large pointed arches supported on responds, all dating to the 15th century, although the north arch crossing can be seen to be built within the earlier one of about 1200. The north transept is also largely work surviving from the original Benedictine abbey church of about 1200. The east wall has an arcade of three round-headed arches providing access to two small chapels with round-headed windows and a niche in between (Fig. 19). The base of a medieval sandstone statue of a cleric, said to be St Columba, now stands in the niche with its upper portion realised as a modern wire installation. In one of the chapels there is a boulder carved with a ringed cross, evidently an early grave-marker, perhaps of the 9th century (Fig. 7). It was found about 1870 some distance to the

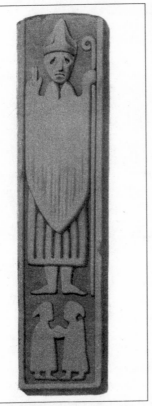

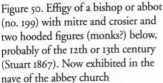

Figure 50. Effigy of a bishop or abbot (no. 199) with mitre and crosier and two hooded figures (monks?) below, probably of the 12th or 13th century (Stuart 1867). Now exhibited in the nave of the abbey church

Figure 51. Grave-slab (no. 137), 14th or 15th century, with a scene of a priest and an attendant saying Mass (Graham 1850). Now exhibited in the nave of the abbey church

northeast of the abbey and has been identified, on no sound basis, as the stone that St Columba is said to have used as a pillow.

The north wall of the choir shows a confusing juxtaposition of a fine door at ground level giving access to a sacristy, and at a higher level an arcade of two openings separated by a cylindrical column supporting pointed arches (Fig. 52). The door is fine work of the 15th century with a cusped head and capitals decorated with figural

Figure 52. The interior of the abbey choir from the south choir-aisle (Pennant 1771). Note the sacristy door in the far wall with an arcade of two openings above it

and foliage work. The arcade is work of about 1220–50 and the carved detail includes dog-tooth decoration. The explanation is that in the 13th century an undercroft was created in the choir, and the floor level of the main church was almost 2m higher than today, with the arcade giving access to a choir-aisle. A drastic change of plan in the 15th century saw the undercroft removed, the arcade blocked up and a sacristy created in place of the north choir-aisle.

The south transept in its present form is 15th-century work, along with the adjacent south choir-aisle. The transept now contains the early 20th-century marble effigies of the 8th Duke of Argyll and his third wife. The choir-aisle is separated from the choir by an arcade with two cylindrical piers supporting pointed archways. The capitals of these piers, the responds and the east arch of the crossing have some of the finest sculptural detail in the whole church. The carver responsible, Donald O' Brolchán, has carved his name on the east arch of the crossing. Amongst the figural scenes are representations of Adam and Eve being expelled from the Garden of Eden, and the Crucifixion. Internally the south choir-aisle is divided into three bays by heavy half-arches (Fig. 53).

The east end of the choir is lit by three large 15th-century

Figure 53. A pier of the south choir-aisle arcade with half-arch (MacGibbon and Ross, 1896–97, vol. 3)

windows. Set in the south wall are a piscina and sedilia. The former has two angels decorating its canopy, the latter an arcade of three ornate, cusped arches (Fig. 54). There are two effigies of abbots and, set in the floor in their original positions, are two medieval gravestones. The earlier of the two effigies (no. 202), to the south, is carved from Carsaig sandstone and is believed to be that of Abbot Dominic, who died about 1465 (Fig. 55), and was probably mostly responsible for the overall appearance of the abbey church as we see it today. It is possibly the work of a Lowland sculptor. The other effigy (no. 203) is clearly labelled on its base as Abbot John MacKinnon, who succeeded Dominic and died about 1498 (Figs 30, 56). It is carved, like the majority of medieval West Highland monumental sculpture, from chlorite schist, and is one of the most accomplished examples of local work of the period. Its design is derived from the effigy of Abbot Dominic. Both effigies were observed in the church by William Sacheverell in the late 17th century, and they may always have been in their present location.

Set in the floor between them is a matrix of Tournai marble for a brass effigy of a knight in armour, of 14th- or 15th-century date (Fig. 57). This would have been an expensive, high prestige import for its time. That fact, along with its position in the centre of the choir in front of the high altar, indicates that it must have

Figure 54. (Below) The piscina and sedilia in the abbey choir, and effigy (no. 202) of Abbot Dominic in the foreground (MacGibbon and Ross, 1896–97, vol. 3)

Figure 55. (Right) Effigy of Abbot Dominic, died about 1465 (no. 202), in the choir of the abbey church (Graham 1850)

Figure 56. (Far right) Effigy (no.203) of Abbot John MacKinnon, died about 1498, in the choir of the abbey church (Graham 1850)

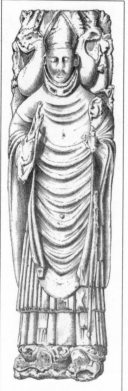

Figure 57. A matrix of Tournai marble for a brass effigy of a knight in armour, 14th or 15th-century, set in the floor of the abbey choir (Graham 1850)

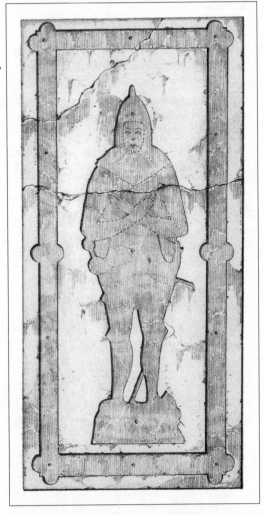

commemorated someone of great importance, for instance John I Lord of the Isles or his son Donald. In the centre of the choir, further to the west, is set a grave-slab (no. 182), now very worn, of a type that probably comes from the general area of Loch Awe in the Argyll mainland (Fig. 26). Its design includes a small image of a warrior, perhaps a Campbell of the 14th or 15th century.

The Abbey Cloisters and Conventual Buildings

The cloisters, heavily restored and rebuilt, are on the footings originally laid out in the early 13th century, unusually to the north rather than the south of the nave of the abbey church. The cloister arcade is all modern work, apart from a reconstructed segment of 15th-century arcading at the southwest corner. At the northwest corner there is, adjacent to the entrance to the abbey shop, the remains of a now blocked doorway, which originally provided access to the late 13th-century refectory, which bounded the north side of the cloisters (Fig. 58). The shop now occupies the refectory undercroft and the heavily restored refectory itself is not normally accessible to visitors. The same applies to the chapterhouse, off the east side of the cloisters. It is entered by a fine 15th-century doorway with a semi-circular arch-head. Inside an arcade of two arches survives from the original work of about 1200, dividing the space into a vestibule and main chamber (Fig. 59).

The main point of interest now about the cloisters is the series of medieval grave-slabs lining its walls, plus one post-medieval slab at the northeast corner, made in 1674 for John Beaton, physician.

Figure 58. The north side of the abbey refectory prior to restoration (MacGibbon and Ross, 1896–97, vol. 3)

Figure 59. The interior of the abbey chapter house (MacGibbon and Ross, 1896–97, vol. 3)

South cloister walk, east to west:

150. The design on this slab of intertwining half-palmettes is typical of a number of works of West Highland sculpture, probably dating to the 15th century, many of them in Iona, Mull and at Lochaline in neighbouring Morvern (Fig. 29). The representation of a galley at the head is particularly fine. The inscription indicates that the slab commemorates 'Angusius, son of Lord Angusius MacDonald of Islay'. This has been taken to be Angus Og, the leader of the MacDonalds who supported Robert Bruce and fought for him at Bannockburn in 1314. This identification is clearly problematical since the slab and its inscription do not appear to be that early. Possibly, however, we are dealing here with a monument erected much later by the MacDonald lords to honour an important ancestor. The slab was formerly in St Oran's Chapel, where Angus Og is said to have been buried.

163. The key characteristic of this slab is the pattern of scroll-work with swirling leaves (Fig. 28). Parallels can be drawn with several other slabs and crosses, mostly located in Islay and Kintyre, where they may have been carved in the late 14th and 15th century.

151. Possibly by the same carver or workshop as no. 150 (Fig. 60). Note the small figure of a warrior incorporated in the foliage design, the galley at the top and the inscription commemorating Malcolm, chief of the MacLeods of Lewis, died sometime between 1515 and 1524.

138. The overall foliage design on this slab, characterised by small leaves, is mostly to be found on other works on Iona, probably dating to the 15th century, including the Maclean Cross (no. 212).

153. The scrollwork on this slab relates to that on no. 163. Note the fine representation of a galley (sculpture with swirling leaves).

159. A slab carved from slate, typically with a sword, but also a cavalryman couching a spear, and below him a kneeling figure – a woman praying with a rosary? – alongside a casket.

158. Some of the scrollwork is similar to that on nos 150 and 151 (sculpture with paired half-palmettes).

155. This slab, commemorating 'John Mac....', is notable for its galley and stag hunt at the foot (Fig. 61).

West cloister walk, south to north:

122. A long-shafted cross with floriate head and semi-circular base, flanked by foliage scroll and a sword. Slabs with long-shafted crosses like this, identified as Iona School class I work, probably date to the late 13th or 14th century. Many of them are to be found in Islay, where they may have originated.

173. A slab with a long, narrow panel of plant scroll. This is typical of a type of slab largely confined to Iona and the Argyll mainland, identified as Iona School class II work.

176. Of the same type as no. 173.

156. Related stylistically to nos 138 and 155. The design includes a galley and stag hunt. All that can be made out now of the inscription at the top indicates that it commemorates someone named Alan (sculpture with small leaves).

Figure 60. Grave-slab (no. 151) commemorating Malcolm, chief of the MacLeods of Lewis, died some time between 1515 and 1524. The design of paired, intertwined, upturned half-palmettes incorporates a small image of a warrior (Graham 1850)

Figure 61. Grave-slab (no. 155) with an untidy design of foliage with small leaves, a galley and a stag hunt (Graham 1850)

148. Related stylistically to nos 150, 151 and 158 (sculpture with paired half-palmettes).

123. Related stylistically to nos 173 and 176 (Iona School class II). It probably dates to the 13th or 14th century but the sword, the hilt of which is carved at the top appears to be an earlier – Viking? – type (Fig. 62). It may not have been part of the original design. Perhaps it represents an ancestral relic of the deceased or is an indication of his ancestry.

128. The cross design of this slab is distinctly different from anything else at Iona, perhaps because it is the work of an Irish sculptor in the 14th or 15th century (Fig. 63). It is, however, made from chlorite schist from Argyll. It appears to be unfinished, the original intention being to cut designs into the blank panels on both sides of the cross-shaft.

118. Related stylistically to no. 122 (Iona School class I).

North cloister walk, west to east:

191. Set within the blocked 13th-century doorway to the refectory this slate slab, from Reilig Odhráin, is one of the most intriguing now in the cloisters (Fig. 42). It cannot be doubted on the basis of the sword carved as the main element of its design that it is any earlier in date than the 14th century, and yet it is possible that it commemorates an earlier ancestor of the MacDonalds, in this case (King) Ranald, son of Somerled. The object placed alongside the sword blade appears to be a wand or sceptre, such as was presented to new kings and Lords of the Isles at their inaugurations. It is possible that the cross to one side of the sword hilt represents the cross that Ranald was believed to have brought back from Jerusalem at the beginning of the 13th century.

184. A worn, and apparently unfinished, slab, from Reilig Odhráin. The main point of interest is the representation of a cloaked figure with a staff, possibly a pilgrim.

143. Related stylistically to nos 150 and 151 (sculpture with paired half-palmettes). There is a pair of shears and a casket at the foot of the slab.

129. Related stylistically to nos 173 and 176 (Iona School class II) (Fig. 25).

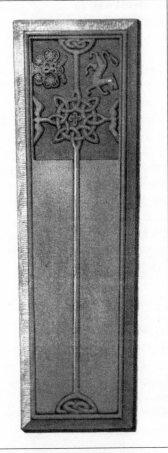

Figure 62. Grave-slab (no. 123), an Iona School class II product, probably dating to the 13th or 14th century, but with the representation of the hilt of an earlier sword (Graham 1850)

Figure 63. The cross design of this slab (no. 128) is distinctly different from anything else at Iona, perhaps because it is the work of an Irish sculptor in the 14th or 15th century (Stuart 1867)

130. Related stylistically to nos 173 and 176.

147. Beneath an inscription panel, now illegible, near the top is a chalice with a rectangular object alongside, probably a book, suggesting that this slab commemorates a cleric. Much of the slab

is covered with a pattern of intertwined plant scrolls with a pair of opposed animals.

146. Related stylistically to nos 150 and 151 (sculpture with paired half-palmettes). The foliage scrollwork includes three anvils at the bottom, one large and two small, indicating that this slab commemorated one or more of a family of smiths or armourers.

119. Related stylistically to nos 122 and 118 (Iona School class I) (Fig. 27). Note the two pairs of shears on a recessed panel at the very bottom.

231. The grave-slab of John Beaton, physician to the Maclean family, died in 1657 aged 63, made by Donald Beaton in 1674 (Fig. 64). It has Beaton arms and a Latin couplet: ECCE CADIT IACVLO VICTRICI MORTIS INIQVE QVI TOTIES ALIOS SOLVERAT IPSE MALIS. SOLE DEO GLORIA ('Behold he who had so often freed others from their ills falls to the conquering dart of overpowering death. Glory be to God alone'). These were Beatons of Pennycross, Donald being the grandson of John.

East cloister walk, north to south:

121. Related stylistically to nos 122 and 118 (Iona School class I).

120. Related stylistically to nos 122 and 118.

149, Related stylistically to nos 150 and 151 (sculpture with paired half-palmettes) (Fig. 65). The inscription panel at the very top commemorated someone called Nicolaus. Below that is a rider followed by a dog and a harpist in a boat. These images are not obviously biblical but may relate directly to Nicolaus' life.

154. Related stylistically to nos 163 and 153 (sculpture with swirling leaves). Note the relatively large representation of a galley.

175. Related stylistically to nos 173 and 176 (Iona School class II).

144. Related stylistically to no. 138 (sculpture with small leaves). This slab was formerly at the nunnery and so probably commemorated a woman.

127. This slab has been dated to the 14th or 15th century but the ringed cross that is the main element in its design seems intended to evoke earlier medieval art (Fig. 66). The layout, with a ship and sword on either side of the cross appears rather crowded.

Figure 64. The grave-slab (no. 231) of John Beaton, physician to the Maclean family, died in 1657 (Graham 1850)

Figure 65. The inscription panel at the very top of this slab (no. 149) dating to the 14th or 15th century commemorates someone called Nicolaus. Below that is a rider followed by a dog and a harpist in a boat (Stuart 1867)

It is possible that it is an earlier cross slab that has been adapted and recut in late medieval times.

132. Related stylistically to nos 173 and 176 (Iona School class II).

172. Related stylistically to nos 173 and 176.

125. Related stylistically to nos 173 and 176 (Fig. 67).

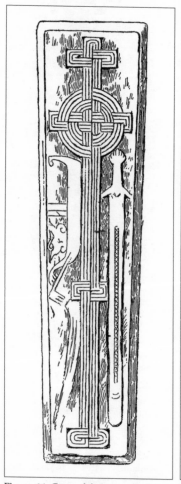

Figure 66. Grave-slab (no. 127) of the 14th or 15th century but with a ringed cross of earlier type (Brydall 1898)

Figure 67. Grave-slab (no. 125), a typical example of an Iona School class II product (Graham 1850)

The Bakehouse and Brewhouse

To the west of the cloister and the reconstructed west range the space within the wall footings of the medieval monastic bakehouse and brewhouse has been converted into a garden.

Michael Chapel

To the east of the north range of the cloister is a free-standing early 13th-century chapel, considerably restored (Fig. 48). It is now called the 'Michael Chapel' although it is not clear if it is the structure so recorded in the 16th century.

Essential viewing

The Abbey Museum

The Abbey Museum occupies a free-standing building to the north and east of the main abbey complex. It is a structure of the 1960s erected on the foundations of what was supposed to be the medieval infirmary of the abbey. It contains an important display on the history of the abbey, illustrated with many of the most significant pieces of surviving sculpture, and some finds, including pottery, glass and metalwork, from excavations. The approach is thematic, looking broadly at the history of the abbey from Columban times onwards, and considering such matters as the monastery in Columba's time, prayer, the sign of the cross and pilgrimage. The highlight of the exhibition are the monumental free-standing high crosses. The sculpture is listed here in the order in which the visitor is likely to encounter it. The identifying numbers are provided from the RCAHMS Iona Inventory.

Columba's Monastery

22. Grave-marker with a 'Chi-rho' monogram (Fig. 8), that is a design derived from the two first Greek letters of 'Christ', in this case with the rho (R) as a small hook on the upper arm of a cross (the chi). The upper edge of the stone has an inscription in Latin, 'The Stone of Echodi'. This is thought to be Eochaid Buide, king

of Kintyre from 609 until his death in 631. He was a son of King Áedán of the Corcu Reti. This stone is the earliest identifiable piece of Christian carving on Iona.

Journey to Heaven

31. Fragment of a cross-slab of Carsaig sandstone with an inscription in Irish, 'A prayer for Fergus', 8th or 9th century. It was found in front of St Columba's Shrine-chapel.

Sign of the Cross

9. Kite-shaped boulder carved with a cross, probably used as a grave-marker, 7th century (Fig. 68).

19. Rectangular slab from Reilig Odhráin with a cross design, 7th century. Note how a simple incised cross has been carved over an earlier one with double volute terminals.

16. Rectangular slab carved with a cross with a circular hollow in each quarter, 7th century.

18. Slab with cross with two cross-bars, perhaps originally intended to be recumbent over a grave. Smaller crosses were later carved on both faces, indicating a change in use, 7th–9th century (displayed above no. 8).

8. Pillar-stone carved on both sides with crosses, 7th–9th century (displayed below no. 18).

20. Grave-marker from Reilig Odhráin with sunken crosses on both sides, 7th century.

Figure 68. Kite-shaped boulder carved with a cross (no. 9), probably used as a grave-marker, 7th century (Brydall 1898)

Place of Pilgrimage

81. Part of the shaft of a large free-standing, ringless cross from Reilig Odhráin, 9th century.

99. Two pieces, originally clamped together, from the top of a composite base for a large cross, from Reilig Odhráin. One piece has later been reused to hold a smaller cross while the other, carved with a ringed cross, has served as a grave-marker.

The High Crosses

80. St Oran's Cross, reconstructed from fragments formerly in St Oran's Chapel; hence the name, which was only given to it in the 20th century. The cross is of massive size, about 2m across its arms and possibly originally rising about 4m above the top of its base (not preserved). It is deemed to be the earliest of the high crosses, dating to the middle or second half of the 8th century. It has rounded armpits and is composite in construction. The side arms were carved as a single piece with mortices (slots) top and bottom to take tenons (projections) on the top of the shaft and the bottom of the upper arm. Much of its decoration consists of panels with bosses, spirals and serpents. On the front, at the top of the shaft, there is a Virgin and Child flanked by Angels, and on one of the side arms a representation of Daniel in the lions' den. On the back one of the side arms has King David playing his harp.

82. St John's Cross, made up from fragments, known to have stood near the west end of the abbey church where there is now a reconstruction of the complete cross (Fig. 10). The first mention of a cross dedicated to St John dates to the late 18th century, but there is no certainty that this is it, or that the name reflects a tradition of much earlier times. It is supposed that this cross was originally similar in form to St Oran's, with the side and top arms carved as one piece separate from the shaft to which it was attached by means of a mortice and tenon joint. As the result of a failure or collapse, the cross was then remodelled with a separate upper portion to its shaft and upper arm and, more significantly, four separate quadrant pieces that together form a ring around the head of the cross (only a fragment of one of them survives). The result-

ing ringed cross was the first ever, and this design was to prove very influential and enduring in Scottish and Irish art. St John's Cross was the biggest at Iona, at least of those that survive, rising above its base to a height of about 4.35m and across its arms about 2.17m. It is decorated all over with panels with bosses, spirals and serpents. On the east side of the shaft there is also a panel of fretwork forming lozenges with key-pattern and rosettes. On the west face there are two circular recesses, one at the centre of the cross, the other near the top of the shaft which may have been intended to hold metal plaques. It is believed to have been both created, and remodelled as a ringed cross, during the 8th century.

84. St Matthew's Cross. Less survives of this high cross than the other two, only a portion of its shaft and a piece of its head and a side arm. Stylistically it is later in date, belonging to the 10th century. It was known as St Matthew's Cross by the 18th century. Its base is still in situ to the west of the abbey church, near St Martin's Cross and the reconstruction of St John's. It was mono-lithic in form with a ringed head. An image of Adam and Eve can be recognised on the shaft.

Close to Columba

45. Slab carved with a ringed cross from Reilig Odhráin, 8th century (Fig. 69). The Irish inscription seeks a prayer for the soul of Éogan.
42. Slab carved with a ringed cross, 8th century.
34. Slab carved with a ringed cross, 8th century.

Between the High Crosses

47. Slab carved with a ringed cross from the paving in front of St Columba's Shrine-chapel, 9th century (Fig. 9a). It has an Irish inscription seeking prayer for Loingsechán, probably an abbot of Iona.

49. Slab carved with a ringed cross, incorporated in the paving outside St Columba's Shrine-chapel, 9th century.

46. Slab carved with a ringed cross from the paving in front of St Columba's Shrine-chapel (Fig. 9b). It has an Irish inscription seeking prayer for the soul of Flann, believed to be Flann mac Maíle-dúin, Abbot of Iona, died 891.

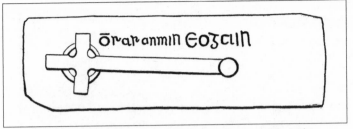

Figure 69. Slab (no. 45) carved with a ringed cross, 8th century. The Irish inscription seeks a prayer for the soul of Éogan (Allen and Anderson 1903, vol. 2)

Turbulent times

26. Large slab with four different cross designs (Fig. 70). It is suggested that this may have been placed over a mass grave in the 10th century following a Viking attack.

70. Cross-slab previously at the nunnery (Fig. 71). Its ringed cross is carved with interlace typical of that produced in other Scandinavian areas of the British Isles, 9th–10th century.

89. Shaft fragment from a free-standing cross from Reilig Odhráin. On one face it has a scene interpreted as two clerics being sheltered by an angel, and on the other it has panels of interlace, 10th or 11th century.

Hallowed ground, sacred spaces

88. The head and shaft of a free-standing sandstone cross, 10th to 12th century.

30. Sandstone slab with a cross carved in relief, 10th century.

85. Fragment from the boss of a free-standing ringed cross, 10th century.

57. Slab from Reilig Odhráin with incised ringed cross.

A strong presence

95. Part of a cross-shaft decorated on one side with an interlace design and on the other side displaying a longship with central mast full of armed warriors (Fig. 11). Above is a smith with his tools

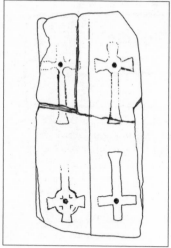

Figure 70. Large slab with four different cross designs (no. 26), possibly from a mass grave of the 10th century

Figure 71. Cross-slab (no. 70) with a ringed cross of Scandinavian type, 9th or 10th century (Allen and Anderson 1903, vol. 2)

and to the right an animal identifiable as an otter. These representations possibly relate to the Sigurd legend. The work is Scandinavian in style, of 10th-century date. The shale rock from which it is carved may come from the Isle of Man.

53. Slab carved with crosses on both sides, one a ringed cross, 9th century.

86. Part of the head of a free-standing, sandstone ringed cross, 10th century.

33. Upper part of a rectangular slab from Reilig Odhráin with a relief carving of a cross, 10th century.

68. Rectangular slab from Reilig Odhráin with an 'expansional cross' design and traces of an inscription, 10th century (Fig. 72).

78. Disc-headed cross-slab, 10th century.

77. Head of a disc-headed cross-slab, 10th century.

65. Two pieces of a sandstone slab from the Nunnery Church with a relief carving of a disc-headed cross, 11th century.

73. Cruciform-shaped grave-marker, 11th century.

Figure 72. Rectangular slab (no. 68) from Reilig Odhráin with an 'expansional cross' design and traces of an inscription, 10th century (Stuart 1867)

24. Grave-marker with an incised cross within a circle, 11th century.

Family funerals

113. Grave-marker, probably of a priest, from Reilig Odhráin, 13th century. It is decorated with a ringed cross flanked by a paten and chalice.

141. The design on this slab of intertwining half-palmettes is typical of a number of works of West Highland sculpture, probably dating to the 15th century, many of them in Iona, Mull and at Lochaline in neighbouring Morvern. At the top there is a cross-head with concentric circles. It was formerly at the nunnery and was therefore most likely a monument to a woman.

207. Warrior effigy of Gilbride MacKinnon wearing an aketon, mail coif over his shoulders and basinet on his head (Fig. 14). His hands are clad in gauntlets and his feet and legs also appear to be clad in armour or protective clothing. Inscriptions on his pillow and along the top edge of the slab record five generations of Mac-Kinnons. According to tradition Gilbride (Gille-Brigde) fought under Angus Og MacDonald at Bannockburn. The effigy itself may date to the mid 14th century.

West Highland warriors

211. Effigy of a warrior clad in typical West Highland armour, principally an aketon and basinet, about 1500 (Fig. 23). This is one of the most accomplished such images from anywhere in the Isles and West Highlands. It is the only such piece that adopts a pose standard throughout the rest of Europe, showing the figure in the act of drawing his sword. On the pillow and continuing down the left-hand side of the slab is an inscription indicating that it is the work of Mael-Sechlainn Ó Cuinn, who also signed an impressive free-standing cross at Oronsay Priory. A 19th-century source (Graham's Antiquities of Iona) identifies this effigy as a Maclean of Coll.

Powerful patrons

215. Part of the head of a disc-headed cross with a crucifixion, 14th or 15th century.

208. Military effigy with a bearded warrior holding a spear and a shield (Fig. 73). He appears to be clad in a hide or leather coat (like the buff-coats worn in the Civil Wars of the mid 17th century). At his right hip there is a whelk-shell (hunting horn?) and a hound beneath his feet. This may be an import from the region about Loch Awe on the Argyll mainland, 14th or early 15th century. The figure was identified by Graham as a Maclean of the Ross of Mull.

209. Effigy of a bearded warrior dressed and armoured similarly to no. 208 (Fig. 74). There is a wyvern crest on his helmet and a hound at his feet. Graham identified him as a Maclean of Duart though this stone may also come from the Loch Awe area, 14th or early 15th century.

210. Effigy of a warrior wearing an aketon with a pose typical of West Highland sculpture, fastening on his sword belt, early 16th century (Fig. 17).

214. Cross-shaft, decorated on both sides with foliage scroll (Fig. 18). There is a griffin, a galley and an inscription indicating that it was commissioned by Lachlan MacKinnon and his son John, Abbot of Iona, in 1489. It is of high quality, related stylistically to the effigy of John still in the choir of the abbey church.

Figure 73. Military effigy (no. 208) of a bearded warrior with a spear and a shield, and a whelk-shell hunting horn (Graham 1850)

Figure 74. Military effigy (no. 209) of a bearded warrior with spear, sword and shield, 14th or early 15th century (Brydall 1898)

204. Grave-slab with the effigy of Anna Maclean, Prioress of Iona Nunnery, who according to the inscription, died in 1543 (Fig. 75). Her pillow is supported by angels, with the towers of the Holy City in the background, and two lap dogs cling to her cloak. The bottom part of the slab is now missing but drawings of it when complete indicate that it had a seated image of the Virgin and Child. Although later in date, it is related stylistically to the cross-shaft 214 and the effigy of Abbot John MacKinnon.

Figure 75. Grave-slab (no. 204) with the effigy of Anna Maclean, Prioress of Iona Nunnery, who, according to the inscription, died in 1543 (Stuart 1867)

Tigh an Easbuig

Tigh an Easbuig is Gaelic for the 'bishop's house', the ruins of which are in a field just to the north of the abbey, outside the area directly cared for by Historic Environment Scotland. It measures about 14m by 7m internally, its walls now all reduced to grass-covered foundations except for the partition wall, standing to a height of 3.7m. From a description of the building, then in ruins, by William Sacheverell in 1688, and the illustration of Iona in Pennant's *Tour in Scotland*, showing it complete but for its roof (Fig. 6), it is possible to deduce much more about its plan. The larger western chamber was the hall, open to the roof and containing a fireplace with a chimney in the west gable. The smaller eastern chamber, described as the buttery, was entered by a door in the cross-wall, and there was an upper chamber here in the roof, possibly reached by a ladder and lit by a window in the east gable. It has been supposed to date after 1499, when Iona Abbey was granted *in commendam* to the bishops of the Isles, possibly even to be as recent in date as the 1630s. Perhaps, however, it is medieval in date, originally a residence of the abbots or for a secular lord. The great hall of the Lords of the Isles at Finlaggan in Islay, as remodelled in the 14th or 15th century, had a similar plan.

Mill site

Excavations were undertaken in 1991 at the stream, Sruth a' Mhuilinn (Gaelic, 'mill stream'), next to the south end of Burnside Cottage, just to the west of the road from the abbey northwards to Clachanach. There is nothing to be seen now, but a rectangular pit was discovered cut into the stream bed, and associated pits for large posts. It is probable that these features belonged to a small horizontal mill, dating to some time between the establishment of the monastery and the 18th century.

The monastic vallum

The best place to view a surviving stretch of the enclosing bank and ditch around the early monastery is adjacent to the west side of the road that passes the abbey, between the Macleod Centre and Clachanach.

4.4 Lochbuie (St Kilda's Episcopal Church):   NM 609 248
slab with outline cross

This slab is said to have been discovered when the church was being built. It is now built into the porch of the church. It is of sandstone, and decorated with a ring-headed cross potent, possibly of the second half of the 8th century. St Kilda's was built in 1876 for Murdoch MacLaine of Lochbuie. The St Kilda dedication only dates to that time. St Kilda was believed to have been an early saint associated with that island.

4.5 Scoor, cave: rock carvings   NM 417 186

This cave is by the shore to the south of Scoor, at the head of a rocky inlet. Several of the carvings are in the form of cup-markings, possibly dating to the Bronze Age. There are also several small incised crosses probably dating to the late 6th–9th centuries.

For other early historic carvings of crosses, see:
5.21 Carsaig: Nun's Cave.

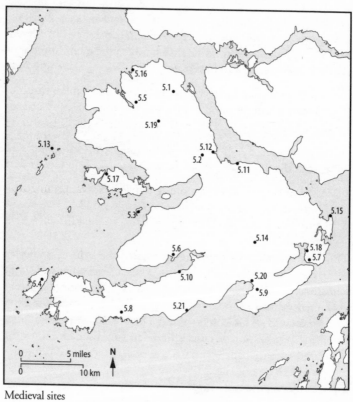

Medieval sites

5. Medieval Sites

CHURCHES, BURIAL GROUNDS AND CROSSES

5.1 Baliscate: chapel and burial ground · NM 496 540

The site lies within a forestry plantation less than 2 miles south of Tobermory. It can be reached by a track leading southwestwards from the back of the Mull Pottery, passing the Baliscate standing stones. It was only identified as a medieval chapel in 2008, an identification confirmed by a small-scale excavation in the following year undertaken by Channel 4's *Time Team*. The site was then subjected to larger scale and more systematic excavation in 2010–2014 through a community archaeology project by Mull Museum, with professional leadership provided by Clare Ellis of Argyll Archaeology.

This work demonstrated that the site had a long, complex history. It sits within a much larger enclosed area of about 1.37 hectares, possibly belonging to an Early Christian monastery, and two small cairns have been identified as the remains of supports for crosses or cross-slabs. Several early, apparently Christian burials, including infants and mature adults, were found in a cemetery in the vicinity of the chapel, dating to the 6th–8th century AD. Immediately to the east of the chapel are the remains of a rectangular stone structure, identified as a *leacht*, or monument commemorating a saint. It probably also dates to Early Christian times but was rebuilt and enlarged, and remained in use as late as the 14th century. Pilgrims lodged white quartz pebbles in it.

The remains of the leacht are still visible at the east end of the chapel, both within a rectangular enclosure. The ruined enclosure wall and chapel are of 14th-century date, but the chapel overlies the remains of a turf and wattle structure, probably a chapel of earlier date. The turf and stone enclosure wall contain an area almost 16m by almost 19m, entered from the east, and the chapel is about 8m by 3.5m internally with walls about 1.9m thick. These are of turf and stone, faced internally with large slabs. The entrance is in the north wall.

There was also evidence from the excavations for a medieval kiln barn. The chapel may not have remained in use for very long for religious purposes, but may have been converted into a domestic dwelling.

Finds from the excavations are on display in the Mull Museum in Tobermory, including pottery, a piece of a decorated quern and an Edwardian penny.

5.2 Cill an Ailein, Aros: church and burial ground

NM 545 455

This medieval church is now reduced to grass-covered foundations within a burial ground enclosed by a 19th-century wall. It is in a clearing in a forest and can be reached from a car park up the track from the Mull Offices of the Forestry Commission, via a signposted forestry walk. It was about 13m by 7m overall with its entrance in its south wall. Some fragments of sandstone dressings observed by the RCAHMS suggest it dates to the 13th century. There is no evidence that it was ever of parochial status but it would have served the holders and tenants of the estate of Aros. It is not clear who the saint is commemorated in the place-name – possibly Fillan. The grave monuments and enclosures mostly date to the 18th and 19th century but there are three medieval grave-slabs (1–3) and a Post-Reformation slab imitating medieval types (Map 4). The author could only find nos 2 and 3 at the time of his visit.

1. A plaited cross at the top, a sword flanked by foliage designs, and possibly a casket and a mirror at the foot, all within a border with nail-head ornament (sculpture with small leaves). This is said to be within the walls of the church.
2. Segment of a medieval slab used as a headstone.
3. Segment of a medieval slab used as a headstone (Fig. 76). The lower part of a sword flanked by scrollwork patterns

Figure 76. Segment of a medieval
slab (no. 3) used as a headstone at
Cill an Ailein (5.2)

is evident. It is in a burial enclosure with a 20th-century
stone commemorating Hendersons.
4. Irregularly shaped slab with a crudely carved sword
of medieval type as the main element in its design. Late
16th or 17th century.

5.3 Inch Kenneth: church   NM 437 354

Visitors have to make their own arrangements to access the ruins
of this 13th-century parish church with its significant collection of
monuments, maintained by Historic Environment Scotland (Fig.
21). It is rectangular in plan with a chancel area clearly marked off
by a step down. Its walls are still largely upstanding, including the
jambs of its doorway in its north wall, and here is use of dressings
of sandstone, possibly quarried on Inch Kenneth. There are two
lancet windows in the east wall above the altar, and two others in
the adjacent north and south walls. There are also aumbries (wall
cupboards) on both sides of the altar and at a higher level stone

brackets, possibly for supporting statues. Another bracket in the south wall with a shallow basin would have served as a lamp. The east end of the church is now supported by two large buttresses of 16th- or 17th-century date.

The dedication of the church is to St Cainnech of Aghaboe, a friend of St Columba. The island of Inch Kenneth and the parsonage of this church belonged to Iona Nunnery. The church probably fell out of use in the late 16th century. When he visited in 1773, Samuel Johnson described how there was on one side of the altar a bas relief of the blessed Virgin, and by it a little bell, cracked and without a clapper.

Inside the church, now arranged against the west wall, are eight medieval grave-slabs, from left to right:

1. A galley at the top, two opposed animals and an overall foliage pattern (sculpture with paired half-palmettes).
2. An interlace panel at the top, a sword surrounded by an overall foliage pattern (sculpture with paired half-palmettes).
3. An interlaced panel at the top, below that a galley and an overall foliage pattern, all within a nail-head border (sculpture with paired half-palmettes).
4. A claymore – a two-handed sword with quatrefoil terminals to its quillons – a circular foliage pattern at the top and foliage scrollwork to both sides. A blank panel may have been intended for an inscription. There is a galley at the bottom. 16th century.
5. An inscription panel at the top, then a galley, a panel of interlace, a sword, plant scrolls and a hunting scene with a dog attacking a stag.
6. An effigy of a bishop or an abbot.
7. An interlace panel at the top, an overall foliage pattern and a casket (?) at the bottom (sculpture with paired half-palmettes).
8. An interlace panel at the top and an overall foliage pattern (sculpture with paired half-palmettes).

Outside the church stands a cross with a small ring-head. It is relatively plain, with a carving of a comb and shears on one side of the shaft. 15th or 16th century. There are also a number of interesting Post-Reformation burial monuments, none more so than a sandstone effigy of a warrior in medieval West Highland style wearing an aketon with mail covering his shoulders, a sword in his belt, and small praying figures above each shoulder. He is, however, carrying a targe, is provided with a dirk in his belt, and wears a morion (a type of helmet) on his head. He holds an object – a cannonball? – in his right hand (Fig. 77). This carving clearly dates to the 17th century.

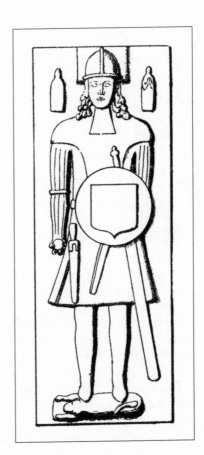

Figure 77. Effigy of a warrior in medieval West Highland style at Inch Kenneth Church (5.3) but dating to the 17th century (MacGibbon and Ross, 1896–97, vol. 1)

5.4 Iona: churches and monuments   NM 285 244

The medieval abbey and other churches on Iona and the large and
important collection of medieval monuments are described in the
previous section of this gazetteer along with the early historic
remains (4.3).

5.5 Kilcolmkill Old Parish Church, Dervaig   NM 436 517

Only grass-covered foundations of this church survive within a
graveyard with 18th- and 19th-century burial monuments. The
church was dedicated to St Columba and remained in use until
1754. A medieval cross-shaft (Fig. 78) from here is now preserved
within the church at nearby Dervaig (7.3).

5.6 Kilfinichen Old Parish Church   NM 496 284

Burial ground with grass-covered foundations of a medieval
church, accessed off the A849 at the head of Loch Scridain, adjacent to a house with public phone box and letter-box. A piece of
a medieval cross-shaft has been removed to the Museum in Tobermory. The remaining monuments are all 18th-century and later.
The name probably commemorates Findchán, a 6th-century priest
who is said by Adomnán, St Columba's biographer, to have
founded a monastery at 'Artchain' in Tiree.

5.7 Killean Old Parish Church   NM 710 284

This church and burial ground overlook a sandy bay on the east
shore of Loch Spelve. Access is relatively easy by boat but by land
is by a track, suitable only for walking, from the A849 to the ruined
settlement of Killean, a distance of over 3km, and then a further
half kilometre cross country. The church itself is about 8m by 15m
overall, with walls reduced to turf-covered stubs. It is first on record
in 1393 and the name indicates a dedication to St John. The
surrounding burial ground, enclosed by a stone wall, is very much
overgrown, but contains several Post-Reformation and modern
monuments, notably two 18th-century armorial headstones, one
with the arms of the Macleans of Lochbuie, with an inscription
on its back commemorating Charles McLaine in Calachilly, died

Figure 78. Medieval cross-shaft from the medieval parish church of Kilcolmkill (5.5), now in Kilmore Parish Church (7.3), Dervaig (from *Proc Soc Antiq Scot* 17,1882–83)

1778. The church may, however, have fallen out of use in the 17th century. There are also several broken medieval grave-slabs (Fig. 79), including a warrior effigy.

Figure 79. Medieval grave-slab, partially exposed at Killean Old Parish Church (5.7), with a sword, a casket and a pair of shears

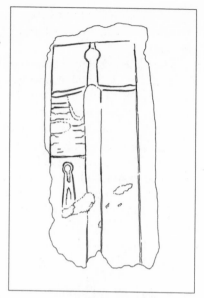

5.8 Kilvickeon Old Parish Church, Ross of Mull   NM 412 196

The substantial ruins of this medieval church stand in a burial ground reached from an unclassified road running ESE of the A849 just to the east of Bunessan. Past Assapol it turns into a track for about two miles, with parking provided near the church. The name is possibly for the church or burial ground of the son of Eogan, in which case Ernán, a nephew of St Columba, may be intended. The church is relatively large by West Highland standards, 8.3m by 15.9m overall. The north and south walls are mostly upstanding and the quality of the stonework with neat courses of large blocks and panels of pinnings suggests a 13th-century date. The dressings around the entrance door in the north wall have all been robbed, but to the east of it, externally, a very worn 'sheela-na-gig' of Carsaig sandstone projects above head height. Sheela-na-gigs are either lewd representations of naked women, or images of women giving birth, depending on one's point of view. Their purpose is not clear but others can be found on West Highland churches, for example Iona Nunnery (no. 4.3) and St Clement's at Rodel in Harris. Socket-holes in the interior surfaces of the north and south walls were probably for a screen separating off the chancel from the nave. The chancel was formerly lit by windows to the north and south.

The substantial burial ground contains many 18th-century and more recent burial monuments, including a fine table tomb commemorating Isabel Cameron, the wife of Donald Campbell, the Bailie of the Ross of Mull, with twinned coats of arms and winged angels. At the time of writing the medieval grave-slab with an inscription to a lady called Mariota had been removed for conservation. Another slab of 15th-century date with a fine effigy of Cristinus MacGillescoil, a Prior of Iona Abbey, was removed from Kilvickeon at some time prior to the mid 19th century and taken to Iona Abbey on the basis that that is where it must have belonged. It is now displayed as no. 205 in the nave of the abbey church (Fig. 49). Perhaps, however, Cristinus was a local boy or had other reasons for wishing to be buried at Kilvickeon.

5.9 Laggan: chapel (Caibeal Mheamhair)　　NM 626 236

This medieval church may at one time have had the status of a parish church. There is no recorded dedication to a saint or Pre-Reformation history. It was substantially restored and reroofed in 1864 as a mausoleum for the Macleans of Lochbuie. It is rectangular in plan, about 6m by 12m overall, and has sandstone dressings, possibly quarried at Carsaig. A blocked window in the south wall with a round head and a rebate for taking glass may be of 12th-century date. The entrance door in the north wall and two other blocked windows are more typical of the 15th century. Inside the chapel are 18th-century Maclean monuments and some recumbent slabs, one with the remains of an inscription that may be 17th-century in date. There are also two stone basins, one perhaps a holy-water stoup or font. The other, octagonal in outline on a square base, may have been a pot quern rather than a font. The church is enclosed in a small burial ground with a stone wall.

5.10 Pennycross: cross　　NM 506 262

The *Crois an Ollaimh*, or Beaton Cross, is enclosed within a fence in a clearing amongst trees, near the north edge of the road from

Bunessan to Pennyghael (Plate 17). It is carved from local rock, set in a plinth, and is undecorated apart from an engraved inscription, GMB 1582 [D]MB, for Gille-Coluim MacBethadh (Malcolm Beaton) and his son Domnall (Donald), successively heads of the Pennycross branch of this medical kindred.

5.11 Pennygown Chapel NM 604 432

Ruined chapel and burial ground, accessible by car off the Craignure to Salen highway. The chapel is of substantial size, about 13.7m by 7m overall, its walls more or less intact apart from the gables, which have been levelled off to the same line as the side walls in a programme of restoration. The masonry has massive sandstone quoins and sandstone dressings round the door in the north side and three lancet windows. One of these is in the west wall; the other two flank where the altar stood against the east gable. There is also a small aumbry in this east wall and two corbels at a higher level.

This church is likely to date to the early 13th century and to have remained in use after the Reformation, but for how long is not clear. It served the north end of the parish of Torosay, and was presumably one of the seven parish churches counted in 1549 by Donald Monro, Archdeacon of the Isles.

Re-erected within the chapel is the shaft of a fine early 16th-century commemorative cross with a crowned and enthroned image of the Virgin Mary with the baby Jesus, and an inscription below, almost all illegible. On the other face of the cross is a galley, sails set, and above that a griffin issuing from a plant scroll. It is related stylistically to the effigy of Abbot MacKinnon at Iona, and particularly the MacKinnon Cross (no. 214) displayed in the Abbey Museum.

In the burial ground there are two worn sandstone slabs with effigies of a man and a woman which, although reminiscent of West Highland medieval effigies, are clearly of much later, probably 17th-century, date. The male appears to have a basket-hilted sword and a dirk. There are also several monuments and tombs of the 18th and 19th century to local landed families. Pennygown means 'the smith's pennyland'.

For other medieval sculpture, crosses and grave-slabs, see:
6.8 Kilninian Parish Church
6.29 Baile Mor (Iona Parish Church)
6.32 Tobermory (St Mary's chapel and the Mull Museum)
7.3 Kilmore Parish Church, Kilmore

CASTLES AND DEFENDED SITES

Essential viewing

5.12 Aros Castle   NM 563 450

Aros Castle can be reached by a walk (cars not allowed) of about half a mile along a private road from the Salen to Tobermory road. The last stage of the walk is a path through woods. 'Aros' is from the Old Norse for the mouth of a river, which describes the castle's location on a rocky promontory on the north side of the bay at the mouth of the Aros River. The most obvious feature of the castle is the large hall-house whose walls are still largely upstanding, though not necessarily for much longer unless some major conservation is undertaken (Plate 18, Fig. 80). It measures 25.3m by 12.5m externally, excluding a small jamb at the north end forming a toilet block. The ground floor was probably given over to storage while the first formed a splendid large hall covered with an open timber roof. It is probable that there was a private chamber or service area at the north end with another chamber above it. There is evidence for a parapet walk crowning the building but no sign of an entrance or internal stairs. Neither the date nor the builder of this great structure is known, although it is safe to assume that it was erected some time in the 13th century, perhaps by the MacDougalls. The hall-house is sited awkwardly at one end of a castle enclosure, its southwest corner projecting into a wide ditch that separates the castle from the adjacent high ground. This suggests that the hall-house was added to a pre-existing residential complex. There are remains of an enclosure wall of unknown date and the grass-covered foundations of two buildings within it. Possibly some of the ruins on the outer edge of the ditch may date to medieval times. Also of medieval date are the substantial remains of a

Figure 80. Aros Castle (MacGibbon and Ross, 1887–92, vol. 3)

harbour just below the point of the headland on which the castle is sited.

In the 14th and 15th centuries Aros was retained by the Lords of the Isles as one of their principle residences. It is described as 'our castle of Dun Aros in Mull' in a charter issued there by Donald Lord of the Isles on 6 December 1410. John II Lord of the Isles issued charters at Aros on 28 June 1469 and 6 December 1492. The large feasting hall (hall-house) and harbour would have made Aros an appropriate residence for the lords, but there must surely also have been large kitchens, storehouses and accommodation for a large retinue, as at Finlaggan in Islay and Ardtornish Castle on the other side of the Sound of Mull.

After the forfeiture of John II Lord of the Isles it became a Crown possession until it passed to the Macleans of Duart, probably in 1543, and then to the Campbells of Argyll in the 1670s. It was described as ruinous and useless by a visitor to Mull in 1688, though that did not prevent a garrison being installed briefly in 1690.

5.13 Cairn na Burgh More and Cairn na Burgh Beg Treshnish Isles: Cairnburgh Castle NM 30 44

These two small rocky islands are at the northeast end of the chain of the Treshnish Islands. They are separated by a narrow stretch of water and both have circuits of fortification, raising doubts as to whether they have always been viewed as two separate castles or one divided into two parts. They have always been difficult of access and few visit them nowadays.

Cairn na Burgh More can be approached from a small beach to the east side of the island through an entrance gate providing access to a gulley sloping up to the summit of the castle. It has the ruins of buildings including a small chapel of late medieval date and a rectangular building about 16m by 6m, evidently a 16th- or 17th-century barracks. It was divided into rooms of unequal size, each provided with a fireplace. It had an attic floor and roof supported on crucks. There are also considerable remains of a curtain wall and evidence for a cistern or catchment pool for collecting water. A 1741 Board of Ordnance plan identifies two other buildings as a store for fuel and a guard house adjacent to the entrance. A gulley separating the main summit area from high ground to the northwest has been walled off.

Cairn na Burgh Beg is divided into a lower and upper bailey and has the foundations of a few smallish buildings and traces of a drystone curtain wall around the lower bailey. The upper bailey is protected by cliff faces except on the side adjacent to the lower bailey where it is defended by a lime mortared wall or breastwork containing musketry loops, and there is an entrance reached by rock-cut steps. Just inside it are the foundations of a small rectangular building, identified on the Board of Ordnance plan as a guard house. There are indications that the lower bailey has been used for agriculture at some time. Cairn na Burgh Beg was apparently accessed from a small boat landing in a gulley at the west corner of the lower bailey where there are also traces of possible boat nousts.

Although none of the walling or other structures on these two islands has been identified as being of earlier date than late medieval times, there is a strong presumption that this was a major

MULL AND IONA

fortification dating back to the Kingdom of the Isles, prior to 1266. Cairnburgh Castle is believed to have been one – or two – of the castles that King Alexander II of Scotland demanded from King Ewen (MacDougall) in 1249 and Cairnburgh is described as an 'exceeding strong' castle in a description of the Scottish Isles contained in the Chronicle of John of Fordun. It dates to the 15th century but the material in it was largely composed at an earlier date. Perhaps in the 12th and 13th centuries a stronghold here could have functioned as a centre of power for kings based in the Isle of Man. In the 16th century King James IV not only showed deter-mination to capture it but apparently also recognised the strategic worth of installing a garrison, under the command of the Earl of Argyll, which continued to hold the place for a number of years.

In later times, Cairnburgh Castle probably served as a bolt-hole for its Maclean owners.

The barracks would have served for the garrison of 30 men under Hector Maclean of Torloisk installed in the castle by General David Leslie after he took it in 1647. The castle continued to be garrisoned, on and off, by Maclean/Jacobite forces and government troops down to the 1740s.

5.14 Caisteal Eòghainn a' Chinn Bhig, Loch Sguabain: Fortified island dwelling   NM 631 307

Inaccessible, except by boat, but a fine view of this site can be got from the A849 through Glen More. The island is oval in shape and enclosed by a substantial, strong drystone wall, standing almost a metre in height. The island, which is about 17m by 29m overall, may be artificial in origin. The only structure visible in the interior, a stone shelter at the north end, is of recent date. It is named for Ewen 'of the little head', a son of John Maclean, 5th of Lochbuy, who was probably its occupant when it was described as 'an inhab-ited strength' by Dean Monro in 1549.

Essential viewing

5.15 Duart Castle NM 749 353

Duart Castle is the ancestral home of one of the most powerful clans of medieval Scotland, the Macleans of Duart (Plate 19, Figs 12, 22). The castle is older than their arrival in Mull and has been supposed to have been a possession of the MacDougalls in the 13th century. It stands on a rocky outcrop at the tip of a small promontory jutting into the Sound of Mull and sheltering a bay ideal for drawing up medieval galleys and birlings. It is mostly of medieval date but was heavily restored in the 20th century with rooms furnished with antiques and clan mementoes. It is open to the public, with good facilities, including parking, a gift shop and a tearoom, and is now one of the major tourist destinations in Mull.

The core of the structure is a rectangular enclosure castle of the 13th century with at least one large rectangular corner buttress, now incorporated in the south corner of the later tower-house, and entrance from the southwest, still in use but heavily restored. The walls have been much damaged, replaced and altered in different building operations over the years. The interior courtyard is lined to the southeast and northeast by ranges of buildings of 16th- and 17th-century date, probably replacing earlier structures. The façade of the northeast range has a door lintel with the initials S/AM for Sir Allan Maclean and the date 1673, the year before he lost his estates to the Earl of Argyll. This northeast range, along with the mid 16th-century southeast range at right angles to it, created a spacious L-plan house which was probably intended as the actual residence for Sir Allan himself rather than the old tower-house.

The massive tower-house of late 14th-century date with four main storeys had been built along the northwest side of the enclosure castle, incorporating some of its walling. It has a jamb on its northeast end, now only one storey high, that contained the original tower entrance. The ground floor was vaulted and there was a hall at first floor level with private rooms on the floors above.

Although the tower-house is clearly of much later date than the rectangular enclosure, it is difficult to believe that the substantial rock platform it is built on could have been left, by design, unoccupied, when the enclosure was erected. The intention would surely always have been to have had a strong tower or hall-block here.

Writing in 1843, James Robertson, Sheriff Substitute of Tobermory, claims there were then around the castle on the land side the vestiges of numerous huts or houses of Maclean followers and clansmen, in an encampment bounded by the remains of a fence.

5.16 Dun Ara Castle, Mishnish   NM 427 577

This castle, a seat of the MacKinnons, is sited on the north coast of Mull and can be reached by a path from Glengorm Castle (Fig. 13). It stands on a large, flat-topped outcrop of rock overlooking the sea, and consists now of a lime-mortared perimeter wall, reduced to its foundations, encircling the foundations of four buildings. The largest, some 15m by 8.3m overall, was probably a hall, with opposed entrances and a service area screened off at one end. The castle summit was reached by a gulley on the east side with rock-cut steps. There are no references to the castle in medieval documentary sources, but it is probable that it dates in its present form to the 14th or 15th century. Around the castle are the grass-covered remains of several houses and rigs, some of which may date back to the time the castle was occupied. About 90m to the southwest is an enclosed harbour for small boats, a pear-shaped basin about 45m by 60m, with a narrow channel giving entry from the sea. A separate canal or passage gives access to two boat-noosts and there is also a recent jetty.

The hall may be compared with another, probably originally constructed in the 13th century, at Finlaggan in Islay, the centre of the Lordship of the Isles. Excavations by the author have shown that it was a ground floor hall with a separate service area at one end and a large fireplace in the opposite gable wall.

5.17 Dùn Bàn, Ulva: residence   NM 384 416

A tidal island sited in the narrow sound between Ulva and Gometra, apparently a seat of the MacQuarries, perhaps known as Glackingdaline Castle. It was connected to Ulva by a causeway and has the remains of a large drystone building, about 5.5m by 11.5m, with opposed entrances in its long sides.

5.18 Eilean Amalaig, Loch Spelve: fortified island

NM 707 299

Adjacent to Eilean Amalaig in Loch Spelve there is a small, tidal, rocky island with remains of a drystone defensive wall, possibly of medieval date, intended to guard the anchorage at the head of the loch. It can be viewed from the track to the old parish church and settlement at Killean.

5.19 Eilean Ban, Loch Frisa: island dwelling

NM 477 493

It is not clear to what extent Eilean Ban is an artificial island or crannog, or else a natural island. There is evidence for a drystone perimeter wall and, on the east side, a small boat inlet. This, and the stonework, might suggest a medieval or later date, though a timber has produced a radiocarbon date indicating it was built some time between about 400 and 60 BC. There is no evidence for a causeway to connect it to the loch side.

5.20 Moy Castle

NM 616 247

This impressive tower-house at the head of Loch Buie was the main residence of the Macleans (or Maclaines) of Lochbuy from its erection in the mid 15th century until the mid 18th century (Fig. 15). It is now a roofless ruin, normally shut up, but its walls are entire to battlement level. It can readily be inspected from the exterior. There is parking for cars by the Lochbuie post office and signposting to a path past the front of Lochbuie House.

The tower-house is square in plan, with sides almost 11m long. It stands on a small rocky outcrop, partially supported by large buttresses. Entrance was from the landward (northeast) side into a vaulted cellar containing a well. On one side of the entrance passage in the wall thickness is a small chamber, and on the other a stair leading up to the hall on the first floor, a vaulted chamber occupying the whole interior space. The second floor, along with other room above in a cap-house (since remodelled), was presumably intended to serve as private or sleeping accommodation. In the late 16th or early 17th century the second floor was adapted into a kitchen by the insertion of a large fireplace suitable for cooking. Prior to this date food preparation may have taken place outside the tower, in since lost buildings in the adjacent barmkin.

The plan of the tower is complicated by several mural chambers, including two entresol ones. One of these is contained in the wall above the entrance and is accessed from the stair from the entrance up to the hall. It intrudes awkwardly into the floor space of the hall, forming a podium along one of its sides. The other entresol chamber is in the thickness of the southeast wall in the haunch of the hall vault, and is entered from a turnpike stair giving access to the upper floors. There are other substantial mural chambers at first- and second-floor level, the former with a trap-door to a pit prison. Fireplaces with flues, however, were not part of the original plan. The hall must have been heated by means of braziers or an open fire, and there are two smoke vents high in the side walls for exiting smoke. A chute for a latrine in the mural chamber at hall level is applied to the exterior face of the main wall. The battlement walk has been remodelled in the late 16th or early 17th century with two round turrets at the north and east corners.

Adjacent to the tower-house is an ovoid-shaped barmkin with traces of an enclosing wall. It would appear to have had a wall walk with access by a now blocked door near the east corner of the tower-house. On the beach below there is a cleared space, bound on both sides by massive boulders, for drawing up boats.

This castle must essentially be the work of Hector Maclean, first of Lochbuy. Samuel Johnson and James Boswell visited the castle in 1773 and were told how the then laird, John Maclean, 17th of Lochbuy, had been fined for imprisoning gentlemen in it. This relates to an event in 1758 when Hector Maclean of Killean and Allan Maclean of Kilmory had been held within its walls for a space of a week, for causing him severe annoyance.

OTHER SITES AND MONUMENTS

5.21 Carsaig: Nun's Cave and quarry   NM 523 204

The cave is in a sea cliff opening on to a raised beach with an exposure of yellow-green sandstone that was quarried in medieval times for building work at Iona and elsewhere. This is one of the very few sources of freestone suitable for building work in the West Highlands and Islands and has also been used in more recent times. The cave, known as *Uamh nan Cailleach* in Gaelic, was probably occupied at various times. Included amongst the carvings on its walls are crosses, some of which probably date to early Christian times.

For other medieval houses and structures, see:
3.9 Dùn na Muirgheidh
5.1 Baliscate

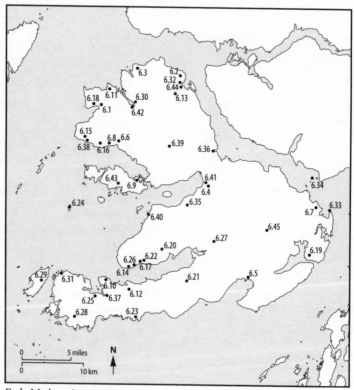

Early Modern sites

6. Early Modern Sites

6.1 Calgary House   NM 377 512

This Gothic Revival mansion overlooking Calgary Bay was built for Captain Allan McAskill, who had purchased land round about from the Argyll Estate in 1817. It may have been designed by the Edinburgh architect James Gillespie Graham, and built soon afterwards as a compact rectangular block of two storeys over a sub-basement, with turrets and a porch. There is an extension dating to the later 19th century. It is now available for let as a holiday home.

6.2 Erray House   NM 504 562

Erray is situated just to the north of Tobermory. The original house, erected in the early 18th century and extended later in that same century, stands in a group of other more recent houses. As originally built it was of five bays, two storeys high with gable ends and a slate roof. It was apparently built for Daniel MacKinnon of MacKinnon, but by 1773, when Boswell and Johnson were entertained there, it belonged to the physician Dr Hector Maclean.

6.3 Glengorm Castle, Mishnish   NM 439 572

A Scottish baronial mansion at the north end of Mull (Mishnish), overlooking the sea, built 1858–60 for James Forsyth by the Edinburgh-based architects, Peddie and Kinnear. It has a prominent, centrally placed square tower and a welter of crow-stepped gables, pedimented windows and turrets with conical roofs. It is now a hotel.

6.4 Gruline: Old Gruline House NM 552 393

This house has had several changes of name. Originally Gruline, a name now attached to a nearby house built in 1861, it was renamed Jarvisfield by its most famous owner, Major-General Lachlan Macquarie, who acquired it in 1804. It is a late 18th-century, two-storey, three-bay house. Some early 19th-century wooden panelling from it is now at Macquarie University in New South Wales, Australia. It is now known as Macquarie House.

6.5 Lochbuie House NM 616 248

The house is an occupied, private residence, but the path from the car park by the post office to Moy Castle goes past the front of the house, providing a good view of this substantial house built for Murdoch Maclean, 19th of Lochbuie in the early 1790s (Plate 20). It has a five-bay, harled, central block of five bays and three storeys with a pediment. There are flanking wings. An earlier two-storey house of 1752 is still preserved at the back.

6.6 Torloisk House NM 410 457

Forming the core of this large Victorian, baronial-style L-plan mansion is a much altered late 18th-century, rectangular, five-bay, three-storey gabled house built by Lachlan Maclean of Torloisk. In the 19th century Torloisk passed by marriage to Lord Compton, later Marquess of Northampton. The house, which is available for holiday lets, is still set in a substantial estate.

6.7 Torosay Castle, Craignure NM 728 352

A Scottish baronial mansion built 1856–8 by David Bryce, an eminent Edinburgh architect, for John Campbell, a prosperous Glasgow merchant. It replaced an earlier house, Achnacroish, and was at first known as Duart House. It has terraced gardens dating to the late 19th or the beginning of the 20th century. Until a few years ago Torosay Castle was a popular visitor destination, with both house and gardens open to the public. It has now reverted to private use.

CHURCHES

6.8 Kilninian Parish Church   NM 397 457

This church and burial ground is adjacent to the B8073, with parking space. The present building is dated 1755, though no doubt on the site of a medieval predecessor. It is now used for Catholic worship. In front of the wall enclosing the burial ground is a cairn erected in 2007 to commemorate a local boy, Allan Maclean (*c.* 1725–98) of the Macleans of Torloisk, 'the saviour of Canada'. He was a career soldier who started out in the Scots Brigade of the Royal Dutch Republic, fought with the rest of his clan in support of Prince Charles Edward Stewart in the 1745 uprising, but spent most of his career in the service of Great Britain, ending with the rank of Brigadier-General. His defence of Quebec against a rebel army led by Benedict Arnold is considered to have preserved Canada from becoming part of the United States of America.

In the vestry at the rear of the church six medieval grave-slabs are displayed, along with a block of stone engraved with a 'mass clock' – a medieval sundial used for telling the times of Mass. The slabs include two effigies of warriors dating to the 16th century, both grasping two-handed swords (nos 6 and 8). The first of these is said to commemorate a member of Clann Duiligh (the Rankins). Another slab (no. 4) has a claymore, the hilt flanked by a casket and a flagon along with a bowl(?). In a panel beneath the sword there is a pair of shears, a comb and a mirror(?) (Fig. 32). Another slab (no. 7a) also has a sword with a casket to one side of its hilt and a mirror and shears to the other side. Slab nos 2 and 3 are examples of sculpture with paired half-palmettes.

Although 'Kilninian' appears to incorporate the name, Ninian, of an early saint based at Whithorn in Galloway, place-name experts point to the fact that Kilninian is a relatively recent form, not recorded prior to the early 19th century. Earlier versions of the name, like Kilnoening in 1561 and Kilninane in 1642, suggest that the original dedication might have been to the nine maidens, said to have been daughters of St Donald in the 8th century.

6.9 Ulva Parish Church

NM 436 398

Ulva Parish Church was erected in 1828, a typical example of a Parliamentary kirk. It is now mostly used as a community centre but retains some of its original pews and a fine two-tier pulpit with a sounding board above, for the minister and the precentor.

RURAL SETTLEMENTS AND FARMING REMAINS

6.10 Achnahaird: corn-drying kiln

NM 391 242

A drystone, D-shaped structure, set against large boulders, with a chamber about 1.2m square. Apparently it was not roofed. The grain for drying was placed inside on a woven mat and hot air drawn in through a flue from outside. It stands on the shore of the loch near the township of Achnahaird.

6.11 Aird, Croig: kiln barn

NM 394 541

This kiln barn, its wall standing up to four courses high, is built into a slope. The top end is rounded and overall the building is about 6m by 7.5m. The kiln bowl in the interior is well preserved, about 1m in diameter, and there are considerable remains of the flue leading downslope from it within the building.

6.12 Airigh a' Bhreac Laoigh, Kilpatrick: shieling huts

NM 423 227

A group of at least eight round or oval huts and platforms, not far above the present head dyke of Kilpatrick, at a height of about 165m above sea level, may be the shieling known as Airigh a' Bhreac Laoigh. The name is Gaelic for 'shieling of the speckled calf'. There is another shieling site with remains of houses on higher ground, not too far distant, at NGR NM 421 223, to which the name might alternatively or also apply.

6.13 Blar Na Fola, Baliscate: shieling huts

NM 498 536

Four shieling huts, one with two chambers, the others single-celled oval or sub-rectangular structures, on a hillside amongst trees about

800m southeast of Baliscate House. This location was formerly part of the Tobermory common grazing. The walls are composed of blocks and boulders, still standing in places to 1m or so in height. The individual cells vary in overall size from 2.1m by 2.6m to 3.6m by 5.2m.

6.14 Burg, Ardmeanach: township

NM 425 265

The large pennyland of Burg was included in the 1390 grant by Donald Lord of the Isles to Lachlan Maclean, the ancestor of the Macleans of Duart. It passed with the other Duart lands to the Earls of Argyll in the late 17th century, and was sold by them to the MacDonalds of Boisdale in 1807. The Burg Estate passed through other hands before being gifted to the National Trust for Scotland in 1936. It was run as an experimental farm until 1948 with the tenants, Duncan MacGillivray and his sister Chrissie, encouraged to develop methods of farming appropriate for the Western Isles.

The boundary with the neighbouring land to the west of Tavool is formed by the Allt na Criche (burn). Upslope from the track, before reaching the farmhouse, are remains of an earlier system of irregular enclosed fields. By 1878 the old township of Burg had been divided into crofts, perhaps five, on the basis of the groups of ruins and dykes visible today. The present farmhouse, to the right of the track, is a corrugated iron-clad timber house, built in 1922. The main cluster of buildings at Burg in post-medieval times was about a couple of hundred metres further on to the southwest. The Ordnance Survey map of 1882 shows 19 unroofed buildings here, four roofed buildings, six enclosures and a sheepfold. The latter was replaced at a later date by sheep pens and a sheep wash. The kiln, with its large cast-iron pot for heating up the wash, is still reasonably intact.

Nearby there are two Bronze Age cairns (2.6) and the Iron Age dun of Dùn Bhuirg (3.23).

6.15 Crackaig and Glac Gugairidh: townships

NM 362 463, NM 363 465

The remains of the houses, rigs and yards of these two townships can be reached by paths from the B8073. Glac Gugairidh is further inland, up the valley of a small stream, than Crackaig. Its name includes 'airidh', Gaelic for 'shieling'. It may therefore represent the colonisation of the shieling ground of Crackaig. There are substantial ruins of nine houses in each settlement, plus an outlier to the southeast of the main group at Crackaig. One of the Crackaig houses has a secondary gable but otherwise all the houses appear to have had hipped roofs and windows, but no fireplaces in the thickness of their walls (Plate 23). They are mostly well-built structures of coursed quarried stones, dating to the 18th century. Both were cleared in 1867.

6.16 Cruinn-leum: township   NM 380 454

Some 17 ruined houses and yards of a township, just to the east and below the dun of Dùn Aisgain.

6.17 Culliemore, Ardmeanach: township   NM 444 276

A substantial number of ruined houses of this township, along with rigs, are visible from the track from Tiroran to Tavool.

6.18 Inivea: township   NM 368 517

The ruined houses and yards of this township are sited on either side of a burn on high ground, about 90m above sea level, in a relatively secluded spot to the north of Calgary Bay (Plate 24). The unenclosed rigs of Inivea are evident to the north and east. There are over 20 buildings, almost all with upstanding walls. The houses are mostly well-built structures, especially four that may have been the dwellings of the main tenants in the 18th century. They have walls of coursed, quarry-dressed stone, rounded corners, and presumably were covered with hipped roofs. They have lintelled windows but all but one with no mural fireplaces. Those buildings with opposed entrances may mostly have been barns. Some less well-preserved structures may be of earlier date, ruined and abandoned prior to the mid 18th century. There may have been a mill on the burn at the north end of the settlement.

Inivea first appears in the documentary record in a charter of 12 July 1390 granted at Ardtornish Castle by Donald Lord of the

Isles to Lachlan Maclean, the ancestor of the Duart family. It was one of the lands that went with the constabulary of the castles of Cairnburgh and 'Isleborg' (perhaps a castle in Tiree). Inivea is given in this document as the pennyland of 'Aeneangboge' (Gaelic, Aoineadh, 'steep rocky place or slope rising from the sea', and a' Bhàigh, 'of the bay'). Two-thirds of it were waste at the time it was transferred to the Earl of Argyll in 1674. Five (male) inhabitants are listed in 1716. It was held jointly by four tenants in 1739, but in 1748 was noted as one of the Mull lands of the Argyll estates which was turning into waste ground. By the late 18th century it had been absorbed into the neighbouring farm of Frachadil. Four families were cleared from it about 1814, the rest of the inhabitants in 1832.

6.19 Killean: ruined township and sheep fank   NM 714 291

The township of Killean has the upstanding walls of several houses of 18th- and 19th-century date, and a large sheep fank that probably superseded them (Plate 25). The ruined medieval parish church of Killean (5.7) is nearby.

6.20 Knockroy: ruined township   NM 480 296

Knockroy (Gaelic Cnoc Ruadh, 'red hill') was a substantial joint tenancy farm when it was abandoned in the 19th century. Its ruins now lie in a substantial clearing adjacent to a track through the Tiroran Community Forest, to the west of the B8035. The west side of the clearing is defined by the settlement's head dyke and there are remains of yards, rigs and some 20 buildings, including houses, barns, byres and a corn-drying kiln. None of these structures, of drystone construction, now stand to any height.

6.21 Pennyghael: sheep fank   NM 513 255

This fank is situated about half a kilometre to the southwest of Pennyghael House, and appears to date from some time between 1819 and 1859. It has one large and four small pens, and there is a row of five turf shearing stools adjacent to the exterior of the south wall.

6.22 Salachry, Ardmeanach: ruined township   NM 450 274

The ruins of a township with seven buildings, lying just to the south of the track from Tiroran to Tavool. Another group of structures – 'Upper Salachry' – lies up the slope on the other side of the road at NGR NM 451 274. This appears to have been a shieling site in origin, although one of the 13 traceable houses may have been a click mill. It is irregular in shape, about 7m by 4m, has drystone walls and a stream flowing through it.

6.23 Shiaba, Ross of Mull: ruined township   NM 437 192

The remains of this substantial township lie almost 2km to the east of Scoor. Vehicles can be left at the car park for Kilvickeon medieval church. The unenclosed rigs of the infield have at a later date been divided into half a dozen long narrow crofts.

6.24 Staffa: cottage   NM 324 354

The ruins of a small stone house stand, centrally, on the flat summit of the island (Fig. 81). It was apparently erected about the beginning of the 19th century as a shelter for the increasing numbers of visitors and tourists visiting the island to view its remarkable geological features.

Figure 81. Ruins of early 19th-century cottage, Staffa

6.25 Suidhe, Bunessan: ruined township   NM 370 219

This ruined settlement, just to the west of Bunessan, is a Scheduled Monument. There is a group of five houses with upstanding walls, dating to the 18th or 19th century (Plate 26). The township had been abandoned by the 1940s.

The prehistoric barrow (2.12) is a few metres to the south.

6.26 Tavool Workers' Houses, Ardmeanach   NM 435 271

The ruins of a settlement cleared in the 1840s for sheep farming, although at least one of the houses remained in occupation into the 20th century. There are remains of at least nine houses, two of them with upstanding walls, on both sides of the track from Tavool to Burg.

6.27 Tenga Brideig: shielings   NM 403 310

There is a sheep fank with a large gathering pen and two smaller holding pens by the north side of the Glen More road at NGR NM 403 306. A path traverses the steep slope behind to the ruins of a small rectangular, drystone house on the bank of a tributary of the Allt Tenga Brideig with an impressive view of the valley below. Around it are the remains of earlier circular shieling huts.

6.28 Tìr Fhearagain (Tireragan): ruined townships   NM 337 188

A two pennyland in the Ross of Mull belonging to Iona Abbey, named for an early abbot, Fergna Britt, who died in 633. It is listed in the abbey lands acquired by Hector, son of Lachlan Maclean of Duart in 1587/8. Tìr Fhearagain, so identified on Ordnance Survey maps, is a cluster of about nine ruined houses and other enclosures. It was known locally as Crò Na Bà Glaise (Gaelic, 'pen of the grey cow'). Round about are traces of unenclosed rigs. About 200m to the north, running NSW–ENE is a sinuous head dyke separating off an area of moorland, Glac Ròineach. Here at NGR NM 331 192 is another ruined settlement with five or more houses surrounded by an enclosure containing previously cultivated ground. This is possibly an old shieling ground that was colonised in the 19th century for year-round occupation. Ordnance Survey maps identify a spot a few 100 metres to the south as Cille Mhuire. It may therefore be that this settlement represents the Kilmorie listed in the Maclean charter of 1587/8. The name indicates that there was a burial ground or chapel dedicated to St Mary.

To the south of Tìr Fhearagain at NGR NM 335 184 is the ruined settlement of Breac-acahdh (Gaelic, 'speckled field') with some eight houses. To the east at NGR NM 3385 1827 is a ruined cottage with evidence for crucks. At NGR NM 3395 1797 is an old sheep fank and other ruined buildings. Ordnance Survey maps supply the name Tòrr Mhic an Fhamhair (Gaelic, 'hill of the giant's son') but it was apparently known as Torran Odhar (Gaelic, 'dun coloured hill'), and may be identified as the successor of the Teirgeyll in the Maclean charter of 1587/8, probably from the Gaelic for 'land of the foreigner or stranger'.

TOWNS AND VILLAGES

6.29 Baile Mor, Iona

NM 286 242

Almost all the 130 or so people who inhabit Iona live in this substantial village, dominated by the ruins of the medieval nunnery and abbey. Its origins can legitimately be traced back to Early Christian times and it was probably out of the ordinary in Post-Reformation times as a substantial, by Scottish standards, village. Thomas Pennant says that it consisted of about 50 mean, thatched houses when he visited in 1772, though he noted there were also the ruins of better constructed ones – mansions dating to an earlier time. The following year James Boswell described the island as fertile, and was told that it exported some cattle and grain. The villagers imported nothing but iron and salt, made their own woollen and linen cloth, and brewed a good deal of beer.

The churches and other monuments on Iona attracted pilgrims and tourists from earliest times. Visits became a great deal easier from 1826 with the commencement of regular links from the mainland by steamers, and as the 19th century wore on, the island became an ever more popular tourist destination. The inhabitants of Baile Mor benefited greatly from this, providing services to visitors, although the majority have for long just been day-trippers.

The island is basically free of cars, and large numbers of tourists are now decanted daily in the summer season at the slipway in the village for the regular ferry service from Fionnphort in Mull, where there are large car parks for cars and buses.

Apart from the medieval ruins and monuments described elsewhere, the village has few buildings of architectural interest. Its present core, a row of houses stretching NNE from the jetty along St Ronan's Bay, dates to the early 19th century. The present parish church was built in 1828 and is a good example of a 'Parliamentary kirk', that is one funded by the Parliamentary Commissioners appointed to build additional places of worship in the Highlands and Islands. It is a simple rectangular structure with a belfry and arch-headed doors and windows (Plate 22). There is a worn medieval grave-slab lying outside it and part of another of 14th- or 15th-century date is kept in the vestry. The adjacent manse, built at the same time as the church, is now occupied by the Iona Heritage Centre.

The Bishop's House, dating to the 1890s, stands at the end of the main street, looking towards the abbey ruins. It is a rectangular block, single-storey with attic and a gablet containing a rose window. It was built as a retreat house for the Scottish Episcopal Church.

Essential viewing

6.30 Dervaig: planned village   NM 430 520

Dervaig is a village planned in 1799 by Alexander Maclean of Coll, with a population of about 80. It consists of a main street of white-washed houses, the original ones, 26 in all, single-storeyed and semi-detached. Immediately to the west is the Bellachroy Hotel, which is claimed to have originated as a drovers' inn in 1608. The present building appears to be no earlier than the 19th century. Also nearby is Kilmore Parish Church (7.3).

6.31 Kintra: village   NM 314 253

A row of houses along the shore. The settlement was founded by the Duke of Argyll in the 1770s for fishermen brought in from Uist and Shetland to encourage the development of a local fishing industry.

Essential viewing

6.32 Tobermory: village

NM 50 55

Tobermory, with a present-day population of less than a thousand, is still the largest and most important settlement in Mull. The name is Gaelic for (St) Mary's well. The site of the well is now marked by a stone cross commemorating the coronation of King Edward VII in 1902, near to the remains of the medieval St Mary's Chapel, within a substantial burial ground at the head of Albert Street at the back of the town (NGR NM 502 553). Only its foundations survive, containing two medieval grave-slabs and part of a third nearby reused as an upright marker for a later burial. In 1843 the Sheriff Substitute of Tobermory, James Robertson, was informed by a local that these were grave-slabs of the chiefs of the MacKinnons. The most complete one is a Group 12 slab of late 15th- or early 16th-century date with two ladies in niches, side by side, below them a foliated cross, and separated from that by a band with a comb two pairs of shears and two mirrors, a foliage design. A band round the edge has traces of an inscription, mostly now illegible (Fig. 82).

The shore of Tobermory Bay, sheltered by Calve Island, was identified by the British Fisheries Society in 1787 as a suitable place to establish a new fishing settlement (Fig. 33). It had long been a favourite place for ships to shelter, including, most famously, one of the ships of the Spanish Armada in 1588. The account of this given over a hundred years later by Martin Martin indicates that there was a settlement around the harbour at that time. The edge of the bay is now lined by a row of houses and shops (Main Street), mostly of 19th-centuy date, attractively painted in a variety of bright colours. They include the splendid Mull Museum. The Co-op supermarket was built as an inn in the 1790s, while the Post Office is the much altered custom house of about the same date. By the harbour there is a rare pillar post-box with insignia for King Edward VIII. Halfway along the street there is also a clock tower erected in 1905 with money left by the noted traveller and writer, Isabella Bird, to commemorate her sister Henrietta.

Behind Main Street is the upper town, on top of a steep escarpment, originally with streets of single-storey cottages.

Figure 82. Grave-slab at the site of the medieval St Mary's chapel, Tobermory (6.32). It is of the late 15th or early 16th century, with representations of two ladies in niches, side by side (from *Proc Soc Antiq Scot* 17, 1882–83)

WRECKS

6.33 The *Swan*   NM 748 354

A small warship, apparently the wreck of the *Swan*, one of the ships of a Cromwellian flotilla lost in a storm off Duart Castle in September 1653. Much of the lower hull survives, as well as debris from the upper hull, and many artefacts. She had three masts, a keel length of 60 feet (18.29m) and oars each side. She would have required a complement of over 100 men, and was provided with ordnance, two guns mounted in her bow, another two at least firing astern, and two firing broadside on each side. In her upper stern she had a small, well-appointed cabin. She was clearly a versatile ship, designed for operating in coastal waters. Indeed, she was very probably a ship built several years earlier for the Marquis of Argyll. Was she, indeed, the ship from which he watched the rout of his men by Montrose at the Battle of Inverlochy on 2 February 1645? There is a rich collection of artefacts and ship fittings now in the National Museum of Scotland, including wooden, ceramic and pewter vessels, items of personal equipment, the remains of the ship's binnacle and fragments of carved wood from the ship's stern, including a warrior's head and a winged cherub. Details of these and information on the ship and its wreck can be found in a recent book by Colin Martin (2017).

The site is a designated historic shipwreck, but divers may visit it on condition that nothing is disturbed or removed, including plant and animal life. For more information on location and access, including a visitor trail for divers, go to: http://www.lochalinedive centre.co.uk/?page_id=1455.

6.34 HMS *Dartmouth*   NM 723 406

The *Dartmouth* was a fifth-rate frigate built in Portsmouth in 1655, lost off Eilean Rubha an Ridire in the Sound of Mull in a violent storm on 9 October 1690. She was rated at 240 tons, had a keel length of 80 feet (24.38m) and mounted up to 32 guns. Some of her keel survives in an intact state and many fittings and artefacts were recovered. They are now in the collection of the National Museum of Scotland though some are sometimes exhibited elsewhere. No visitor's licence is necessary for divers to visit the wreck. For more information go to: http://www.lochalinedivecentre. co.uk/?page_id=1451.

INDUSTRIAL AND MISCELLANEOUS SITES

6.35 Abhainn na h'Uamha: whisky still   NM 517 358

This site was identified as a whisky still by locals. It is about a mile up Gleann na Beinne Fada from the shore of Loch na Keal. At the end of an island formed by the dividing river are the ruins of a rectangular building. Nearby, hidden amongst rocks, are the remains of four smaller structures.

6.36 Aros: bridge
NM 556 448

A single-span stone bridge across the Aros River, adjacent to the road bridge in use today. It was probably built about 1790 when the road from Aros to the ferry at Grass Point was constructed (Fig. 35). There is a similar bridge of about the same date at Auchnacraig, across the head of Loch Don at NGR NM 727 328 on the unclassified road from Lochdon to Grass Point.

Essential viewing

6.37 Bunessan: corn mill
NM 385 218

The substantial ruined remains of this mill are in the care of the Ross of Mull Historical Society (Plate 27). When it was first erected by the Argyll Estate in the late 18th century it was of a single storey, but was later remodelled in 1830 to its present form with an upper storey. The pit for an overshot wheel survives, and some of the gearing, but not the wheel itself. There is a solid millstone within the ruin, probably quarried locally, and the remains of two composite ones. The mill remained in use until about 1910.

6.38 Crackaig: Whisky Cave
NM 3479 4612

As the name suggests, this cave, well hidden down by the shore, near the chapel and township of Crackaig in Treshnish, was used for illicit whisky distilling. There is the stone-lined bowl of a kiln in a platform set in the midden deposits of the cave floor.

6.39 Druim Tighe Mhic Ghill Chatain, Tenga: fairground
NM 489 454

The name is Gaelic for 'ridge of the son of Chattan's servant'. The place, now buried in forestry just to the south of the road from Dervaig to Tenga, is an old market and meeting place where cattle and horses were bought and sold as late as the early 19th century. There are the remains of over 50 small rectangular, turf structures, presumably the footings for temporary shelters or tents.

6.40 Gribun: millstone quarry NM 449 349

There is evidence for millstone quarrying in the Triassic sandstone outcropping on the shore next to the boat-slip for Inch Kenneth. One unfinished stone, about 1.5m in diameter, remains *in situ* (Fig. 83). It is said that 20 or 30 millstones were produced here annually.

Essential viewing

6.41 Gruline: mausoleum NM 549 398

The mausoleum of Major-General Lachlan Macquarie, Governor of New South Wales, 'The Father of Australia'. It is signposted off the B8035 at the head of Loch Na Keal by a sign erected by the National Trust of Australia. There is parking adjacent to the road and the monument can be reached by a short walk. It is built of ashlar, solid with a slabbed gabled roof, clasping buttresses and inscribed marble panels in each gable wall (Plate 28).

Macquarie is believed to have been born in Ulva in 1762 (the inscription on the mausoleum says 1761) and embarked on a military career at the age of 14 or 15. He took part in the American War of Independence and later served in India and Egypt. He was appointed Governor of New South Wales in 1810 in the wake of a serious rebellion, and despite opposition from the free settlers and lack of support from the British Government set out to transform what was a penal settlement into a free colony. He relied on and promoted emancipated prisoners to positions of power and authority. Hobart in Tasmania and Sydney both owe their street plans to him. He established a coinage, encouraged the creation of the Bank of New South Wales and sponsored exploration. He was responsi-

Figure 83. Unfinished millstone on the shore at Gribun (6.40)

ble for the adoption of the name Australia. His detractors pushed him into resigning in 1821 and he died in London in 1824. His enlightened policies, however, survived him and have been recognised as underpinning the modern state of Australia.

6.42 Loch a' Chumhainn: fishtrap   NM 428 516

The head of this loch near Dervaig is cut off by a low drystone dyke which trapped fish as the tide receded.

6.43 Ormaig, Ulva: corn mill   NM 409 391

This mill, some distance from the deserted township of Ormaig on the island of Ulva, is a small ruinous rectangular building of about 1800. The wheel and other machinery have gone; only two mica-schist millstones remain. One of the main points of interest of this mill is the evidence it retains for a cruck-framed roof, the cruck couples having been housed in recesses in the walls.

6.44 Tobermory: Distillery   NM 504 551

Also known as Ledaig, this still functioning distillery is situated at the bottom of Eas Brae, at the south end of the village of Tobermory. There is a visitor centre and guided tours are available. The 19th-century works were largely reconstructed in 1970–72. The two-storey Iona Cottage adjacent to the main gate is the manager's house. Across Eas Brae at the back is an impressive late 19th-century four-storey warehouse, now converted to housing. The distillery was founded in 1798 by a local merchant, John Sinclair, and remained in operation until 1837. It was re-established in 1878 but again closed in 1930. It reopened yet again in 1972.

6.45 Torness: market place   NM 648 326

There is a ruined byre adjacent to the south side of the A849 and just to the east of a forestry plantation. Below the house, just to the northwest of it, are several rectangular, heather-clad mounds, evidently the market place marked on John Thomson's 1824 map of the Northern Part of Argyll. A market was held here annually for horses, perhaps no later than the 1830s.

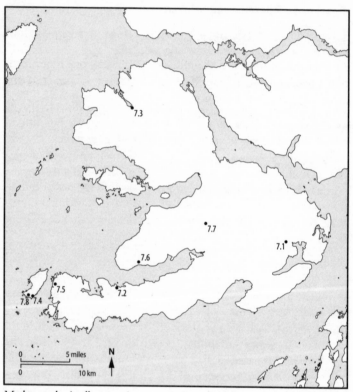

Modern and miscellaneous sites

7. Modern and Miscellaneous Sites

7.1 Ardura: monument to Dugald MacPhail   NM 684 307

At the turn-off from the A849 for Lochbuie is a stone monument to the poet and writer, Dugald Macphail (1818–87), born at nearby Strathcoil. His best known work is the Gaelic song 'An t-Eilean Muileach' ('The Isle of Mull'), known as the 'Mull National Anthem'.

7.2 Bunessan: monument to Mary MacDonald   NM 406 231

By the side of the A849 about a mile and a half to the east of Bunessan stands a small stone monument to Mary MacDonald, who lived at Ardtun in the 19th century. She was the writer of a Gaelic hymn translated into English as 'Child in the manger'.

7.3 Dervaig: Kilmore Parish Church   NM 436 518

This white-harled church, set on a low hill near Dervaig Village, forms a striking landmark. The church is the successor of the medieval parish church of Kilcolmkill, in use until it was replaced by a church on this site in 1755. It in turn was superseded by the present building, designed by Peter MacGregor Chalmers, in 1904–05. It is in Irish Romanesque style with a semi-circular apse, rectangular nave and round tower at the west end. It has seven stained glass windows by Stephen Adam, 1905–10. Inside there is part of the shaft of a commemorative cross dating to the 14th or 15th century (Fig. 78). It comes from the burial ground at the nearby site of the medieval parish church of Kilcolmkill (5.5).

7.4 Rubha na Carraig Géire, Iona: marble quarry   NM 268 217

Although marble has been quarried on Iona since medieval times, as witnessed by the table top of the high altar in Iona Abbey, the evidence of quarrying at the southeast tip of the island to be seen today dates largely from a much later phase of activity from 1907 to 1918. The quarry can be reached by following a path southwards from the golf course, past the east end of Loch Staoineig almost to Port na Curaich; then left, up a small valley, where there are the overgrown ruins of a house, possibly that of an 18th-century quarry manager, and then down a steep gulley to the sea. A substantial vein of marble, partially worked, is exposed, along with much debris. The marble is white, streaked with yellowish-green serpentine. A large iron cutting frame by G. Anderson of Arbroath remains *in situ*, with adjacent to it a producer-gas engine by Fielding and Platt of Gloucester with two tanks behind it. There were two derricks, one adjacent to the cutting frame, and the other on a nearby quay, mostly of natural rock, for lifting and moving blocks and other material. There is also evidence of a short length of railway and the remains of a four-wheeled bogie. The quay, difficult of access even for the 'puffers' that used it, was the only practical means of getting supplies in and out.

7.5 Tormore: granite quarries   NM 305 240

Quarries where the distinctive red Ross of Mull granite was extracted and processed on an industrial scale in the 19th century are to be found in several locations at the western end of the Ross of Mull. Quarries and other evidence of workings can be seen from the sea along the west coast to the north of Fionnphort. At Camas Tuath (North Bay, NGR NM 352 242) to the northwest of Bunessan quarries were opened in 1839 to provide stone for the building of Skerryvore Lighthouse. There are still ruins of the quarriers' houses, other industrial buildings, and the steep ramp which had a railway track to transport blocks of stone down to a jetty. On Erraid are the houses, reoccupied in recent times, of the shore station established for the building of the Dubh Artach lighthouse, 14 miles to the southwest, from 1866. The rock for it was quarried on Erraid.

Quarries at Tormore (Tòrr Mòr), just to the north of Fionnphort, were developed from the 1850s and carried on into the early 20th century. The pier used to ship the blocks of quarried stone from Mull can be seen, along with evidence for rail tracks, houses, a smiddy and powder store, and the rock faces which were extensively quarried. The track providing access down to the houses at the jetty is the bed of a railway. Stone abutments on either side supported a bridge for another railway that went to a waste tip (Plate 29).

MISCELLANEOUS

7.6 Airigh Thearlaich, Ardmeanach: coffin cairns   NM 447 274

Below Airigh Thearlaich, on a rise beside the track leading towards MacCulloch's Fossil Tree, are four coffin cairns, heavily reconstructed in recent times. These mark a traditional point at which funeral parties rested when taking bodies for burial at Kilfinichen Parish Church. Each cairn is said to represent a generation of the MacGillivray family which farmed at Burg.

7.7 Carn Cul Righ Albainn, Mam Clachaig   NM 553 332

There is a cairn on top of Mam Clachaig in what is now a remote location but which overlooks a path, formerly an important routeway connecting Loch Bà with Glen More and the head of Loch Scridain. Mam Clachaig is the top of a ridge over which the path traverses. The cairn is named on Joan Blaeu's map of Mull published in Amsterdam in 1654, but based on the survey work of the Scotsman Timothy Pont, undertaken 50 years or so earlier. The map actually shows a mountain surmounted by a cross, with to the north the name 'Karn culri Allabyn', and to the south 'Karn culri Erin'. These names are Gaelic, respectively, for 'cairn with its back to Scotland' and 'cairn with its back to Ireland'. Neither the latter cairn nor a cross have been located. All this suggests that the surviving cairn is a boundary marker rather than a prehistoric burial. It possibly originally marked one end of the lands belonging to Iona Abbey, just as Càrn Cùil ri Éirinn on Iona (7.8) marked the other end.

7.8 Port na Curaich, Iona

NM 263 217

The name is Gaelic for the 'harbour of the curragh'. It refers to a small bay at the south end of Iona where St Columba is supposed to have first landed. It was believed that a low grass-covered mound, some 22m by 7.5m, was modelled on his boat. It appears, however, to be natural. Less than 1km to the northwest is the summit of Druim an Aoineidh (NGR 257 223), surmounted by a cairn of no great age. It is called Càrn Cùil ri Éirinn (Gaelic, 'cairn with its back to Ireland'). This relates to the tradition that St Columba chose Iona as his place of exile since it was the first reached in his travels from which Ireland was not visible.

Somerled and some of his descendants, including the MacDougalls

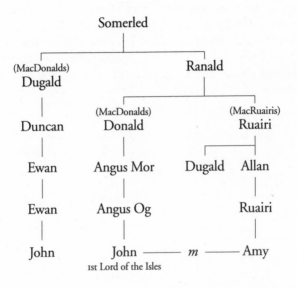

Somerled

(MacDonalds)
Dugald

Ranald

Duncan

(MacDonalds)
Donald

(MacRuairis)
Ruairi

Ewan

Angus Mor

Dugald   Allan

Ewan

Angus Og

Ruairi

John

John ——— *m* ——— Amy
1st Lord of the Isles

The Macleans of Duart

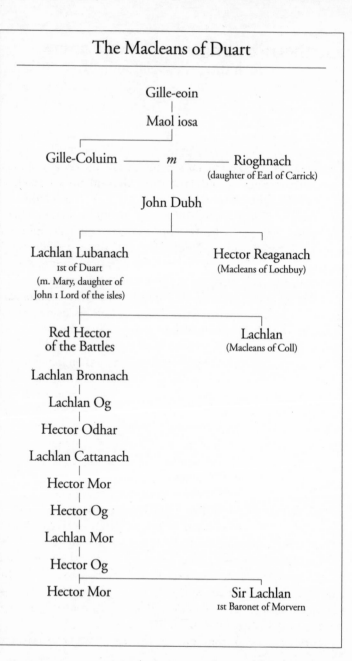

Gille-eoin
|
Maol iosa

Gille-Coluim ——— *m* ——— Rioghnach
(daughter of Earl of Carrick)
|
John Dubh

Lachlan Lubanach
1st of Duart
(m. Mary, daughter of
John 1 Lord of the isles)

Hector Reaganach
(Macleans of Lochbuy)

Red Hector
of the Battles

Lachlan
(Macleans of Coll)

Lachlan Bronnach
|
Lachlan Og
|
Hector Odhar
|
Lachlan Cattanach
|
Hector Mor
|
Hector Og
|
Lachlan Mor
|
Hector Og

Hector Mor

Sir Lachlan
1st Baronet of Morvern

Further Reading

The essential general survey of the monuments and antiquities of Mull and Iona are the *Inventories* published by the Royal Commission on the Ancient and Historical Monuments of Scotland (RCAHMS). The information they contain, and much more, can be accessed via the Canmore database – https://canmore.org.uk – the online catalogue to Scotland's archaeology, buildings, industrial and maritime heritage. Also from RCAHMS is the valuable book of essays on the prehistory of Argyll edited by Ritchie (1997) and the two surveys of medieval sculpture by Steer and Bannerman (1977) and Fisher (2001). *The Proceedings of the Society of Antiquaries of Scotland* contains many reports on excavations, fieldwork and artefacts from these islands. Volumes and indexes can be accessed online from the Society's website: http://www.socantscot.org.

Final publication on the extensive excavations on Iona directed by Charles Thomas is still awaited, but those reported by Barber (1991) are particularly important. Work on the short stone rows of northern Mull is published by Martlew and Ruggles (1996), and the excavation of Croig Cave by Mithen and Wicks (2012). The final report on the wreck of the *Swan* is provided by Martin (2017) and Baliscate can now be found online (Ellis, 2017).

Early histories and chronicles of particular relevance to these islands include *The Chronicles of the Kings of Man and the Isles* (Broderick, 1996), and two MacDonald histories printed in Cameron (1894, 148–217) and Macphail (1914, 5–72). McDonald (1997) is an important modern history for the Kingdom of the Isles, and for the history of the West Highlands and Islands in the 16th century Gregory's work of 1836 remains essential. Useful accounts have been left by early travellers including Monro in 1549 (Munro, 1961), Sacheverell in 1688 (1859), Martin at the end of the 17th century (1994) and Pennant in 1772 (1774).

Surviving acts of the Lords of the Isles have been gathered

together by Munro and Munro (1986). Rentals of Mull lands in 1509 and 1541 when in the hands of the Crown can be found in the *Exchequer Rolls of Scotland*. A rental for the Duart Estates in 1674 is given in Macphail 1914, 277–95. Vital for later times are the lists of Mull inhabitants in 1715 and 1779 (Maclean-Bristol 1998 and Cregeen 1963) and the instructions issued by the 5th Duke of Argyll for his Mull estates (Cregeen 1964). There is much significant information about Mull and the local economy in the works of early agricultural writers, especially the Rev. John Walker (McKay, 1989), Smith, (1798) and Macdonald (1811).

For Mull and its people, particularly in the 18th and 19th centuries, there is the indispensable book by Jo Currie (2001). Just as important for Iona is the 1990 study by Mairi MacArthur. A reliable source of information on some of the main Mull families and individuals is the *Oxford Dictionary of National Biography*. The Macleans are well served by a 19th-century clan historian (MacLean, 1889) and more recent studies by Nicholas Maclean-Bristol (1995, 1999). The two *Statistical Accounts* are invaluable for detailed information on a parish by parish basis for the late 18th and early 19th century. Tom Devine's 1988 analysis of the great 19th-century famine is of considerable importance for understanding major changes at that time, including clearances and emigration.

Allen, J.R. and Anderson, J., 1903, *The Early Christian Monuments of Scotland* (Edinburgh, Society of Antiquaries of Scotland).

Allardyce, A. (ed.), 1888, *Scotland And Scotsmen in the Eighteenth Century from the MSS of John Ramsay, Esq. of Ochtertyre*, vol. 2 (Edinburgh, Blackwood).

Baker, R., 1999, *The Terror of Tobermory. Vice Admiral Sir Gilbert Stephenson* (Edinburgh, Birlinn).

Bannerman, J.M.W., 1974, *Studies in the History of Dalriada* (Edinburgh, Scottish Academic Press).

Bannerman, J.M.W., 1986, *The Beatons* (Edinburgh, John Donald).

Barber, J., 1981, 'Excavations on Iona, 1979', *Proc Soc Antiq Scot* III: 282–380.

Barnard, A., 2003, *The Whisky Distilleries of the United Kingdom* (Edinburgh, Birlinn).

Boyd, J.M. and Bowes, D.R. (eds), 1983, *Natural Environment of the Inner Hebrides* (The Royal Society of Edinburgh).

Broderick, G. (ed.), 1996, *Cronica Regum Mannie et Insularum. Chronicles of the Kings of Man and the Isles* (Douglas, Manx National Heritage).

Brown, O.M. and Whittaker, E.J, 1988 *A Walk Round Tobermory*.

Brydall, 1898, see MacMillan, 1898.

Burl, A. 1976, *The Stone Circles of the British Isles* (New Haven and London, Yale University Press).

Caldwell, D. H., 2007, 'Having the right kit: West Highlanders fighting in Ireland', *in* Duffy, S. (ed.), *The World of the Galloglass: kings, warlords and warriors in Ireland and Scotland, 1200–1600* (Dublin: Four Courts Press), 144–68.

Caldwell, D. H., 2014, 'The Kingdom of the Isles', *in* Caldwell, D. H. and Hall, M. A. (eds), *The Lewis Chessmen: new perspectives* (Edinburgh, National Museums Scotland), 70–93.

Caldwell, D. H., Hall, M. and Wilkinson, C., 2009, 'The Lewis Hoard of Gaming Pieces; a re-examination of their context, meanings, discovery and manufacture', *Medieval Archaeology* 53: 155–203.

Caldwell, D. H., McGibbon, F. M., Miller, S. and Ruckley, N. A., 2010, 'The image of a Celtic society: medieval West Highland sculpture', *in* O'Neill, P. (ed.), *Celts in Legend and Reality: papers from the sixth Australian conference of Celtic studies, University of Sydney, July 2007* (Sydney, series in Celtic studies 9; University of Sydney), 13–59.

Caldwell, D.H. and Ruckley, N.A., 2005, 'Domestic Architecture in the Lordship of the Isles', *in* Oram, R. and Stell, G. (eds), *Lordship and Architecture in Medieval and Renaissance Scotland* (Edinburgh, John Donald), 96–121.

Campbell, E., 1999, *Saints and Sea-Kings. The First Kingdom of the Scots* (Edinburgh, Canongate with Historic Scotland).

Campbell, F., 1871, 'Note On An Artificial Island and Ancient Canoe Found in Draining A Loch Near Tobermory, Mull', *Proc Soc Antiq Scot* 8 (1868–70), 465.

Campbell, J. L. and Thomson, D., 1963, *Edward Lhuyd in the Scottish Highlands 1699–1700* (Oxford, Clarendon Press).

Cameron, A., 1894, *Reliquae Celticae*, vol. 2 (Inverness, Northern Counties Newspaper and Printing and Publishing).

Cameron, J. S. 2013, *A History of the Ross of Mull* (Bunessan, Ross of Mull Historical Centre).

Clare, J., 2010, *Guide to the Historical Features of the Ross of Mull* (privately printed).

Collectanea De Rebus Albanicis, consisting of Original Papers and Documents relating to the history of the Highlands and Islands of Scotland (Edinburgh, Iona Club, 1847).

Cowan, I. B. and Easson, D. E., 1976, *Medieval Religious Houses Scotland* (London, Longman).

Cregeen, E. R. (ed.), 1963, *Inhabitants of the Argyll Estate, 1779* (Edinburgh, Scottish Records Society, vol. 91).

Cregeen, E. R. (ed.), 1964, *Argyll Estate Instructions, Mull, Morvern, Tiree, 1771–1805* (Edinburgh, Scottish History Society).

Currie, J., 1998, *Mull Family Names for ancestor hunters* (Tobermory, Brown and Whittaker).

Currie, J., 2001, *Mull: The Island & Its People* (Edinburgh, Birlinn).

Curle, A. O., 1924, 'A note on four silver spoons and a fillet of gold found in the nunnery at Iona, and on a finger-ring, part of a fillet and fragment of wire, all of gold, found in St Ronan's Chapel, the Nunnery, Iona', 1924, *Proc Soc Antiq Scot* 58 (1923–24), 102–11.

Daniell, W., 1820, *A Voyage Round Great Britain Undertaken in the Summer of the Year 1813*, vol. 3. London.

Devine, T. M., 1988, *The Great Highland Famine* (Edinburgh, John Donald).

Discovery And Excavation in Scotland. Published annually by Archaeology Scotland; also available online.

Douglass, M., 2003, *Lost Townships, silent voices: a field study of Mull* (Dunoon).

Drummond, J., 1881, *Sculptured Monuments in Iona and the West Highlands* (Edinburgh, Society of Antiquaries of Scotland).

Dumville, D.N., 2002, 'Ireland and North Britain in the Earlier Middle Ages: Contexts for *Míniugud Senchasa Fher nAlban*', *in* Baoill, C.Ó. and McGuire, N.R. (eds), *Rannsachadh na Gàidhlig 2000* (Obar Dheathain, An Clò Gaidhealach), 185–211.

Dunbar, J., 1981, 'The Medieval Architecture of the Scottish Highlands', in *The Middle Ages in the Highlands* (Inverness Field Club), 38–70.

Duns, Prof. 1879, 'Notice of a Bronze Penannular Brooch from the Island of Mull', *Proc Soc Antiq Scot* 13 (1878–79), 67–72.

Edwards, K.J. and Ralston, I.B.M. (eds) 2008, *Scotland After the Ice Age. Environment, Archaeology and History, 8000 BC – AD 1000* (Edinburgh University Press).

Ellis, C., 2017, *Monks, Priests and Farmers: A Community Research Excavation at Baliscate, Isle of Mull 2017* (Scottish Archaeological Internet Report no 68), available through the website of the Society of Antiquaries of Scotland (https://socantscot.org).

Environmental Resources Management, 1996, *Landscape assessment of Argyll and the Firth of Clyde* (Scottish Natural Heritage, Review no. 78).

Exchequer Rolls of Scotland 1878–, ed. by J. Stuart *et al.* (Edinburgh, HM General Register House).

Fairhurst, H., 1962, 'An Caisteal: An Iron Age Fortification in Mull', *Proc Soc Antiq Scot* 95 (1961–62), 199–207.

Faithfull, J., 2004, *The Ross of Mull Granite Quarries* (Iona, New Iona Press).

Fawcett, R., 2011, *The Architecture of the Scottish Medieval Church 1100–1560* (New Haven and London, Yale University Press).

Finlayson, B., 1999, 'Understanding the Initial Colonization of Scotland', *Antiquity* 73: 879–84.

Fisher, I., 2001, *Early Medieval Sculpture in the West Highlands and Islands* (Edinburgh, RCAHMS and the Society of Antiquaries of Scotland).

Fowler, E. and Fowler, P. J., 1988, 'Excavations on Torr an Aba, Iona, Argyll', *Proc Soc Antiq Scot* 118: 181–201.

Fraser, J.E., 2009, *From Caledonia to Pictland: Scotland to 795* (The New Edinburgh History of Scotland, Edinburgh University Press).

Garnett, T., 1800, *Observations on a Tour through the Highlands and Part of the Western Isles of Scotland.* Vol. 1 (London).

Giblin, C., 1964, *Irish Franciscan Mission to Scotland 1619–1646* (Dublin, Assisi Press).

Gibson, J. G., 2002, *Old and New World Highland Bagpiping* (Montreal, McGill-Queen's University Press).

Graham, H. D., 1850, *Antiquities of Iona* (London).

Graham-Campbell, J. and Batey, C.E., 2005, *Vikings in Scotland, an Archaeological Survey* (Edinburgh University Press).

Gregory, D., 1836, *History of the Western Highlands and Isles of Scotland from A.D. 1493 To A.D. 1625* (Edinburgh, William Tait).

Haggarty, A. M., 1988, 'Iona: some results from recent work', *Proc Soc Antiq Scot* 118: 203–13.

Haldane, A.R.B., 1952, *The Drove Roads of Scotland* (Edinburgh, Nelson).

Harden, J. 1996, *An Archaeological Survey of lands on Burg Estate, Mull, in advance of Millennium Forest Work* (prepared for NTS. Copies available in HES Library and the Pennyghael in the Past Historical Archive).

Henshall, A.S., 1972, *The Chambered Tombs of Scotland*, vol. 2 (Edinburgh University Press).

Hughes, M., 1998, *The Hebrides at War* (Edinburgh, Canongate).

Hunter, J. (ed.), 1986, *For the People's Cause: From the Writings of John Murdoch* (Edinburgh, HMSO).

Johnson, S. and Boswell, J., 1993, *A Journey to the Western Islands of Scotland and The Journal of a Tour to the Hebrides* (London, Penguin reprint of editions of 1775 and 1786).

Jones, R., 2007, *Tea With Chrissie – The Story Of Burg And Ardmeanach On The Isle Of Mull* (Aros, Craigmore Publications).

LeMay J. 1998 *Ardmeanach: A Hidden Corner of Mull* (Isle of Iona, The New Iona Press)

LeMay, J. and Gardner, J., 2010, *Glen More: a drive through history* (Tobermory, Brown and Whittaker).

Loudon, J. B., 2001, *The Mull Diaries. The Diary of James Robertson, Sheriff Substitute of Tobermory 1842–1846* (Dunoon, Argyll & Bute Library Service).

MacAlister, R. A. S., 1914, 'An inventory of the ancient monuments remaining in the island of Iona', *Proc Soc Antiq Scot* 48 (1913–14), 421–30.

MacArthur, E. M., 1990, *Iona. The Living Memory of a Crofting Community 1750–1914* (Edinburgh University Press).

MacArthur, E. M., 1995, *Columba's Island. Iona from Past to Present* (Edinburgh University Press).

MacCormick, J., 1934, *The Island of Mull Its History, Scenes And Legend* (Glasgow, MacLaren).

Macdonald, F. A., 2006, *Missions to the Gaels, Reformation and Counter-Reformation in Ulster and the Highlands and Islands of Scotland 1560–1760* (Edinburgh, John Donald).

Macdonald, J., 1811, *General View of the Agriculture of the Hebrides or Western Isles of Scotland* (Edinburgh).

McDonald, R.A., 1997, *The Kingdom of the Isles Scotland's Western Seaboard, c. 1100 – c. 1336* (East Linton, Tuckwell).

McGeachy, R. A. A., 2005, *Argyll 1730–1850* (Edinburgh, John Donald).

MacGibbon, D. and Ross, T., 1887–92, *The Castellated and Domestic Architecture of Scotland*, 5 vols (Edinburgh, Douglas).

MacGibbon, D. and Ross, T., 1896–97, *The Ecclesiastical Architecture of Scotland*, 3 vols (Edinburgh, Douglas).

McKay, M.M. (ed.), 1980, *The Rev Dr John Walker's Report on the Hebrides of 1764 and 1771* (Edinburgh, John Donald).

MacKenzie, A., 2002, *Island Voices. Traditions of North Mull* (Edinburgh, Birlinn).

MacKenzie, D. W., 2011, *As it was, Sin Mar A Bha, An Ulva Boyhood* (Edinburgh, Birlinn).

McLauchlan, T., 1864, 'Notice of Monoliths in the Isle of Mull', *Proc Soc Antiq Scot* 5 (1862–64), 46–52.

MacLean, J. P., 1889, *A History of the Clan MacLean* (Cincinnati, Clarke).

MacLean, J. P., 1923, *History of the Island of Mull*, 2 vols (Greenville, Jones).

Maclean-Bristol, N., 1995, *Warriors and Priests. The History of the Clan MacLean 1300–1570* (East Linton, Tuckwell).

Maclean-Bristol, N., 1998, *Inhabitants of the Inner Isles Morvern and Ardnamurchan 1716* (Edinburgh, Scottish Record Society).

Maclean-Bristol, N., 1999, *Murder Under Trust: The Crimes and Death of Sir Lachlan Mor MacLean of Duart, 1558–1598* (East Linton, Tuckwell).

MacMillan, A, 1898, *Iona: Its History, Antiquities, Etc* (London); including Brydall, R., *Its Carved Stones*.

Macnab, P., 1998, *Traditional Tales of Mull* (Tobermory, Brown and Whittaker).

Macnab, P. A., 2008, *Mull & Iona* (Newton Abbot, David and Charles).

Macniven, A., 2015, *The Vikings in Islay: The Place of Names in Hebridean Settlement History* (Edinburgh, Birlinn).

Macphail, J.R.N., 1914, *Highland Papers*, vol. 1 (Scottish History Society).

Macquarrie, A., 1983, *Iona through the ages* (Society of West Highland and Island Historical Research).

Marsden, F., 2001, *Lachlan Macquarie: from Mull to Australia* (Tobermory, Brown and Whittaker).

Martin, C., 1978 'The *Dartmouth*, a British frigate wrecked off Mull, 1690.5. The Ship', *International Journal Nautical Archaeology and Underwater Exploration* 7/1: 29–58.

Martin, C., 1998, *Scotland's Historic Shipwrecks* (Historic Scotland and Batsford, London).

Martin, C., 2017, *A Cromwellian Warship Wrecked Off Duart Castle, Mull, Scotland, In 1653* (Edinburgh, The Society of Antiquaries of Scotland).

Martin, M., 1994, *A Description of the Western Islands of Scotland circa 1695* (Edinburgh, Birlinn).

Martlew, R. D. and Ruggles, C. L. N., 1966, 'Ritual and Landscape on the West Coast of Scotland: an Investigation of the Stone Rows of Northern Mull', *Proceedings Prehistoric Society* 62: 117–31.

Marshall, R.K. 2013, *Columba's Iona, A New History* (Dingwall, Sandstone Press).

Mithen, S., 2010, *To The Islands: An Archaeologist's Relentless Quest To Find The Prehistoric Hunter-gatherers Of The Hebrides* (Uig, Lewis, Two Raven Press).

Mithen, S., and Wicks, K., 2012, 'Croig Cave: a Late Bronze Age ornament deposit and three millennia of fishing and foraging on the north-west coast of Mull, Scotland', *Proc Soc Antiq Scot* 142: 63–132.

Moir, P., and Crawford, I., 1994, *Argyll Shipwrecks* (Wemyss Bay, Moir Crawford).

Morton Boyd, J. and Bowes, D.R., (eds), 1983, *Natural Environment of the Inner Hebrides.* The Royal Society of Edinburgh (*Proceedings*, section B, vol. 83).

Munro, J. and Munro, R.W., 1986, *The Acts of the Lords of the Isles* (Edinburgh, Scottish History Society).

Munro, R.W., 1961, *Monro's Western Isles of Scotland and Genealogies of the Clans 1549* (Edinburgh, Oliver and Boyd).

Nelson, J., 2016, *The Story of Glengorm* (privately printed).

Ó Carragáin, T., 2010, *The Archaeology of the Early Irish Church* (New Haven, Yale).

O'Sullivan, J., 1994, 'Excavation of a women's cemetery and early church at St Ronan's medieval parish church, Iona', *Proc Soc Antiq Scot* 124: 227–65.

O'Sullivan, J., 1994, 'Excavations on the mill stream, Iona', *Proc Soc Antiq Scot* 124: 491–508.

O'Sullivan, J., 1999, 'Iona: archaeological investigations, 1875–1996', *in* Broun, D. and Clancy, T.O. (eds), *Spes Scotorum Hope of Scots: Saint Columba Iona and Scotland* (Edinburgh, T. and T. Clark).

Oxford Dictionary of National Biography. Oxford: Oxford University Press (http://www.oxforddnb.com/).

Pennant, T., 1774, *A Tour in Scotland and Voyage to the Hebrides, 1772* (Chester).

RCAHMS, 1980, *Argyll Volume 3: Mull, Tiree, Coll & Northern Argyll* (Edinburgh, RCAHMS).

RCAHMS, 1982, *Argyll Volume 4: Iona* (Edinburgh, RCAHMS).

Riddell, C., 1996, *Tireragan – A Township on the Ross of Mull.*

Ritchie, G. (ed.), 1997, *The Archaeology of Argyll* (Edinburgh University Press).

Rixson, D., [Blog], Land Assessment Scotland (http://las.denisrixson.com/)

Ruggles, C., 1999, *Astronomy in Prehistoric Britain and Ireland* (New Haven and London, Yale University Press).

Sacheverell, W., 1859, *An Account of the Isle of Man ... with A Voyage to I-Columb-Kill*, ed. T. Brown (Douglas, Isle of Man, The Manx Society).

Sellar, W.D.H., 2000, 'Hebridean Sea Kings: The Successors of Somerled, 1164–1316', *in* Cowan, E.J. and McDonald, R.A. (eds), *Alba, Celtic Scotland in the Medieval Era* (East Linton, Tuckwell), 187–218.

Shetelig, H., 1954, 'The Viking Graves', *in* Curle, A.O., Olsen, M. and Shetelig, H. (eds), *Viking Antiquities in Great Britain and Ireland, Part 6* (Oslo), 67–111.

Sinclair, C., 1953, *Thatched Houses: A contribution to the social history of the old Highlands* (Edinburgh, Oliver and Boyd).

Smith, J., 1798, *General View of the Agriculture of the County of Argyll.*

Smith, R., 2001, *The Making of Scotland: A Comprehensive Guide to the growth of Scotland's Cities, Towns and Villages* (Edinburgh, Canongate).

The Statistical Account of Scotland by the Ministers of the Respective Parishes, vol. 7, 1845 (Edinburgh). Kilfinichen And Kilviceuen, pp. 296–339; Kilninian And Kilmore, pp. 339–59.

Steer, K.A. and Bannerman, J.W.M., 1977, *Late Medieval Monumental Sculpture in the West Highlands* (Edinburgh, RCAHMS).

Stephenson, D., 2005, *Mull And Iona; A Landscape Fashioned by Geology* (Perth, Scottish Natural Heritage).

Stevenson, R.B.K., 1966, *Sylloge of Coins of the British Isles. National Museum of Antiquities of Scotland, Edinburgh. Part I. Anglo-Saxon Coins* (London, British Academy).

Stuart, J., 1867, *Sculptured Stones of Scotland Volume Second* (Edinburgh, Spalding Club).

Teignmouth, Lord, 1836, *Sketches of the Coasts and Islands of Scotland and the Isle of Man* (London).

Thompson, J.D.A., 1956, *Inventory of British Coin Hoards A.D. 600–1500* (London, Royal Numismatic Society).

The Statistical Account of Scotland ed, Sir John Sinclair, 1794 (Edinburgh). Torosay, vol. 3, pp. 265–96; Kilninian, vol. 14, pp. 139–56; Kilfinichen And Kilviceuen, vol. 14, pp. 170–211.

Wadden, P., 2016, 'Dál Riata *c.* 1000: Genealogies and Irish Sea Politics', *Scottish Historical Review* 95/2, no. 241 (Oct. 2016): 164–81.

Walker, F.A., 2000, *The Buildings of Scotland. Argyll and Bute* (London, Penguin).

Walker, M. J. C. and Lowe, J. J., 1985, 'Flandrian Environmental History of the Isle of Mull, Scotland', *New Phytologist* 99: 587–610.

Whyte, A. C., 2014, 'Gruline, Mull, and other Inner Hebridean Things', *Journ Scot Name Studies* 8: 115–52.

Wilson, N., 1985, *Scotch and Water. Islay, Jura, Mull, Skye. An illustrated guide to the Hebridean malt whisky distilleries* (Moffat, Lochar).

Wilson, N., 2003, *The Island Whisky Trail. An illustrated guide to the Hebridean Distilleries* (Glasgow, The Angel's Share).

Woolf, A., 2007, *From Pictland to Alba 789–1070* (The New History of Edinburgh, Edinburgh University Press).

Yeoman, P. and Scott, N., 2014, *Iona Abbey and Nunnery* (Historic Scotland, Official Souvenir Guide).

Index